Values in Social Work

Reshaping Social Work Series

Series Editors: **Robert Adams, Lena Dominelli, and Malcolm Payne**

The **Reshaping Social Work** series aims to develop the knowledge base for critical, reflective practitioners. Each book is designed to support students on qualifying social work programmes and update practitioners on crucial issues in today's social work, strengthening research knowledge, critical analysis, and skilled practice to shape social work to meet future challenges.

Published titles

Anti-Racist Practice in Social Work Kish Bhatti-Sinclair
Values in Social Work Jane Fenton
Spirituality and Social Work Margaret Holloway and Bernard Moss
Social Work Research for Social Justice Beth Humphries
Social Work and Social Policy under Austerity Bill Jordan and Mark Drakeford
Social Care Practice in Context Malcolm Payne
Critical Issues in Social Work with Older People Mo Ray, Miriam Bernard, and Judith Phillips
Social Work and Power Roger Smith and Jo Campling
Doing Radical Social Work Colin Turbett
Adult Social Work Law in England John Williams, Gwyneth Roberts, and Aled Griffiths
Social Work and Community Development Catherine Forde and Deborah Lynch

Forthcoming titles

Globally Minded Social Work Practice Janet Anand and Chaitali Das

Invitation to authors

The Series Editors welcome proposals for new books within the *Reshaping Social Work* series. Please contact one of the series editors for an initial discussion:

- Lena Dominelli at lena.dominelli@durham.ac.uk
- Malcolm Payne at macolmpayne5@gmail.com

Reshaping Social Work
Series Editors: **Robert Adams, Lena Dominelli, and Malcolm Payne**
Series Standing Order ISBN 978–1–4039–4878–6
(outside North America only)

You can receive future titles in this series as they are published by placing a standing order. Please contact your bookseller or, in the case of difficulty, write to us at the address below with your name and address, the title of the series and the ISBN quoted above. Customer Services Department, Macmillan Distribution Ltd, Houndmills, Basingstoke, Hampshire, RG21 6XS, UK

Values in Social Work

Reconnecting with Social Justice

Jane Fenton

 palgrave

First published 2016 by
PALGRAVE

Palgrave in the UK is an imprint of Macmillan Publishers Limited, registered in England, company number 785998, of 4 Crinan Street, London, N1 9XW.

Palgrave Macmillan in the US is a division of St Martin's Press LLC, 175 Fifth Avenue, New York, NY 10010.

Palgrave is a global imprint of the above companies and is represented throughout the world.

Palgrave® and Macmillan® are registered trademarks in the United States, the United Kingdom, Europe, and other countries.

ISBN 978–1–137–52832–2 paperback

This book is printed on paper suitable for recycling and made from fully managed and sustained forest sources. Logging, pulping, and manufacturing processes are expected to conform to the environmental regulations of the country of origin.

A catalogue record for this book is available from the British Library.

A catalog record for this book is available from the Library of Congress.

Printed in China

This book is dedicated to my parents,
Irene and Arthur McIntosh

Contents

Acknowledgements		ix
1	**Introduction**	**1**
	Neoliberalism	2
	Values	3
	Social Justice	4
	Theme 1: Reconnection to Social Justice	9
	Theme 2: Ethical Stress	12
	Structure of the Book	14
2	**The Social Work Context**	**18**
	Development of Social Work	18
	Consequences of the Contemporary Context: Ethical Stress-Inducing Characteristics	30
	Developing a Political Standpoint	39
3	**Them and Us**	**41**
	A Very Brief Economic History	41
	The Underclass	45
	Inequality	55
	There Is No Alternative (TINA)	55
	The 'Something for Nothing' Culture Must Be Tackled!	56
	Individuals as Representative of an Entire Class	56
	Hegemony	57
4	**Current Ethical Approaches and Care**	**62**
	Recap of Thinking So Far	62
	Care and Compassion	74
	The Ethics of Care in Practice	75

5 **Connecting an Ethics of Care with Ethical Stress: As Easy As It Sounds?** **80**
Ethics of Care and Ontological Anxiety 84
Identify and Act on Ethical Stress 95
Further Difficulty with Ethics of Care Implementation 98

6 **Social Justice** **102**
Radical Social Work 104
Critical Social Work 110
Anti-oppressive Practice 112
Human Rights-Based Practice 113
An Eclectic Social Justice Approach 114

7 **Relationship-Based Practice** **121**
Empathy 122
Emotional Intelligence 125
Purposeful Relationship-Based Practice 136

8 **Ethical Stress, Anxiety, and Professional Practice** **138**
Ethical Stress – Ethical Action 140
Ontological Anxiety – Coping 148
Professionalism 152

9 **Conclusion** **157**
The Journey So Far 157
Applying the Practice Model 160
Application of the Practice Model to Contemporary
   Examples of 'Good Practice' 168
Concluding Comments 170

References 173
Index 183

Acknowledgements

I would like to thank Erika Cunningham and Richard Ingram who have supported and generously encouraged me through the process of writing this book. Thanks should also go to Peter Hooper and Louise Summerling from Palgrave whose reassurance and support have been indispensable. Contributions, real-life 'stories', and kindly shared struggles from academic staff, students, social workers, and service users should also be acknowledged as the inspiration for many of the ideas in the book. Finally, I would like to thank my family, Steve, Gina, and Adam, for listening to my ideas and tales of progress (or not!) with humour, patience, and love.

1 Introduction

Overview

This chapter introduces the reader to the key terms and ideas that will be used throughout the book. Neoliberalism, values, ethics, social justice, and ethical stress will be defined and explained, thereby giving a common understanding and meaning which will be essential as ideas are expanded on and explored in subsequent chapters. Some evidence for the utility of the book will also be introduced. Finally, descriptions and rationales for forthcoming chapters will be presented.

This book is designed to assist students and practitioners to navigate their way through the application of social work values and, in particular, to reconnect to the fundamental value of a commitment to social justice. In July 2014 the International Federation of Social Workers (IFSW) and the International Association of Schools of Social Work General Assembly agreed on the following global definition of social work:

> Social work is a practice-based profession and an academic discipline that promotes social change and development, social cohesion, and the empowerment and liberation of people. *Principles of social justice, human rights, collective responsibility and respect for diversities are central to social work.* Underpinned by theories of social work, social sciences, humanities and indigenous knowledge, social work *engages people and structures* to address life challenges and enhance wellbeing.
>
> (IFSW 2014, np, emphasis added)

This book takes as its starting point the idea, apparent in the above definition, that principles of social justice lie at the heart of the social work profession. The *activity* of social work can be located within the statement that social work acts to 'promote social change and development, social cohesion, and the empowerment and liberation of people' and 'engages people and structures' (ibid.). This is what social work is meant to *do*. Furthermore, principles such as social justice and human rights are central to these activities – and these can be understood as the underpinning *values* upon which the practice is based.

The British Association of Social Workers' (BASW) *Code of Ethics for Social Work* is entirely in sympathy with the ethos presented in the global definition, for example:

> Social workers have a responsibility to promote social justice, in relation to society generally, and in relation to the people with whom they work.
>
> (BASW 2012, p9)

So far then, it is clear that the ethical framework within which social work operates is concerned with social justice. Because a basic premise of this book is that neoliberalism makes connecting with social justice difficult, neoliberalism itself needs attention and definition.

Neoliberalism

'Neoliberalism' is a term used to describe a system of economic and social governance that liberates businesses from state interference and allows the market to run and regulate itself. The idea is that prioritising the market leads to profit maximisation, so everyone will benefit as the wealth trickles down. Within that market-based thinking, however, the state is reluctant to support people or to allow 'dependence' – individuals must step up, look after themselves, and take responsibility. Making things difficult for those who struggle to do this is a way to incentivise people to work harder and to be responsible.

Parton (2014, p22) describes neoliberalism as follows:

> For the neoliberal New Right, the problems in the economic and social spheres were closely interrelated and the approach stressed the importance of individual responsibility, choice and freedom and supported the disciplines of the market against the interference of the state. However, while the vision was of a 'minimal state', when it did intervene...[it] should be strong and authoritative.

As a political framework, neoliberalism, of course, impacted very significantly on social work policy and practice. I. Ferguson (2008) notes that its introduction led to the import of a pro-business ideology (known as New Public Management or managerialism) into the public sector, bringing a transfer of directly provided services to privately provided 'contracted-out' services, micro-management of, and reduced autonomy for, social workers, less direct work by social workers, an emphasis on performance indicators and external measures of 'success', and a real emphasis on cost cutting (reducing the role of the state). An easy way to think about this is to consider managerialism as the operational arm of neoliberalism.

Neoliberalism and its effects on practice will be explored throughout this book, but some neoliberal ideological principles to keep in mind as you read further are as follows:

- The welfare state and 'dependency' should be severely curtailed (austerity measures and public service cuts).
- Society and community are not important; individual responsibility is.
- The market is the best organising concept for society (and where markets don't exist, they should be created, e.g. social care).
- Authoritarian law and order is necessary when people do not fulfil their individual responsibilities.
- Effects of structural difference are downplayed as excuses; anyone can be a success if he or she works hard enough.

This book takes an explicitly oppositional position to neoliberalism, as will become apparent. To achieve the goal of helping social workers reconnect with social justice, it is necessary to expose the fact that neoliberalism makes social justice-informed social work very difficult indeed.

Values

'Values' can be a problematic term, due to its many uses and definitions. The definition Banks (2012, p7) arrives at gives us clarity about values from the outset and is useful as a point of reference throughout this book; that is, 'values can be regarded as particular types of belief that people hold about what is worthy or valuable…the use of the term "belief" reflects the status that values have as stronger than mere opinions or preferences'.

Biestek (1961), a Jesuit priest, made the first attempt to list social work values and to define a 'value base' for social work. Values were characterised by the individual-level casework relationship and included individualisation, self-determination of clients, non-judgementality, and acceptance. Radical and anti-oppressive thinkers took the analysis beyond the individual level with the incorporation of structural understanding of oppression and disadvantage, thus leading to the inclusion of an explicit commitment to social justice. The influence of human rights thinking and legislation and of deontology in the form of 'respect for persons' (see Chapter 4 for more on this) can also be identified in contemporary writing about social work values.

Social work values, then, are a set of underpinning beliefs about what the profession deems to be worthy or valuable. BASW (2012) defines that set of underpinning beliefs as follows:

1. Value: Human rights
    Ethical principles: Upholding and promoting human wellbeing and dignity; respecting the right to self-determination; promoting the right to participation; treating each person as a whole; identifying and developing strengths.
2. Value: Social justice
    Ethical principles: Challenging discrimination; recognising diversity; distributing resources; challenging unjust policies and practice; working in solidarity.
3. Value: Professional integrity
    Ethical principles: Upholding the values and reputation of the profession; being trustworthy; maintaining professional boundaries; making considered professional judgements; being professionally accountable.

We can see from the above that ethical principles or ethics are distinct from values, due to their concern with behaviour and what social workers should *do*. As Banks (2012, p5) points out, one use of the word 'ethics' is as 'a plural term referring to the norms or standards of behaviour people follow concerning what is regarded as good or bad, right or wrong'. For the purposes of this book, therefore, we will retain the distinction that values concern underpinning beliefs and ethics concern behaviour. In terms of the BASW *Code of Ethics*, social workers should be able to say 'I believe in human rights, social justice, and professional integrity' (values) and 'I will try to uphold and promote human wellbeing and dignity, respect the right to self-determination, and practise all the other ethical principles' (behaviour).

In terms of values, then, this book takes social justice as a central focus. So, what is actually meant by the term 'social justice'?

Social Justice

Doel (2012, p27) outlines two definitions of social justice: 'The reformist wing of social work subscribes to equal opportunity, but the radical and social democratic wing goes further towards redistributive justice, for example using progressive taxation to reallocate wealth in society.'

It might be that some social workers believe in equality of opportunity and would subscribe explicitly to the reformist wing of social work but also believe that our society is characterised by a benign meritocracy where everyone already *does* have equal opportunity to access to resources. We have free health care and education, for example, and anyone can take advantage of that if they so wish. To suggest that divisions in our society might impact on opportunities to do this might lead to the question 'what divisions?' Everyone can work hard at school and get qualifications and thus a good job – it is just down to the individuals and their choice to work hard. If they don't, they can qualify for benefit – but this too should be a qualified right as, again, people just need to apply themselves more diligently, and we need to beware of the 'something for nothing' culture (Cameron, cited in *Daily Mail* 2008). The reformist understanding of social justice can, therefore, be interpreted in a way that is congruent with this type of individualistic or neoliberal thinking.

In order to challenge that world view, ideas from the radical/social democratic interpretation of social justice can be introduced. Some students, however, on exposure to the ideas that wealth should be redistributed and that people have a right to basic provision, might respond by asking why wealth should be redistributed if people are simply not applying themselves enough to the opportunities on offer. Wouldn't that just encourage the 'dependency culture' (Levitas 2005)? This hypothetical student response is based on what Marston (2013, p132) calls a 'moralizing self-sufficiency discourse' and is illustrated very well by his example of housing problems in Australia. In the mid-1990s, social housing tenants were rebranded as 'customers', which signalled increasingly market-led responses to housing shortages. In parallel, a governmental and media representation of social housing 'customers' as 'bad tenants' was increasingly delivered to the public to defend and justify policies in favour of landlords – less secure tenure, for example. According to Marston, this directed attention away from structural problems and causes of problems in Australia's housing system such as 'increasing income inequality, rising land prices in metropolitan areas, long waiting lists for public housing and discrimination in the private rental market' (ibid.). The consequence of this type of 'framing' of the situation was that individual tenants were held solely responsible for the difficult situation they were in. This neoliberal way of viewing social problems, that is, blaming the individuals in the situation *for* the situation (poverty is not the problem, the poor are!), is a natural consequence of a belief in a benign meritocracy that gives everyone equal chances. If this type of understanding is held by some students, then radical ideas introduced as a blunt attempt to challenge it will have no purchase and might well be dismissed as 'woolly, liberal, outdated nonsense'. Accepting that social work education has a real challenge on its hands to confront and dispel some deeply held neoliberal and oppressive ideas is necessary before educators can work out exactly how to face that challenge (Fenton 2014b).

Since the mid-1990s, there has been an increasingly strident 'moral underclass discourse' (MUD), arising from the politics of New Labour (Levitas 2005, p14). Levitas explains that the fertile ground for the growth of MUD can be found in the market neoliberal economics of the 1980s and the parallel neoconservative strengthening of the state, which was required to uphold order and morality. She calls this the 'dual character of the new right' (Levitas 2005, p14), and it was this character that brought about the shift from welfare being seen as a necessary and good thing (for some recipients anyway) to welfare construed as 'dependency' – a bad thing that sapped people's motivation and incentive to work. Benefits were beginning to be seen as bad for people. This discourse of a 'culture of dependency...took over the public domain' (ibid.) and led to the idea of the existence of a moral underclass. Thus, we can see, again, the shift from understanding social problems as having structural causes to understanding them as the products of poor behaviour by an underclass. The 'bad tenant', for example, in Marston's example. This absolute pervasive discourse in political thinking has gained in strength from the time of New Labour and is now the accepted 'common sense' view of the world. It is reinforced daily by appeals to 'hard-working families' and media coverage of benefit scroungers depleting a country's hard-earned capital (O. Jones 2011). And so, in terms of social work, if this world view is accepted, what should be the object of a social worker's attention? It must be the individual and interpersonal level of change, because social problems have behavioural causes and thus aberrant behaviour must be tackled. People simply need to be helped, encouraged, or coerced to overcome their personal weaknesses and to take up the opportunities available to us all.

The idea missing from the neoliberal picture above, of course, is that inequality, poverty, and structural differences *affect* the way that people are able to engage with the opportunities available. They also make for fewer available opportunities – poorer schools, poorer housing, more pressure and anxiety, etc. So, we need to link radical ideas about the effects of inequality and poverty (for example, Wilkinson and Pickett 2010) to reformist ideas about the difficulty people have in engaging with opportunities and the opportunities themselves not being equal. For example, people who have the opportunity to attend public school, despite comprising only 7 per cent of the general population, are very much over-represented (50 per cent or over) in occupations such as top barristers, top journalists, top civil servants, finance directors, and politicians (O. Jones 2011). As Marston (2013, p132) states, overlooking the true picture of difference in condition and opportunity 'assumes that the background conditions that...people face are not unjust and that structural difficulties have been overcome through the march of modernity and the achievements of a range of social movements'. It is clear from the evidence that this is simply not the case.

In terms of a radical/social democratic understanding of social justice we must first of all ensure that such an interpretation has a basis in the underlying principles of social work as a profession. Does the profession endorse a radical/social democratic definition of social justice? To find out, we should look, once again, to the global definition of social work. The concern with 'structures' as well as individuals would suggest a radical/social democratic frame of reference. Also, the *Code of Ethics* (BASW 2012) states unequivocally that 'social workers have a responsibility to promote social justice in relation to society in general' and to 'bring to the attention of their employers, policy-makers, politicians and the general public, situations where resources are inadequate or distribution of resources...are oppressive (or) unfair' (BASW 2012, p9). Furthermore, the standards that student social workers must meet include requirements to 'understand, identify and apply in practice the principles of social justice, inclusion and equality' (College of Social Work 2012) or to 'respond...to...structural inequality' (Scottish Government 2003, px). It is difficult to see how social workers or students could meet these requirements whilst adhering to a reformist, and potentially neoliberal, interpretation of social justice.

The aim here, then, is to define social justice in a way that encompasses both interpretations – equality of opportunity and reduced inequality, poverty, and discrimination – and to help students understand that dual interpretation. This is difficult when students are steeped in the 'common sense' of neoliberalism and the idea that we all have similar opportunities. As Marston (2013, p135) goes on to say, 'it is also the case that beginning social workers are likely to be influenced by the dominant discourse of self-sufficiency and the muted political agency that this discourse gives rise to'. So, new social workers and social work students might simply believe that less successful people don't take advantage of the opportunities equally on offer to all of us, due to their own failings and characteristics (MUD discourse). Also, it suits the beneficiaries of the existing structural configuration of society to promote this way of thinking. As O. Jones (2011, p137) states:

> What if you have wealth and success because it has been handed to you on a plate? What if people are poorer than you because the odds are stacked against them? To accept this would trigger a crisis of self-confidence among the well-off few. And if you were to accept it, then surely you would have to accept that it's the government's job to do something about it – namely by curtailing your own privileges. But, if you convince yourself that the less fortunate are smelly, thick, racist and rude by nature, then it is only right that they should remain at the bottom. Chav-hate justifies the preservation of the pecking order, based on the fiction that it is actually a fair reflection of people's worth.

Given the weight of propaganda and the 'propping up' of a neoliberal, individualised, self-sufficiency discourse by the establishment, it is unsurprising when people who are not aware of an alternative picture simply believe this as the unquestioned truth. According to Pease (2013, p31), it is most important that 'social workers reject the notion of state and the welfare apparatus within it...as neutral or benign. It is essential that critical social work education develops analyses to interrogate the power of the state and its extension into the community and develops strategies to enable social workers to find spaces within which to challenge that power.' Pease also acknowledges, however, that 'neoliberal ideas have penetrated the psyche of social workers', thus posing a greater challenge to educators today than in the past. Social work students are entering programmes with their frames of reference often very much shaped by neoliberal thinking – including a belief in a neutral state with equal opportunities and the resulting individualising of failure and problems – which requires a robust and challenging response from educators. Some doubt, however, has been cast on whether social work education is indeed up to this neoliberal challenge (Fenton 2014b).

So, rejecting the neoliberal view of society above, our definition is that equality of opportunity can only be possible if people have enough access to good opportunities and if there is sufficient equality of condition (via wealth redistribution) to liberate people from obstacles that would prevent them from taking advantage of those opportunities. Currently, however, poverty, inequality, and lack of opportunity are becoming more and more severe. Students need to be exposed to, and helped to understand, the true picture.

What do we expect from students and social workers who *do* have a robust connection with social justice? As Gray and Webb (2013, p7) state, 'front-line social workers are unorganised and do not usually have the time, energy, resources or assertiveness to take up active political roles. This exposes the weakness of social work as a professional pressure group.' So if there is, in reality, little political agitating social workers feel they can do, do we only aspire to *understanding* the political landscape and injustice faced by many service users? According to Gray and Webb, this might indeed be the aspiration: 'critical social work...is more often a form of critique than a direct emancipatory practice. ... Its goal is not so much to offer tangible, practical ways of meeting the pressing, crisis-oriented, micro needs of service users...and informal carers, which practitioners encounter on a daily basis, but to enlarge their critical thinking' (ibid.). However, this book is designed to help students and social workers apply their social justice knowledge to those micro needs, and this will be demonstrated by the case examples throughout the text. Social justice-underpinned practice must be applicable to the daily encounters of social workers in order that it remains, or becomes, relevant and central to our next generation of practitioners. In other words, this book argues that there is a direct practice connection with an understanding of social justice – engagement with services users looks very different if a worker employs a MUD discourse as opposed to a radical social justice discourse. Via relationship-based practice, understanding, and emancipatory practice, this book will guide students and social workers towards just such a Practice Model. The first theme around which the new model is constructed is a reconnection to social justice, and we turn to that now.

Theme 1: Reconnection to Social Justice

In Sheedy's (2013, p22) chapter on 'Values in social work' his opening line is 'Please, take a seat in the "uneasy" chair'. He describes the application of values as a difficulty in finding comfort and ease – and draws attention to the many dilemmas that a social worker encounters and that are so very difficult to reconcile. This is, perhaps, a fitting introduction to the idea that for all our understanding of social work values, their application is much less straightforward. From my own experience as an academic teacher on social work programmes, and echoing Sheedy's observation that students often present the subject of values in a simplistic way, I have read assignments giving many examples of how students say they have implemented their values by being non-judgemental, promoting self-determination, and recognising diversity, whilst any competing value tensions or any ethical dilemmas have been overlooked, deliberately omitted (for ease), or simply not recognised. So, for example, an unannounced home visit may be described as value based due to the student social worker on placement treating the adults in the household with respect ('Mr and Mrs Smith, would you mind...'), being non-judgemental about the poor condition of the house, and promoting self-determination by giving choices about where to meet next – home or office. Consideration of values issues such as just turning up for a visit without notice or lack of choice in actually meeting again with the social worker (Human rights? Social justice? Professional integrity?) are simply not considered, because the visit is *necessary* and therefore must be *right*. No further exploration is required, and values are expressed within the narrowly defined boundaries of the necessary home visit. McLaughlin (2008, p56) describes this idea as a 'narrowing of politics to the interpersonal level', that is, the location of practice within the sphere of interpersonal relationships and the concern with individual, interpersonal values only. He suggests that this could lead to, for example:

> social workers demonstrating their 'anti-oppressive' credentials by admonishing the asylum seeker for using sexist language, while at the same time refusing them services, or taking their children from them, because they are not considered 'one of us'.
>
> (McLaughlin 2008, p56)

The social worker or student above could make the case that he or she was 'challenging discrimination' (one of BASW's ethical principles) by challenging the language, and yet he or she is missing the discriminatory and oppressive policy shaping the social worker's task of gatekeeping access to services. In other words, he or she is missing the link between the task required and social justice definitions of redistribution and opportunity.

The preoccupation with values on the individual or interpersonal level is, perhaps, exacerbated by the frameworks that regulate social work practice in Wales, Northern Ireland, and Scotland. The regulatory bodies for these countries – Cygnor Gofal Cymru/Care Council for Wales (2004), Northern Ireland Social Care Council (2004), and SSSC (2004) – share the same codes of practice, albeit with different titles. An analysis of these codes finds a distinct lack of reference to social justice and an overall concern with individuals and the role social workers have in helping them to promote their own interests via respect for their opinions and the promotion of equal opportunities. The codes, therefore, create an impression of the social work role as concerned with the empowerment of service users' individual endeavour and a social work practice underpinned by respect for the individual. Where is attention to the underpinning values of human rights and social justice? Arguably, professional integrity as a value could encompass many of the codes' statements, but the same cannot be said for the others. On a more hopeful note, the Professional Capabilities Framework (College of Social Work 2012, np), which regulates practice in England, makes several references to social justice within the domain of 'Rights, justice and economic wellbeing: advance human rights and promote social justice and economic wellbeing'. For example, at the qualifying social worker level, the first capability in this domain is: 'understand, identify and apply in practice the principles of social justice, inclusion and equality'. The fourth capability is: 'Recognise the impact of poverty and social exclusion and promote enhanced economic status through access to education, work, housing, health services and welfare benefits'.

Reamer and Shardlow (2009) point out that the Welsh, Scottish, and Northern Irish codes are codes of *practice* and, in contrast to the BASW Code of *Ethics,* are narrow managerial tools concerned with the regulation of behaviour rather than the application of values. They argue that there is a dissociation from the morality inherent in social work, so morality and practising ethically are no longer the driving forces, having been replaced by the imperative to abide by the rules and follow procedures.

So, what is really going on here? It would seem that there is a suggestion that social workers are dislocating their practice (including values expression) from wider societal issues, such as social justice, discrimination, and structural influences. Certain roles, rules, tasks, policies, etc. are accepted as necessary and are therefore unquestioned. Values operate within these established frameworks about and to which a social worker has little to say or object, and as long as respect, empowerment of an individual's own endeavour, and adherence to the rules of practice are achieved, social workers perhaps see little else they *should* be doing.

A further feature of this theme is that this shift away from social justice appears to have become more apparent in recent years. Fenton (2014b) found, in her study of criminal justice social workers in Scotland, that newer, younger social workers objected significantly less than their older, more experienced colleagues to: lack of autonomy, risk aversion, and lack of time/space for relationship-based practice and helping. In her paper, she links these elements to the neoliberal societal shift that has occurred over the last three decades and that has led to a far more managerial, task-driven, and bureaucratic type of social work. Her suggestion is that people who have grown up knowing no alternative to neoliberal thinking accept, far less critically, the neoliberal characterisation of contemporary social work; this will be explored more fully in Chapter 2.

Similarly, P. Gilligan (2007) found that a certain age group of applicants to a social work programme were significantly more likely to rate societal problems as the 'fault' of individuals and their poor choices, rather than as arising from societal divisions and oppressions. The age group were what the author termed 'Thatcher's Children', and it may be congruent, in age terms, with the younger workers in Fenton's study. Lafrance, Gray, and Herbert (2004, p336) found that practice educators in their study were clear that a value position congruent with social justice aims was fundamental to the social work profession, but they 'expressed concern about students who failed to understand the social conditions that affect their clients, or to address the systemic issues that come to their attention'. Practice educators were also concerned that students over-identify with 'the bureaucratic imperatives and lose sight of their allegiance to the goals of social work' (ibid., p337). Woodward and Mackay (2012) also found that social work students in year one had difficulty in applying values arising from structural and social justice issues, and yet could apply individual-level values relatively easily. One year on, although students could recognise structural and social justice issues, they still struggled to apply them to their practice.

So, to endorse a book for social work students, practice educators, and practitioners with a central theme of 'reconnecting to social justice' we simply need to consider the persuasive body of evidence above and to reflect on Sheedy's (2013, p6) view that 'a number of social work students commence their studies claiming no knowledge of politics, or more worryingly, no interest in politics. The danger of such an approach is that one focuses on "helping people" to the exclusion of consideration of the broader contexts within which this vocational task is carried out.' The task of reconnecting with social justice when social justice per se does not feature significantly in students' frames of reference is a challenging and yet necessary one.

Much has been written about the neoliberal and managerial character of contemporary social work, which would be very congruent with social workers practising in a managerial, neoliberal way, concerned with values on the individual level only. However, there is also a body of literature that demonstrates some social workers' deep disquiet and unhappiness with that world. C. Jones (2001), for example, describes extremely unhappy and disillusioned local authority social workers who found themselves working as gatekeepers, struggling to have time for relationship-based practice or to be able to express their values through their practice. Preston-Shoot (2003, p10) echoed these findings, with social workers reporting 'demoralisation and disillusionment' because they felt 'unable to uphold the knowledge base and values of a competent professional'. This is a further piece to an emerging, complex values jigsaw and leads us to the next theme central to this book: ethical stress.

Theme 2: Ethical Stress

Ethical stress is the stress produced when workers feel they cannot base their practice upon their values. The concept of 'ethical stress' emerged from Fenton's (2014a) research study, conducted with 100 local authority, criminal justice social workers in Scotland. In the study, workers' experiences of two types of internal conflict or stress related to value/behaviour incongruence were measured. One type was 'disjuncture', a feeling of conflict experienced when practitioners cannot base their practice upon social work values and thus cannot put their values into action (usually due to workplace restrictions and demands) (Di Franks 2008). The other type of internal conflict measured was 'ontological guilt', that is, the negative feeling experienced when a person cannot base his or her practice on what he or she feels is 'right' or in line with his or her conscience (Taylor 2007). Of course, both concepts overlap, and the extent of their overlap was enough for them to be brought together as complementary aspects of the same concept, named as 'ethical stress'. Statistically, the combined scale measuring 'ethical stress' had a Cronbach's coefficient alpha measure of .817, meaning it had very good internal consistency and that each element (question) was tapping into the same phenomenon – ethical stress. This statistical measure gives an indication that the measure of ethical stress was very reliable, that is, measuring what it set out to measure. An easy way to think about ethical stress is that it is the consequence of conflict between what the person thinks is the *right* thing to do (in terms of social work values and one's own conscience) and the constraints/priorities/rules of the workplace.

The research demonstrated that the experience of ethical stress is influenced by the managerial culture of the agency, risk aversion, heavy workloads, and a changing 'ethical climate' (Fenton 2014a). The change in ethical climate may be illustrated by the erosion of welfare and 'helping' approaches to social work and a greater concern with risk management, defensive practice, and gate-keeping resources – a shift in a neoliberal direction, in effect (C. Jones 2001; I. Ferguson 2008; Preston-Shoot 2003; etc.). It should be noted once again, however, that newer, younger workers in the study suffered less ethical stress than their older, more experienced colleagues, because they objected less to the neoliberal and managerial shifts. Reviewing the literature mentioned above about students' unquestioning acceptance of a neoliberal ethos permeating social work, it is hardly a surprise that less ethical stress is experienced by 'Thatcher's Children'. And yet, ethical stress can be an extremely useful emotive indicator of when practice 'feels wrong' and, thus, should be questioned. We need to encourage and grow the experience of ethical stress as an emotionally intelligent way of reconnecting with our inner values and using the discomfort caused when they are compromised as a guide. From my own experience of teaching social work students, I have found the majority of them to be responsive to understanding and recognising the experience of ethical stress, despite having never named it or consciously thought about it as a 'thing' previously. For example, after a lecture on ethical stress a student sent me an email that said: 'I've been chatting about some of the feelings that you mentioned, for example, the feelings of frustration and the conflict between my values and the procedures and policies of my placement, while in supervision; although I haven't been able to really pinpoint what I'm trying to say or explain how I'm feeling. I've just been aware that things weren't sitting comfortably with me.'

One of the key themes in the experience or avoidance of ethical stress is being able to care for services users. Kosny and Eakin (2008) found that workers in their study experienced very little ethical stress because of key features of the three agencies studied, namely: practice being congruent with a clear agency mission; the belief that people deserved to be treated with care and compassion; the acceptance of people as they are; and the underpinning belief that the service users were in the situations they were in due to an unfair and unjust society. So, a clear statement of belief in a radical definition of social justice but also a belief in *care* as a central feature of practice went a long way to ameliorate feelings of ethical stress. One of the reasons C. Jones (2001) found such unhappy and disillusioned workers was because of the inability to care for service users in the way workers felt they wanted to. Gregory (2010) in a study of experienced probation officers also found that they saw care as central to their work. Caring and finding connectedness, even to people who had done some terrible things, were, in the eyes of the probation officers, absolutely key. Although this practice was being eroded by managerial and technicist approaches, the workers were still able to find a means of adhering to their care values. In essence then, not to be able to care for the service users we work with is a central feature of ethical stress, and experiencing ethical stress is likely to happen when workers feel they cannot care in the way they want to.

Explicit recognition of ethical stress, and using it as a guide for moral questioning or action, is a necessity in social work if we are to avoid blind, rule-bound, procedural work, which carries the potential for uncaring and oppressive practice, discrimination, and the ignorance of social justice. We therefore must, as social work educators, help to create the conditions in which ethical stress can be experienced, that is: educate students about what it is and how it feels and emphasise that it is a *positive* trait to be able to experience and use the feeling; help students really reconnect with individual-level values and see the worth in compassion and care; and help students reconnect with social justice as an underpinning value for all of their practice. If we can achieve some success in this regard, then we will be helping students to dust off and recalibrate their moral compasses.

Structure of the Book

This book is designed to help students and social workers reconnect their practice to a radical/social democratic interpretation of social justice. This involves understanding social justice issues and how they affect the lives of the people we work with and, as a consequence of that understanding, developing a responsive social work practice cognisant of that context. Furthermore, the book will explore individual-level 'on the ground' practice and its links from care and compassion to relationship-based practice and, ultimately, to social justice. By the end of the book, students should be able to analyse their practice through a coherent framework that links all of those elements. As BASW (2012, p11) states in relation to the Code's ethical practice principles:

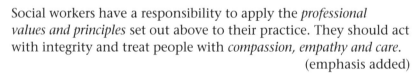

> Social workers have a responsibility to apply the *professional values and principles* set out above to their practice. They should act with integrity and treat people with *compassion, empathy and care.*
> (emphasis added)

The book will achieve its aim by a logical progression of ideas, whilst organising the information around two key themes as already mentioned: reconnection to social justice and ethical stress. Chapter 2 begins this process with an exploration of 'the changing social work context'. What are the ethical stress-inducing features of contemporary social work, and how have they evolved? The development of social work from post-war welfarism to a current preoccupation with individualism will be explored. Furthermore, the chapter will explore how the emphasis on individualism actually impacts on day-to-day social work practice. Success or failure as attributable to individual choice or weakness only can shape social work practice in a controlling and punitive manner, and this will be highlighted. By the end of this chapter, readers should be able to see some of the shifts in social work practice that might otherwise have been taken for granted or gone unacknowledged. Moving beyond work on the individual level and the ethical stress-inducing features therein, Chapter 3 ('Them and Us') will take the reader's thinking into the area of practice concerned with the application of social justice understanding. Addressing the tendency to *disconnect* from social justice and attempting to explain why this is happening, this chapter will explore: 'underclass' and populist thinking, including caricatures such as 'chavs', 'junkies', etc.; the link between an individualist way of understanding social problems and neoliberalism; the idea that there is no alternative to the current neoliberal 'common sense' way of thinking; and neoliberal hegemony, including media stereotypes and lack of attention to alternative discourses.

The book at this point, then, has begun an exploration of the two themes: ethical stress when individual-level values are thwarted; and an exploration of why social work is disconnecting from social justice, including the powerful, neoliberal forces that shape the disconnection. Chapter 4 considers 'current ethical approaches' and their interface with those two themes. Utilitarianism, deontology, virtue ethics, and ethics of care will be explored. The practice example given in Chapter 3, which exemplifies neoliberal, controlling practice, will be linked to the different ethical approaches to illustrate how students and social workers *can* justify their practice, even if it is value poor, via blunt understanding of these approaches. It will become clear, however, that an ethics of care approach cannot be applied to such practice and, thus, an ethics of care approach will be promoted as the most useful in guarding against neoliberal, controlling, and managerial practice.

Next, Chapter 5 ('Connecting an Ethics of Care with Ethical Stress: As Easy As It Sounds?') will consider the reality of implementing an ethics of care approach in the current managerial context of social work. The chapter will also differentiate between healthy ontological anxiety and ethical stress and will discuss how the experience of each should be a guide to further action. A model illustrating the interconnectivity of those elements will be presented. The reader has now been introduced in a basic way to a model of individual-level, caring social work practice that should serve as a starting point. Finally, the chapter will look at situations where empathy, care, and compassion are less easy to apply and will investigate how social workers, perhaps left without a reference point in these situations, can still utilise the model.

Chapter 6 will explore the next theme of the book: social justice. Ways of working underpinned by models of social justice-informed practice will be considered, namely radical social work, critical social work, anti-oppressive practice, and positive human rights approaches. The aim of this chapter is to help students understand *how* social justice understanding can inform actual practice, and a further iteration of the Practice Model, including the social justice dimension, will be outlined. As Gray and Webb (2013, p28) state: 'minimally, social workers can avoid pathologising service users and holding them responsible for problems shaped by structural and material conditions'. The basic understanding and application of the model will achieve this, but the book will also take readers further, from understanding and not-blaming (minimum), to social justice-informed day-to-day practice (goal).

Chapter 7 ('Relationship-Based Practice') introduces and explores the central ring of the new model, which is, essentially, the 'glue' that holds the entire model together. The preceding chapters should come together and make further sense in the light of this final, vital part of the jigsaw. Chapter 8 ('Ethical Stress, Anxiety, and Professional Practice') builds on the ideas covered in Chapter 5 and looks in more detail at the horizontal aspects of the Practice Model. Concepts that contribute to the ethical stress/ethical action connection and those that contribute to the ontological anxiety/coping link will be discussed further. A conceptual understanding of professionalism, congruent with the Practice Model, will also be investigated.

Finally, Chapter 9 will provide the conclusion to the book by summing up the key messages and looking to the future. The chapter will analyse the Practice Model in a detailed application to the practice example from Chapter 3. The new approach will be contrasted with the original neo-liberal approach used by the social worker. Ideas of what might be considered 'good practice' in the contemporary social work context will also be compared to the essential elements of the Practice Model. Once again, this should augment the reader's critical understanding of the social work context.

Chapters will contain practice examples, 'stop and think' sections, and messages from research and will end with a summary of the main points. The book is intended as a useful guide for anyone who wants to shape, re-shape, or re-invigorate his or her practice. I hope you will enjoy it.

main points

- Social justice is a core social work value, although there appears to be a creeping disengagement from social justice-informed practice.

- Younger social workers and social work students appear to be the group in which this disengagement is most apparent.

- The tendency to individualise social problems and to view them as problems of character or individual behaviour is a significant part of the disengagement from social justice. Explanations of social problems in terms of poverty or inequality are viewed as excuses.

- The current social work context can encourage social justice disengagement but can also produce ethical stress for workers when they feel they cannot base their practice on their values.

- Ethical stress is a positive experience which can allow workers to identify that things are, perhaps, not 'right' in terms of values.

taking it further

- BASW (2012) *Code of Ethics for Social Work* (Birmingham: BASW) and IFSW (2012) *Statement of Ethical Principles*, http://ifsw.org/policies/statement-of-ethical-principles/ (accessed 10 May 2015). See both documents to really understand the basic requirement for engagement with social justice in the social work profession.
- Ferguson, I. (2008) *Reclaiming Social Work: Challenging Neo-liberalism and Promoting Social Justice* (London: Sage). An informative account of the impact of neoliberalism on social work.
- Gray, M., and Webb, S. A. (eds) (2013) *The New Politics of Social Work* (Basingstoke: Palgrave Macmillan). A collection of works gathered together on the basis of a shared belief in radical and anti-neoliberal practice.
- Sheedy, M. (2013) *Core Themes in Social Work: Power, Poverty, Politics and Values* (Maidenhead: OU Press). An accessible text from a social work educator, encouraging critical thinking in social work students.

2 The Social Work Context

Overview

This chapter explores the contemporary social work context, with a particular focus on those features that contribute to the experience of ethical stress. How have those developments emerged over time and how have we arrived at the current picture? This chapter will attempt to answer these questions by tracing the development of social work from the Enlightenment and emergence of modern values to the present day. A contemporary, neoliberal picture of the social work landscape will be explored, featuring managerialism, individualism, participationism, and privatisation, and the chapter will examine how the consequences of this picture for social work practice can result in ethical stress for workers.

Development of Social Work

Social work is not a neutral profession, operating in a vacuum and unaffected by political and social developments. Quite the opposite, in fact, with the impact of changes in the demography of society having extremely significant consequences for social work provision. Think about the amount of discussion going on at the present time about the 'ageing population' and what this means for the provision of social care in the future. Think about the change in family structure and the increased need for childcare provision as more women enter the employment market. Alongside these and other demographic changes, political changes and imperatives also lead to changing emphasis on where social work should target its efforts. This leads, in turn, to shifts and changes in everyday social work practice. This section will briefly trace the main developments and changes in the social work context from the Enlightenment to the present day.

Morality period

Social work has its roots in the charitable endeavours of the Church. In fact, Horner (2012) states that the closest equivalent services to modern social work were organised and run entirely by religious people. Secular developments then emerged during the sixteenth and seventeenth centuries with the enactment of Poor Laws, and clear distinctions were made between the deserving and undeserving poor. It is interesting to note that this tension persists through history, including social work history, and has emerged in a very much reinvigorated form in the present day. In the eighteenth century poor houses were expanded, due to the perceived threat of the poor and disabled 'underclass'. Poor houses accommodated people with a range of needs and, again, the core idea was that people should be encouraged or coerced into work and to be self-reliant (Horner 2012).

According to Barnard (2008, p9) the emergence of 'modern values' was brought about by the Enlightenment (early eighteenth century): the cultural and scientific movement that led to the promotion of values of tolerance, understanding, progress, and enquiry coupled with a dominant scientific and rational narrative, as opposed to the previous religious authoritarianism. Utilitarianism and deontology emerged as a result of this shift, as philosophy grappled with questions such as 'what is the right thing to do?' (ibid.). The erosion of religious decree in these matters left a space for philosophy to develop new theories, some of which still have influence in ethical thinking today (see Chapter 4 for more on these philosophical paradigms).

The Charity Organisation Society (COS) was set up in 1869 to organise and direct the myriad of charitable organisations then in operation. The COS was very clear in its underpinning philosophy – that social problems were a result of the failed moral character of the poor. Any endeavour to help, therefore, would target the intervention on the moral character of the recipient (Horner 2012).

The nineteenth century also saw the development of further Poor Laws, workhouses, and asylums. Workhouses were deliberately harsh places, intended to be uninviting and to act as a deterrent against lazy, work-shy behaviour, thereby encouraging improved moral character. Specialist institutions, however, were then developed in line with scientific thinking and 'expertise' in each field and took hold towards the end of the nineteenth century.

Barnard (2008, p10) refers to all of the above as the 'morality period'. The roots of social work are to be found here – with the emphasis well and truly on correcting the poor's low moral standards. It is somewhat ironic that this value position was the primary one taken at the very beginning of the emergence of social work and yet has absolute resonance with the current, and relatively new, value position of neoliberal thinking! Keep this in mind...

Emergence of 'War on Want'

In the early 1900s, the focus of attention to social problems shifted from a concern with the morality and failings of feckless individuals to structural influences such as poverty, poor housing and sanitation, and unemployment (Barnard 2008), in recognition of the worst consequences of the industrial revolution. Furthermore, the economic depression of the 1930s and the enormous and devastating effect on all of the population of both world wars led to a realisation that the government had a responsibility to (and owed a debt to?) ordinary – often poor – people. This manifested itself in Beveridge's War on Want and the consequent emergence of the welfare state, with the aim of realising a guaranteed decent standard of living for people for life. The National Health Service, National Insurance, and the welfare system were all features of the new society.

Using Evers (sec. 6.20, in Munday 2003) as a guide to the development of social work from the perspective of service-user involvement, post-war stages and themes will now be examined and critiqued.

The following section critiques the above chronological phases (from Welfarism to Participationism), with a focus on the changing value base within each one. In particular, values relating to *causes* of people's problems, the targets for social work action, will be explored.

Welfarism

During the welfare phase, people had universal rights and access to help and welfare. The state could meet needs and the determination of need was thought to be best made by social workers. So, although the spirit of ensuring a decent life for people and assisting with difficulties was realised, there was a paternalistic element to the provision of welfare and an arrogance about the skill and knowledge of social workers (Turbett 2014). During this time, the key reports that shaped social work in the UK were published: the Seebohm Report (1968) in England and Wales and the Kilbrandon Report (1964) in Scotland, leading to legislative and organisational changes that created Social Services departments in England, Northern Ireland, and Wales and Social Work departments in Scotland.

During the 1950s and 1960s, scientific and psychiatric advances were made that heavily influenced social work – looking for explanations for human weakness or maladaptive behaviour in the psyche of individuals. Bowlby's seminal work on attachment was published at this time, alongside other key concepts that still influence social work casework, such as separation and loss, trauma and deprivation (Doel 2012). So, although located within a welfare state, social work refocused once again on individual causes and explanations of problems – although there was a clear emphasis on explaining and understanding as opposed to simple

Welfarism	Professionalism	Consumerism	Managerialism	Participationism
hierarchical governance of service systems	case management	competition	managed care	collective self-help
full coverage/uniform services	upgrading of educational levels	individual choice	target setting	volunteering
equal standards	upgrading professional advice and consultancy	market research	upgrading managerial and economic concerns	strengthening user- and community-based service providers
boards and commissions for corporate governance	quality control through professional self-control	vouchers	external quality management	strengthening local embeddedness
quality control by state inspection	public service ethos	customer orientation	complaint management	orientation towards empowering users
social rights and patients' charter		consumer lobbying		more service dialogues
		consumer protection		more user control in designing and running services

(From Evers sec. 6.20, in Munday 2003)

imputations of moral weakness. Psycho-social casework was the conduit through which social workers employed their skills and knowledge, targeting individual psychology whilst acknowledging the effects of wider social issues.

This phase also saw the rise of radical social work. The radical movement drew attention to structural differences and poor circumstances as the reason that people had problems. The radical movement was also a reaction to the psychodynamic and individual focus of casework described above. Explaining the grip of psychoanalysis and its dangers, Bailey and Brake (1975, p6) state:

> Psychoanalysis provided a skill which was rewarding for the social worker, who felt helpless before problems which were the result of political decisions and material deprivation. It encouraged a feeling that something could be done, and gave to the newly emerging profession a distinct skill distinguishing them from the layman and the amateur. Social problems became individualised and the profession became immersed in an ideology which devalued collective political action. The poor and the deviants had progressed from moral inferiority to pathology.

Adding to that view, Barnard (2008, p12) points out that at this point in social work's history:

> The ideological smokescreen of social work was to 'blame the victim' and locate social problems as instances of individual failing, not structurally defined problems. The central concern of the value base of radical social work was a focus on equality, understood in the Marxist sense of redistribution of income and wealth and a notion of justice built on that redistribution.

Herein then, we can identify a congruence between the radical movement of the 1970s and the definition of social justice used in this book. Inequality of income and wealth and structural difference provide the fertile ground for social problems and must be tackled to allow for better opportunities for people and to create the circumstances whereby people are able to take advantage of those opportunities (see Chapter 1).

Professionalism

During the 1970s some high-profile cases of social work failure hit the headlines, beginning with the death of Maria Colwell in 1973. One of the consequences of those tragedies was that social work education was seen as requiring improvement, including increased attention to applied ethics. For example, BASW (1975) drew up its *Code of Ethics*, which included acting without judgementality and supporting self-determination. Further child deaths in the 1980s, for example Jasmine Beckford in 1985 and Tyra Henry in 1986, brought a loss of public confidence in social workers and vilification of them in the media. This led to a phase characterised by increasing managerial control, increased emphasis on professionalism, and increasingly tight procedures and processes. At the same time as significant negativity towards social work, there was a push towards real recognition of it as a 'profession'. In order, perhaps, to regain some respectability and reputation, the particular brand of professionalism concerned qualifications for managers and increasing control being placed in managers' hands; increasing managerialism, in other words. As Meagher and Parton (2004) point out, various feminist writers have viewed 'professionalism' as a masculine construct, in the same vein as bureaucracy. The authors argue that culturally defined masculine ideals of separateness, 'objective' decision-making, and emotional detachment feature in notions of professionalism. Phillips and Cree (2014) point out that professionalisation brought with it attempts to attract and employ more men in social work, thus supporting the idea that professionalism and masculinity are indeed related. They also note that many of those men recruited went on to positions of management in a very much female-dominated world. It might be suggested, then, that this has aided the increasing bureaucratisation and managerialism of social work – in an attempt to heighten a masculine idea of professionalism and thus restore confidence in a beleaguered profession. Meagher and Parton (2003) also suggest that, despite these attempts, social work has never reached the kind of professional status enjoyed by, for example, medicine, but has remained a 'bureau-profession', with bureaucratic tasks and systems often characterising social work activity. So, a picture is emerging of social work as a managerial, bureaucratic, semi-profession, with 'profession' being defined in a masculine way. It is not unusual in social work education to meet students who believe that social workers need to be unemotional, detached, and logical – and who use 'professionalism' and 'professional boundaries' as terms for notions that encapsulate these requirements.

In contrast to this, Etzioni (1969), who first used the term 'semi-profession' to describe teaching, social work, and nursing, suggested that there should not be a need to aspire to full 'professionalism'. The idea that training is shorter, autonomy somewhat curtailed, and status lower should simply be accepted and absorbed as part of the semi-profession understanding. It is the absence of a properly recognised semi-profession niche (between blue-collar workers and the 'full' professions) that leads employees to seek the status of a 'full' professional. Notwithstanding Etzioni's argument, social work now has a longer period of higher-level education and a set of values in common, and it still aspires to real professionalism. It could also be suggested that accepting a semi-professional status with elements of less autonomy and shorter 'training' would very much suit the neoliberalisation of social work and would make reconnecting to social justice far more difficult. (See 'the rise of neoliberalism' in Chapter 3 for some thoughts on the neoliberalisation of social work education and how 'training' for tasks has been the direction in recent times.) A social work 'professionalism' is needed to properly enact our value base. (See Chapter 8 for a further discussion of professionalism.)

Consumerism

Evers (in Munday 2003) describes the next phase of social work development as consumerism. During this era, 'clients' became 'customers' and had more choice in the services they received. On the surface, this looks positive and in keeping with the promotion of values such as self-determination. Also, clear links can be seen between consumerism and its newest branding, 'personalisation'. In critiquing the ideology of consumerism, however, I. Ferguson (2008), whilst recognising the potential for stronger service-user voices in the provision of social work services, points out that the diversion of accountability (from service provision to assessment only), the imbalance of power when service users attempt to exercise their procedural rights, the involuntary status of many service users, and the increasingly high thresholds that people have to meet to qualify for services (unless they self-fund) conspire against the realisation of true consumerism. As for personalisation, I. Ferguson (2008, p80) points to the underlying neoliberal premise that encouraging lifestyle changes and independent agency should be the chosen method of solving social problems. The neoliberal abhorrence of dependency is the underpinning value of consumerism and personalisation, alongside the idea that everyone should be *able* to step up to independence and agency:

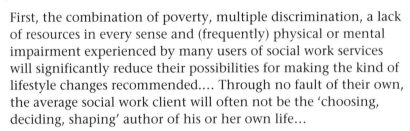

> First, the combination of poverty, multiple discrimination, a lack of resources in every sense and (frequently) physical or mental impairment experienced by many users of social work services will significantly reduce their possibilities for making the kind of lifestyle changes recommended.... Through no fault of their own, the average social work client will often not be the 'choosing, deciding, shaping' author of his or her own life...

The fact that we are all likely to be 'dependent' at some point in our lives for various periods of time has led to the suggestion that 'interdependent' be used as a less pejorative and more accurate term. The constant media and political barrage about the horrors of 'dependency' and 'the benefit culture' leads to the general promotion of the neoliberal idea that dependency is simply bad and that people must always take responsibility for their own circumstances. This can be experienced by service users 'not as empowering but as punitive' (ibid.). Once again, then, we see the persistence of a focus on the individual rather than on collective, structural issues.

Managerialism

As already mentioned, the 1980s saw the rise of New Public Management (or managerialism) and the import of private sector management techniques into the public sector (Barnard 2008). This involved increased emphasis on external measures of success, such as audits and key performance indicators, rather than internal (between the service user and worker); privatisation of services; preoccupation with efficiency and best value; and managers as decision-makers. Whether to start or end work with a service user was now determined by managers and via eligibility criteria. As Doel (2012, p37) states: 'The managerialist approach prioritises procedures and targets over professional values and standards and it stresses compliance and rule-governed behaviour rather than critical analysis and reflection.' It is interesting to refer back to Reamer and Shardlow's (2009) point that the codes of practice are managerial tools to encourage workers to follow the rules (see Chapter 1). As Ingram et al. (2014, p6) note: 'A critical analysis of the codes reveals that there is no mention of reflection: it is not a requirement that social workers in Northern Ireland, Wales and Scotland reflect, analyse or critically examine their practice.'

The era of case management saw the tendering of direct work to other, often private, agencies. Social workers became 'case managers' and did direct work less and less. Managerialism and the type of professionalism discussed earlier can be encapsulated in the vision of a suit-wearing social worker, carrying a briefcase and concerned with financial matters, thresholds, and commissioning services. Yes, communication skills are important here, but there would not appear to be much space for relationship building, helping, or tackling matters of injustice. The practice is efficient, well documented, procedural, and divorced from values. As Dustin (2006, p229) suggests, care managers require skills over and above existing traditional casework and communication skills, which she details as including: risk assessment skills; 'constructing a case' skills; skills in the use of management information systems; IT skills; management skills in terms of groups of service providers (rather than doing direct social work); and financial skills such as accounting. Within this set of new skills, theory was viewed by care managers as superfluous and, as Dustin states, 'practice was not theory-driven, but was instead driven by procedure.... this is consistent with the managerialism characteristic of current SSD [social services departments] organizations in the public sector'.

The above features of social work practice can still be easily recognised in the current landscape. Managerialism, therefore, is well and truly alive and, indeed, appears to be increasingly supplanting the core social work features of reflection and application of values.

Participationism

Personalisation and self-directed support are probably the strongest examples of participationism in the contemporary social work context. I. Ferguson (2008, p77) describes personalisation as 'the most recent development of consumerism within public services'. The critique of consumerism above, therefore, can also be applied to the personalisation phase – can people really be the 'choosing, deciding, shaping authors' of their own futures? Ferguson adds a caveat to this statement by reminding readers not to 'understate the resilience that many poor people exhibit in the face of oppression and material hardship' (ibid.), but his point stands that not every person can step up to independence quite as easily as others.

The participationism phase could be argued to employ a different 'smokescreen'. This time, there appears to be more choice, more empower-ment, and more self-determination for service users (very much supported by the codes of practice, see Chapter 1), which, it could be argued, serves to disguise massive cuts in provision of services, much higher thresholds to qualify for services, and organisations providing services for profit, leading to poorer care – 15 minutes per home-care visit, for example (BBC News 2013).

Lymbery (2014) identifies two lenses through which to view and under-stand personalisation and direct payments or self-directed support. One is what Evers (sec. 6.20, in Munday 2003; see table above) would describe as an 'orientation towards empowering users' or, in Lymbery's (2014, p299) terms, 'citizenship and rights'. In essence, this is a consequence of activists and pressure groups who do not want to be viewed as in need of services but rather as full citizens with equal rights, who require facilitation at some times and in some circumstances. Helping people to achieve full citi-zenship would, as Lymbery points out, require a commitment to resources that successive governments have failed to make. So, once again, we can see the effect of ever greater neoliberal squeezing of public fiscal resources, curtailing further and further hope of full citizenship and the realisation of rights. The other lens is what Lymbery (2014, p299) terms 'an extension of neoliberal political ideology' to encompass social work by supposedly helping people to act on their rights in the private marketplace. No longer should society be looking after people, but people should be helped to help themselves, thus minimising dependency on the state. Once again, Ferguson's scepticism about the ability of everyone to enact this is impor-tant to remember. So lack of real choices, choice-making being asked of people at a time when they might not have the personal resources to make those choices, extremely high thresholds to qualify for help, and the actual unlikelihood of choices being realised due to squeezed public services are the features that make up the view of personalisation through Lymbery's second lens.

Another theme to consider when thinking about participationism or personalisation is 'inclusiveness'. In order to take part in the participationist project, people need to be 'included'. The idea of social inclusion/exclusion became prominent with the rise of New Labour in the 1990s. As Levitas (2005) notes, however, the rhetoric around 'social exclusion' served to mask the true picture of divisions in our society. 'Social exclusion' creates a persuasive impression that there is really only one division of note – the one between the 'excluded' (benefit claimants, marginalised people, substance misusers, offenders, etc.) and the rest of us, the 'included'. Combine the idea of a group of 'socially excluded' people with a 'moral underclass discourse' (MUD), which is growing in strength (see Chapter 1), and we can quite clearly see the concept of an underclass forming. This is an idea that is then given credence by media reporting of lazy and feckless people on the dole. Yet another smokescreen is being employed here, because, as Levitas reminds us, there are further, and far more damaging, divisions in society. For example, the 'exclusive' group of super-rich at the top end of the economic hierarchy: financial and multinational company CEOs and institutions that 1) lose the country money in tax evasion; 2) have required bailouts from the tax payer; and 3) often employ people at the minimum wage, on zero-hour contracts, or in part-time or insecure employment. This division has disappeared within the 'included' category, where the exclusive remain hidden among ordinary, working people. Webb (2006) also points out that real inclusion means people having a decent standard of living, housing, comfort, opportunities, and so on, but suggests that the term has been narrowed down to mean 'employed' or included in the job market. The excluded are the feckless unemployed – there due to their own faults. Participation in many areas of life for people in the 'excluded' group is, as Ferguson notes, maybe far less easy than the rhetoric would suggest.

Participationism, then, is the final phase in Evers's framework of the development of social work, and it brings us right up to date and presents us with a partial picture of social work in the current context. It is suggested, however, that there are other important features of social work today, which can be described as 'individualism' and 'privatisation'.

Individualism

At the extreme end of individualism, social workers simply see individual service users as the architects of their own misfortune, usually because of poor behaviour that needs to be rectified. This neoliberal stance negates the influence of societal factors such as poverty, inequality, and oppression and requires social workers to simply focus on correcting the individual. As already pointed out in Chapter 1, younger social workers and social work students appear to be embracing this approach, perhaps because of a lack of awareness of an alternative paradigm, or perhaps because of an uninformed belief in a benign society with equal opportunities for everyone. This position is encouraged by the current government; for example in 2013, Michael Gove, the then education secretary, was reported in the *Telegraph* (2013) as follows:

> Social workers are abdicating their responsibility by viewing individuals as 'victims' of injustice rather than making them stand on their own two feet... Too many frontline social workers have been filled with 'idealistic' left-wing dogma that allows people from troubled backgrounds to 'make excuses' for their behaviour...

Here is a clear political and value position from the current government. We should be taking an extreme neoliberal view of service users: they are responsible for their own circumstances and we should not view them as victims. Presumably, Mr Gove wants social workers to ignore the fact that people have been significantly affected by society's deep divisions and accept that considering them as 'victims' of an unfair and unequal society is unhelpful to promoting improved behaviour. In a reply to Mr Gove, the social work academic community stated:

> Social work is an evidence-based profession, however. When highly respected research studies such as Wilkinson and Pickett's *The Spirit Level* show the extent to which inequality contributes to social problems – and even when a former Conservative prime minister laments the lack of social mobility in the UK – then social workers need to recognise this in their practice. The alternative is the kind of victim-blaming and scapegoating of poor and disabled people that too often characterises current government attacks on people on benefits.
>
> (*Guardian* 2013a)

Adopting Mr Gove's perspective, therefore, would mean believing that people who break the law, indulge in substance misuse, or are involved with social work due to safeguarding processes in relation to children or adults or family breakdown need to be dealt with by a tough social work force who will 'make them stand on their own two feet'. It follows that these deviants should also be punished harshly in order to deter future misbehaviour. Within this ideological stance the primary role of the state can be seen. Although much of the current picture is one where the state plays a decreasing role (privatisation of services, for example), in terms of law and order the role increases and strengthens – to deal with the increasing numbers of people who will not toe the line. So, as people have less and less of a stake in society and feel less and less connected or engaged, resultant symptoms such as crime, substance misuse, family breakdown, levels of imprisonment, and mental health problems increase (Wilkinson and Pickett 2010) and must be dealt with increasingly harshly. As Rogowski (2014) suggests, putting increasing responsibility on people for their own misdemeanours – which of course people must be responsible for, even whilst we recognise social and political context *has an effect* – means that an increasingly punitive response is required. Rogowski describes the role of the state as 'the "invisible hand" of deregulated labour markets, conjoined with the "iron fist" of a diversifying, expanding and increasingly intrusive penal apparatus' (Rogowski 2014, p8). Rather than viewing crime as a symptom of an unhealthy society – a view that would lead to efforts being made to restore the health of the society – the neo-liberal dogma is that crime is a choice made for rational actors' own ends. The correct response in *that* case is, therefore, harsher punishments. The idea that crime is among a plethora of symptoms created by an unequal, deeply divided, and unhealthy society (Wilkinson and Pickett 2010) will be explored in more detail in Chapter 3.

Privatisation

> Justice Secretary Chris Grayling said changes will help reduce reoffending. 'These reforms are all about changing lives. We cannot go on with a situation where thousands of prisoners are released onto the streets every year with no guidance or support, and are simply left to reoffend', Mr Grayling said. 'These reforms will transform the way in which we tackle reoffending.'
>
> (BBC 2014)

The passage quoted above is from a BBC report on the proposed privatisation of the Probation Service in England. The plans (which at the time of writing, March 2016, have largely gone into effect) were to sell off sections of the service to private companies, retaining only work with 'high risk' offenders within the nationalised service. It is interesting that Mr Grayling seems to imply that a private company would do a more thorough job of supervising offenders. It is not clear what the rationale for this might be when, as was pointed out earlier in this chapter, private companies undertaking personal care do a far more superficial and quick job in 15 minutes than their council-paid predecessors – presumably to cut costs, increase efficiency, and make profit for the company owners. Might the same not apply to those companies that win tenders for probation work? Also, if it *is* the case that private companies would do a better job, why leave high risk offenders in the, obviously shoddy and incompetent, hands of the probation service? The patent illogicality of the proposal adds weight to the suggestion that this is yet another example of the advancement of a neoliberal ideology. Where markets do not exist, they should be created (Doel 2012) as a matter of ideological principle and an opportunity for yet more money-making and profiteering.

Essentially, the Conservatives in the early 1990s introduced a shift away from councils providing social services to opportunities for the private sector to do much more of this. This privatisation of services led to social workers becoming managers of care packages and private companies providing services (I. Ferguson 2008). This increasingly privatised world has gained more and more ground, the Probation Service simply being the most recent example.

<table>
<tr>
<td rowspan="2">Exercise 2.1</td>
<td>

What influences my practice?

Think about the development of social work themes through time and think about the current picture. The influence of these developments and strands can still be felt to varying degrees in contemporary practice. Think about your own practice and the ethos of your agency – what influences from historical development or current context are experienced? If you are a student, think about your last Practice Learning Opportunity (PLO). What influences on the agency and on your own practice can you detect? Make some notes and reflect on why the agency has the characteristics it has. Why does your practice?

</td>
</tr>
</table>

Consequences of the Contemporary Context: Ethical Stress-Inducing Characteristics

This chapter has traced, in quite a simple and condensed way, the development of social work over its history. We have seen that 'managerialism, individualism, participationism, and privatisation' form the current ideological framework, and this section will now explore the influence of that ideology on daily social work practice and will suggest that the roots of ethical stress can be found in that influence. It should be acknowledged at this juncture, however, that there is a false reductionism in the binary 'old social work = good/new social work = bad' understanding of the development of social work. In tracing the different periods of social work, it is clear that there have been moralising, punitive, and controlling aspects throughout social work's history and, of course, there has always been bad practice. There will always be good practice too, and the suggestion being made is simply that the contemporary framework brings its own unique difficulties in undertaking 'good' value-based social work.

Weakening of the welfare state

An acquaintance from my village describes herself as a 'home help' and she is employed by our local council. The mostly elderly service users she visits have to pay a charge to the council for her services, and she bemoans the days when her services could be paid for by our taxes. She is about to be made redundant, and the people she works for are having to find, and pay for (or be given a budget for), their own services, which they will have to find in the private sector. Privatisation of care has taken hold. A good number of my acquaintance's service users have asked her to continue privately (they know her, trust her, and have a relationship with her), but she cannot do that without setting up her own business. She does not want to do this, cannot contemplate how she would do it, and sees it as an unrealistic option. The people she works for are despairing and worried about the future.

The public sector is receiving ever-reduced budgets and is being asked to make savings on the provision of services. Since the beginning of 'austerity measures', the local government budget has been cut by 31 billion pounds (Duffy 2014). Social work departments are, therefore, often short of staff; thresholds for services are constantly raised, so people making necessary but modest requests are turned down; councils are closing down care services or selling them off to the private sector; and councils are also cutting the financial contributions they make for voluntary sector services.

Ethical stress might be experienced, therefore, due to having to say 'no' to people in need who require services (see Practice Example 2.1); being unable to undertake preventative work of any kind due to lack of available staff and having to prioritise 'high risk' cases; witnessing the closure of voluntary-sector services people you work with rely on; witnessing older and vulnerable people losing their home-care services and having to grapple with complicated self-directed support measures (with the 'choice' often failing to materialise and the dawning awareness that real choice is illusory); and feeling helpless in the face of people asking for help and there being no resources with which to actually help. Preston-Shoot (2003, p10) notes that social workers 'reported "demoralisation and disillusionment" because they felt "unable to uphold the knowledge base and values of a competent professional"'.

At the same time as the developments above impact on social work, benefits are being cut, plunging more and more people into further poverty. By 2015–16, benefits were cut by 15.6 billion pounds. Cuts have been felt most keenly by people already in poverty, disabled people in poverty, and people who need social care help (Duffy 2014). Even as people are plunged further into poverty, the attitudes towards poor people that hardened in recent decades remain the same (JRF 2014; Chapter 3 will explore this further). Might a worker feel ethical stress due to these politically driven benefit cuts? There may be times when workers see people they work with battling against adversity and yet getting less and less money, and this would be extremely hard to bear. It is unlikely that social workers who *know* the service users and know the reality of their lives would feel that the cuts and increasing financial hardship were 'deserved' by anyone they worked with. Witnessing the reality of the effects of these policy decisions might well be difficult to tolerate. At the same time, being thwarted in trying to help, unable to obtain money or assistance, and powerless to alleviate circumstances might lead to deeply felt ethical stress.

So, the weakening of the welfare state, including the availability of much-needed supports and services and the further impoverishment of people they work with, might indeed see social workers experiencing ethical stress and feeling hopeless in the face of such political brutality.

The compliance culture

In the new neoliberal world, against a backdrop of managerialism, individualism, participationism, and privatisation, social work becomes more and more concerned with getting people to comply with defined courses of action. So, for example, the young man 'Tony' involved with criminal justice social work in Scotland states that 'a lot of the boys just do the programmes...' (*The Road from Crime* 2012). External measures of success – key performance indicators (KPIs), for example – will measure completion rates and attendance figures for the programmes, but service users' voices saying that they do not *help* are not really listened to. Other programmes in criminal justice social work such as 'Constructs' are often mandatory for service users and yet are evaluated as having patchy and inconclusive benefits (CJDCS 2009). Once again, however, KPIs will measure external factors such as completion and social workers will be designated as referrers or group workers, with little time or space for individual helping or welfare work. Indeed a study in this field found that social workers *did* feel ethical stress when the agency did not allow time for individual work beyond group work and bureaucratic tasks. Interestingly, however, the actual emphasis on group work did not cause workers ethical stress as they saw it uncritically as necessary and the right thing to do (Fenton 2014a). This is a similar view to the one taken by the social work student doing an unquestioned and necessary unannounced home visit in Chapter 1. No ethical stress results, because the task simply has to be done, and the social work job is to do it. Interestingly, in the study social workers saw lack of time to do the relationship-based work they wanted to do as a practical and technical issue rather than an ethical one. And younger workers were more likely to see it as a technical matter and less likely to experience ethical stress as a result (Fenton 2014b). Banks (2012, p20) suggests that 'what is regarded as a technical matter for one person (simply applying the rules) may be an ethical problem for another'. In the study, the younger workers were the ones who did not define the issues as ethical. Once again, it can be suggested that social work education needs to highlight and promote critical thinking beyond simply doing the task and to encourage students to question procedures, assumptions, and the way people are treated and experience social work. If this can be achieved, perhaps younger workers and students would begin to experience ethical stress to a greater extent and to use it as a guide. In the absence of this critical thinking, social workers become part of the 'strong and authoritative' (Parton 2014, p22) state, with enforcement as their primary aim.

Preoccupation with risk assessment and management

Fenton's (2014a) study of ethical stress among criminal justice social workers in Scotland found that ethical stress was significantly related to perceptions of how risk averse the worker's agency was perceived to be. Social workers wanted to be 'allowed' the freedom to use judgement and not be completely rule-bound by the formal tools and processes of risk assessment. Ethical stress was reduced when workers felt they had this flexibility, and they made comments such as:

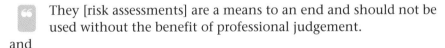 They [risk assessments] are a means to an end and should not be used without the benefit of professional judgement.

and

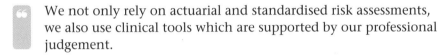 We not only rely on actuarial and standardised risk assessments, we also use clinical tools which are supported by our professional judgement.

However, as stated above, there were many cases where social workers perceived their agencies to be very risk averse, and this resulted in the social workers experiencing ethical stress. So, why is it that within a context of managerialism, individualism, participationism, and privatisation, social work in all fields has become so preoccupied with risk? Beck (1992) suggests that we now have what he terms a 'risk society' where people are preoccupied with risk, and especially with protection from future risk. Furedi (1997) calls this a 'culture of fear' and cites our obsession with risks associated with lifestyle, health, and dangers caused by other people as examples of this. Much has also been written about the public's distorted view of risk – we tend to think risks are far greater than they actually are, due to constant media attention and preoccupation with risk (*Independent* 2013). I. Ferguson (2008) points out that many genuinely serious risks have actually come about as a result of neoliberalism's overarching concern with wealth creation – global warming as a result of huge industrialisation and companies' refusal to take eco-measures (and governments' refusal to insist on this), for example.

Factors causing ethical stress

In her study of criminal justice social workers in four local authorities in Scotland, Fenton (2014a) undertook a quantitative analysis of the relationship between features of contemporary social work and the experience of ethical stress. She found that the more risk averse the approach to social work and the more 'value empty' the ethical climate of the agency, the more significant the experience of ethical stress for workers. In other words, the *neoliberal* characterisation of the agency affected workers' feelings of ethical stress.

So, against a backdrop of increasing preoccupation with risk, social work has itself become increasingly concerned with risk minimisation and risk management. Banks (2012) points out that social work's reliance on tools and procedures and the idea that social work can always make the right decision, lead to social workers being blamed when decisions result in poor outcomes. She stresses that even good decisions can have extremely bad outcomes, because social work decisions are so often the choice between two unwelcome courses of action. As the blame culture persists, so does the temptation to adopt defensive and risk-averse practices – usually implemented in a managerial way and for the protection of the agency. Social workers need to demonstrate they have done everything 'properly' just in case something goes wrong. Although it would be understandable if social workers found that approach quite comfortable, Fenton (2014a) shows that defensive, risk-averse agency cultures often cause social workers to experience ethical stress, as described above.

Once again, the influence of individualism can be seen. If societal problems and causes of social problems are ignored, the only legitimate target for social work efforts is individual behaviour. If a person is posing a risk, the behaviour must be controlled and managed. Understanding the behaviour – listening to what the service user has to say and employing empathy and compassion – is de-prioritised. The social worker is only concerned with assessing risks and then managing the behaviour.

This narrow, risk-prioritised version of social work will also grow in strength as inequality within our society increases. As Wilkinson and Pickett (2010) demonstrate, levels of trust between people diminish with increasing inequality. Thus, people in higher positions in the social status hierarchy look down on, and fear, the people further down the hierarchy and want them to be managed and controlled as much as possible. There is resonance here with the fears about the masses experienced in Victorian times! Couple this to evidence from the Joseph Rowntree Foundation that attitudes to poor people are hardening (JRF 2014) and the level of scrutiny brought to bear on the risk practices of social work agencies becomes increasingly understandable.

In summary, then, social workers exist in a blame culture (which is part of a risk society) where managerialism has taken hold and created rigid procedures and processes for risk assessment and management that leave little room for responsivity or relationship-based practice. The resultant rigid practice has been shown to cause ethical stress for social workers. In fact, it might be said that it takes courage and sometimes defiance to withstand said culture. For example, Sawyer (2009) interviewed mental health social workers in Australia about their perceptions of risk assessment and management. One worker gave the example of a suicidal service user whose dog had to be euthanised. The service user had previously commented that the dog's impending death would bring on suicidal feelings, but asked the worker for some time alone to say goodbye to his dog. The worker, undoubtedly feeling anxious, agreed with the request because she felt it was the right thing to do and stated 'I felt confident enough to say "I'm going to take the risk"' (Sawyer 2009, p454). Had the worker, out of risk aversion driven by fear of something going wrong and getting into 'trouble' or because of a restrictive policy, not given the service user time with his dog, she might well have gone on to experience (unhealthy) ethical stress though less (healthy) anxiety. It is also apparent that the worker required confidence to 'take the risk' and to resist the dominant culture. Another social worker felt obliged to ignore a policy that workers should not engage with any service user who is intoxicated. The social worker felt that the policy was excessively risk averse and did not allow for individual circumstances, the worker's knowledge of and relationship with the service user, and the service user's vulnerability. When faced with this situation, the choice for this particular worker would appear to be: follow the procedure and live with the ethical stress of not having 'helped' when he felt he needed and wanted to help; or ignore the policy (and risk himself and his job) and act in accordance with his values and conscience and help the service user. The worker consistently chose the latter. A policy that controls workers and situations in such a managerial and homogenising way may well put workers in the most difficult position, and this worker chose active resistance at his own expense. Should something go wrong, the worker would shoulder the full weight of 'blame' and the agency would be exempt, able to say that the worker should have followed the policy. On the other hand, the worker, knowing the service user, simply could not leave him/her to suffer or be in danger. This serves to illustrate the strength of the toxic nature of ethical stress and the lengths that some people will go to avoid it and do what they feel is 'right'.

Gate-keeping

Privatisation and a shrinking welfare state have led to high thresholds for people in need to obtain services funded by the local authority. Preston-Shoot (2003) found that one consequence of very high thresholds and the inability to grant requests for modest help was 'internalised oppression' (Preston-Shoot 2003, p12). In other words, workers felt that any attempts to relieve the hardship of service users' lives were futile, so why should they continue to try? Preston-Shoot considered this to be a 'resigned accept-ance' (ibid.), a state of mind that might well be a consequence of long-term ethical stress; a method, albeit an unhealthy one, of coping.

As mentioned earlier, Dustin (2006) points out that care managers require 'new' skills, often accountancy and managerial, over and above traditional social work skills. Overall it seems that procedures drive out theory in the practice of care management. Care managers are working out ways to 'construct a case' for the people they work with, to obtain services in increasingly tight budgetary organisations. They are also prioritising procedural methods of working and turning less and less to theory. As a consequence of these developments, social workers are becoming resign-edly accepting (Preston-Shoot 2003) or extremely unhappy and disillu-sioned (C. Jones 2001). Ethical stress abounds.

Crisis response rather than prevention

Munro (2011) in her review of child protection in England strongly advo-cates for a change in culture from a crisis 'protection'-focused service to one that emphasises prevention and early help. At the moment, however, there is very little space and time for prevention and help before things reach crisis; that is, when the risk to children becomes so high that statutory measures might well be required, and workers are immediately thrust into the territory of risk assessment and management – with the potential for risk aversion and ethical stress that such measures bring. In addition, because voluntary agencies are subject to funding cuts, referrals to those agencies that might have undertaken 'preventative' work are becoming a less available choice.

As a result of the austerity cuts to public funding, social workers have more and more to do and, of necessity, their caseloads become heavy with child protection/crisis cases, and preventative work is again thwarted. C. Jones (2001) points out that, because of increasing inequality and poverty, service users are more troubled and distressed than before, but there is less help. Caseloads are therefore full of heavy-end cases, service users feel hopeless, and rehabilitation and prevention efforts have gone. Even when social workers are inclined to help and want to do so, their efforts are often thwarted and ethical stress might well result.

Agency culture

Finally, Fenton (2014a) demonstrates that the ethical climate, or culture, of the agency significantly affects workers' experience of ethical stress. C. Jones (2001) and Preston-Shoot (2003) also make reference to this in their discussions of managerialism, restrictive micro-management, and lack of resources. On a smaller scale, Fenton suggests that discussion in the office (addressing values or ignoring them?), supervision, decision-making, and workload issues could all play a part in causing or reducing ethical stress. So, even the impact of the wider policy issues can be either ameliorated somewhat or exacerbated by the aspects of the agency culture experienced daily by workers. The first-line manager has been found to play a key role in terms of what kinds of discussion go on, what 'basic underlying assumptions' (Schein 2010) underpin the agency values, and what kind of supervision is on offer. All of these factors significantly affect the experience of social workers and, of course, are elements of the social work context that can be affected by the people who work in the agency. It is, perhaps, in this closer environment where social workers can make a difference and can withstand some of the effects of neoliberalism.

Schein (2010) advocates for an analysis of workplace culture. He defines three levels of culture, which can be seen in the illustration below. Thinking about these different levels, we can perhaps identify where and how social workers can make a difference:

Schein's (2010) three levels of culture:

1. Artifacts
- Visible and feel-able structures and processes
- Observed behaviour

– Difficult to decipher

2. Espoused beliefs and values
- Ideals, goals, values, aspirations
- Ideologies
- Rationalisations

– May or may not be congruent with behaviour
and other artifacts

3. Basic underlying assumptions
- Unconscious, taken-for-granted beliefs and values

– Determine behaviour, perception, thought, and feeling
(Schein 2010, p24)

Espoused values are most often the rhetoric around social work values. However, if underlying assumptions are actually neoliberal and punitive values are held by the first-line manager as well as by team members, then social work values will remain as rhetoric only – actually living them will be difficult if not impossible. The true underlying basic assumptions will translate into neoliberal, punitive, and managerial practice as already discussed. However, this internal culture, whilst not impacting on the wider social work context, can be subject to influence if enough workers and first-line managers have a real belief in social work values and have under-pinning basic assumptions in tune with them. For example, Kosny and Eakin (2008) studied three not-for-profit agencies in Canada that worked with socially excluded groups of people. The 'mission' of the agencies and the underlying basic assumptions were very much in tune – the agency's philosophy, and that of the workers therein, held that people on the margins of society were victims of an unjust and harsh society. They did not 'blame' the service users for their predicament but, rather, understood their situations with real compassion and empathy. Workers in these agencies reported very little ethical stress, even though resources were difficult to come by and financial restrictions made helping very difficult. Could this, then, transfer to statutory social work in the UK? The wider context would still be characterised by procedures, tight budgets, and managerial practice, *but* if the agency culture was aware of and resistant to that, if social workers were encouraged to help service users stand up to that context, and if service users were viewed as victims of an unfair society, would that ameliorate ethical stress for workers? Would they feel that they were on 'the same side' as the service users and helping them with their daily struggles? The workers in Jones's and Preston-Shoot's studies above might have had very different experiences if the culture of the agencies within which they worked had been akin to that of the agencies in Kosny and Eakin's study.

All of the above is well and good, and quite hopeful, *but* depends completely on workers and first-line managers sharing radical underpinning assumptions. Once again, social work education needs to find a way to bring the importance of this home to the new workers of tomorrow.

2.1 Gate-keeping resources

practice example

A care manager wants to provide an older couple with a new walk-in shower so that the elderly man can continue to help his disabled wife with personal care. At the current time he is using a bucket to wash her. The care manager has been told the couple are not priority and there is no funding for the structural work that would have to be done. The couple simply do not meet the high threshold for services. The care manager experiences considerable ethical stress in this situation and feels that her values are completely at odds with her next task, which is to return and tell the couple she cannot help them.

Exercise 2.2

Look back at the contemporary features of a neoliberal ideology. Can you identify any of these features in Practice Example 2.1? Go through them individually and try to locate them within the example.

Developing a Political Standpoint

Hopefully, this chapter will have helped readers to identify and understand some of the neoliberal features of contemporary social work practice. This understanding means that some aspects of social work that might have otherwise been taken for granted as 'just the way things are' can be analysed and critiqued from a more informed position. Why is it so important that social workers and social work students can do this? Why is it so important that they, in Sheedy's (2013, p5) words, develop a 'world view'? Well, as Sheedy states:

> The way in which we construct people's problems and the solutions we offer through our professional interventions will largely depend on our view of how the world we live in operates... we should at least develop a clear idea of how we think society operates to gain a fuller understanding of the aetiology of the problems faced by the service users and their lived experiences.
>
> (ibid.)

Social workers need to understand that shifts in our society have made life more difficult for service users. The absence of that understanding might lead to an uncritical acceptance of how things are, to an increasingly punitive and judgemental response on an individual interaction level, and to a further disconnection from social work values. The presence of that understanding, on the other hand, should lead to an increasing experience of ethical stress, the recognition of that ethical stress as a legitimate and useful feeling, and a consequent impetus for questioning the status quo and taking action.

stop and think

The practice example just given in this chapter raises other ethical tensions. When the worker returns to the couple to give the bad news, does she:

- Blame the system?

- Blame her manager or the panel that made the decision?

- Defend the decision out of loyalty to her agency, 'pretending' she agrees?

What if the culture is one that demands that type of loyalty (Preston-Shoot 2003)?

main points

- Social work has changed over time and is shaped by the prevailing socio-political context within which it operates.

- The contemporary context is characterised by managerialism, individualism, participationism, and privatisation.

- Ethical stress may be generated by these features of contemporary social work.

- In particular, a weakened welfare state, an emphasis on compliance, a preoccupation with risk, gate-keeping resources, and a crisis- rather than prevention-driven service may all generate ethical stress for workers.

- From an increased understanding of the current, complex picture of social work and its developments over time, readers should be able to come to a political awareness and standpoint.

taking it further

- Bailey, R. and Brake, M. (Eds) (1975) *Radical Social Work* (London: Edward Arnold). A classic collection of essays discussing radical social work. Still very relevant.
- Fenton, J. (2014a) 'An analysis of "ethical stress" in criminal justice social work in Scotland: The place of values', *British Journal of Social Work*, 10.1093/bjsw/bcu032. A study exploring which features of contemporary social work might contribute to ethical stress.
- Munro, E. (2011) *The Munro Review of Child Protection: Final Report* (London: TSO). A key report on the future of child protection which highlights the features discussed in this chapter, including proce- dures, risk preoccupation, and lack of autonomy for social workers.

3 Them and Us

Overview

This chapter explores why neoliberalism might, in fact, be acceptable to social workers and students. In what way might social workers absorb the principles of neoliberalism uncritically and unquestioningly and, thus, avoid the important experience of ethical stress? The chapter will also look at some of the ways in which the public are convinced that the neoliberal world view is the correct one and will help students and social workers critique the perceived 'common sense'.

The previous chapter explored the ethical stress-inducing features of the contemporary social work landscape and highlighted the importance of social workers developing a 'world view' and an understanding of the effects of neoliberalism on their work and on service users. However, the point was also made in the preceding chapters that younger social workers and social work students might experience less ethical stress than their older colleagues, as they may be far more uncritically accepting of neoliberalism. They may find the neoliberal 'version' of social work a reasonably comfortable one. This chapter will explore why that might be and will help readers understand why social work practice may be becoming increasingly congruent with Michael Gove's vision whereby social workers 'make' service users 'stand on their own two feet' and stop them making 'excuses for their behaviour' (*Telegraph* 2013).

A Very Brief Economic History

A recurring theme in this book is that younger workers steeped in '30 years of neoliberalism' are, as a consequence, more accepting of neoliberal social work. To explore this issue further it is important to contextualise those 30 years. What came before neoliberalism? What happened to bring it about? Economics is perhaps not a subject of great interest to social workers, so this section will attempt to outline in a relatively easy way economic changes from World War II onwards. This will illuminate, for younger workers and students, the economic philosophy their older colleagues grew up with and will highlight that things have not always been the way they are now.

World War II

Prior to World War II, during the 1920s, a global economic depression occurred. The economic framework of the time was a traditional liberal one comprising very little state intervention and unregulated property and wealth accumulation rights (Crouch 2011). This meant that factories and industries were controlled by a very small but extremely powerful property-owning class, upon whom workers were completely dependent and to whom they were generally subservient. In the absence of financial protection from unemployment, no free health care, or any other 'safety net', people had to work for extremely low pay (to maximise financial profit for the owners) or literally starve. This unhappy situation was changing, however, as ordinary working people increasingly began to seek rights and liberty from their employers. At the same time, socialist thinking was gathering strength (Garner, Ferdinand, and Lawson 2009) with the aim of contesting capitalist power and property ownership. Both thinkers and workers looked to the state to play a role in changing things, and moves began to be made towards universal suffrage. The wealthy ownership class very much feared the emergence of democracy, because if the working class had voting rights, the old order that so privileged their interests would certainly be dismantled.

After World War II, things changed dramatically, but the old liberal ideas did not disappear, as the ideology of unregulated money-making, property ownership, and low taxes remained extremely appealing to the very wealthy. The ideas did retreat, however, and might be said to have remained waiting in the wings...

Keynesian economics

After World War II there emerged a new political and economic framework called 'social democracy' (Crouch 2011). This was a compromise centre-left form of governance where private ownership of business and property was accepted but was regulated by the state. The state played an important role in protecting people from fluctuations in the market by, for example, investing to keep unemployment low. The basis of the economic philosophy was:

> Confident, secure working-class consumers, far from being a threat to capitalism, could enable an expansion of markets and profits on an unprecedented scale. Capitalism and democracy became interdependent.

(Crouch 2011, p11)

The new economic framework was known as 'Keynesian demand management' (ibid.) after the British economist John Maynard Keynes. In essence, when the country performed poorly economically, the government would borrow money to invest (to prevent redundancies or cuts in wages, for example) and would then pay back their debts when the country was performing well. This was a benevolent form of governance that protected people from the ruthlessness of a purely market-driven system.

At the same time, a system of national insurance, welfare, national health service, and universal employment emerged as part of an overarching philosophy that saw the government as having the duty to ensure that every person in the country had a decent minimum standard of living (Turbett 2014). This is very important, because the interpretation of that philosophy is that people had a *right* to a minimum standard of financial security, housing, health care, education, etc. – the elements that make up a decent standard of living. Also it is of note that this applied to everyone; whether working or not, everyone had a right to those basic resources.

This very positive and inclusive state of affairs lasted until the 1970s, when the economic crisis caused by rising oil prices uncovered Keynesian demand management's weakness.

What happened?

The UK form of Keynesian demand management, unlike that of some countries, was weak on neo-corporate industrial relations (Crouch 2011). In other words, there were no agreements about negotiations between unions and owners such that workers would not take action or make demands that would contribute to inflation. So, when the oil crisis hit, unions did demand more money in line with increasing inflation, which brought further economic problems. This is where the mantra of the right that the 'unions were far too strong' in 1970s Britain has its roots, and where Margaret Thatcher was able to garner support for the crushing measures she took when dealing with the unions.

The response to the above problem, then, was not to make changes to the Keynesian philosophy that had served the country well but to completely abandon it in favour of a new version of that old liberal ideology that had been waiting just off stage.

The rise of neoliberalism

According to I. Ferguson (2008) the above crisis led to three main outcomes: 1) mass unemployment; 2) cuts in public spending; and 3) Keynesianism replaced by monetarism, the precursor to neoliberalism. In short, the resurgence of a free market economy. Low taxes, unregulated accumulation of capital and property, and disempowered unions and curtailment of workers' rights all resurfaced, much to the delight of the wealthiest in the country.

The promise of neoliberalism was that the prioritisation of wealth creation would benefit everyone, as said wealth would 'trickle down' from the richest to the poorest (I. Ferguson 2008). Looking at the picture today, that simply has not happened. The country embraced neoliberalism 30 years ago and it is still very strong today, with very little political opposition up until recently, even from traditional opponents such as the Labour Party who, via 'third way' policies, had shifted to the right and were also characterised by neoliberal philosophy until Jeremy Corbyn won leadership of the party in September 2015. Corbyn and his supporters (inside and outside the party) are now mounting a vigorous challenge to the neoliberalism of so-called New Labour. See Chapter 1 for a definition of neoliberalism.

Garrett (2010, p350) explains how neoliberal hegemony has subsumed social work practice by the injection of more vocational, practical training in social work education, alongside a de-prioritisation of critical, social science education and a tightened, more regulated curriculum. Garrett suggests that these shifts have had the aim of producing neoliberal social workers who have the 'correct' mind-set to carry out social work tasks or to 'prepare students for the reality of becoming a social worker'. Garrett concludes by suggesting that social work education does not, adequately, help student social workers to critically understand the neoliberal context in which they will operate; thus, neoliberal 'common sense' social work is perpetuated:

> Since the 1970s the neoliberal project to define social work's essence and thematic boundaries has been reflected in the constant to shape and mould its dominant perspectives, ways of *thinking* and *acting*. Nevertheless, within the field of social work education there has been, on the whole, a failure to see this 'bigger picture'. Consequently, there appears to have been an inability to grasp how, oftentimes, even the micro and molecular can, although seemingly lacking any pattern of association and connecting threads, be rooted in more structurally embedded neoliberal shaping mechanisms.
>
> (Garrett 2010, p352)

This book should be utilised by readers to help understand that very thing – the *patterns* of social work daily practice that are unrecognised in their connections to, and perpetuation of, neoliberal hegemony.

Return to Chapter 2 and trace the different periods of social work history – can you map the different phases against the economic changes above? Doing so will give you a real understanding of the links between economics and social work.

Hopefully, by this point, the reader will understand more about neoliberal economics and ideology. This is the ideology to which many younger people know of no alternative. So, in addition to the persistence and dominance of that economic ideology and its links to the contemporary context of social work (see Chapter 2: managerialism, individualism, participationism, and privatisation), how else might people be influenced to unquestioningly accept neoliberalism as the 'common sense' truth?

The Underclass

In 1990 the American sociologist Charles Murray wrote about the 'emerging British underclass' (Murray 1990). In his book he very clearly outlines his premise that there is an underclass in Britain who are unemployed, criminal, dropping out, neglectful of their children, and predominantly single parents or the product of single-parent households. The picture he paints is of a nasty rabble whose behaviour is the only factor in causing the raft of social problems that coexist in these 'underclass' communities. Completely congruent with neoliberal thinking, the social problems in these communities are exaggerated and generalised, then blamed on the behaviour, lifestyles, and characteristics of individual people. Of course, once this interpretation of the situation is accepted, the logical response is to target and punish the individuals concerned in an attempt to change the perceived root causes – the bad behaviour and poor lifestyle choices. As Tyler states in relation to how Nicolas Sarkozy referred to the disaffected young people in the areas of urban degradation in France: 'racaille...infinitely more pejorative than "scum"...characterizing an entire group of people as subhuman, inherently evil and criminal, worthless' (Tyler 2013, p38).

So, how are some groups of people, often the traditional recipients of social work services, portrayed? How have the public become convinced that the neoliberal view of these populations is the correct one?

Poor people and chavs

In his influential text *Chavs: The Demonization of the Working Class*, O. Jones (2011) very eloquently describes how notions of the traditional 'working class' have been replaced by a caricature of an underclass – the caricature of the 'chav'. Jones outlines very clearly how there has been a shift from a shared understanding about collective and societal notions of responsibility for social problems to a very much individual one, as already covered. The political message that people are simply responsible for their own behaviour and poverty was promoted with an incredible amount of force, as illustrated by Margaret Thatcher's famous comment in an interview with *Woman's Own*: 'There is no such thing as society' (*Guardian* 2013b, np). Even more direct is her summing up of the problem of poverty in an interview with the *Catholic Herald* in 1978:

> Nowadays there really is no primary poverty left in this country.... In western countries we are left with the problems which aren't poverty. All right there might be poverty because they don't know how to budget, don't know how to spend their earnings, but now you are left with really hard fundamental character-personality defect.
>
> (*Catholic Herald* 1978, np)

The nub of this matter, then, is the claim that there is no poverty in the UK. This is something that, as a social work educator, I hear students ask – 'How can service users be poor? They all have brand name trainers for their kids/flat screen TVs/phones/money for cigarettes and alcohol, etc.' It is important that we address this, otherwise the Thatcher philosophy above does indeed seem to make sense...

Relative poverty is defined by the European Union as 60 per cent less than the median income of the country (JRF nd, a). Absolute poverty (which Margaret Thatcher is using as her definition when she says there is no 'primary poverty' in the UK) is defined as when people do not have enough of the basics to survive, for example shelter, food, and warmth (JRF nd, a). So, in some ways Margaret Thatcher is right about that – there are shelters and food kitchens for the very poorest and homeless people among us, and it is unlikely people would be allowed to starve on the streets. Resurrecting the absolute measure as *the* measure of poverty has had some support from conservatives over the years. For example, expressing a common view held by the Conservative Party in the 1980s, John Moore, the then social security secretary, stated that what the

> [r]elative definition of poverty amounts to in the end...is that however rich a society, it will drag the incubus of relative poverty with it up the income scale. The poverty lobby would find poverty in paradise.
>
> (Lansley and Mack 2015, p10)

John Moore wanted a return to accepting absolute poverty as the true measure and thus recognising that capitalism had actually wiped out the 'stark want of Victorian Britain' (ibid.). The idea he is expressing, that how wealthy a country is does not matter because the relative poverty line moves up with increasing overall wealth (so that the poor will always be identified as such), is actually a misunderstanding of the maths involved. The measure is 60 per cent of the median (not the average), that is, the mid-point person if everyone was lined up in order of income. So, if wealth increased across people at the bottom of the scale, they would still be lined up in the same way but would simply *not* be 60 per cent less than the median (Lansley and Mack 2015). So it is perfectly possible to wipe out relative poverty, but it would depend on increasing equality and improving the circumstances of the poorest in the county. If we were to go along with John Moore's idea that absolute measures are more useful, then we are simply agreeing that 'those on low incomes [do] not have a right to participate fully in growing prosperity' (Lansley and Mack 2015, p11). The issue is an ethical and moral one: in a wealthy country, should we tolerate huge disparities in wealth to the extent that so many people are excluded from being able to take part in 'normal' family life, when the richest in the country continue to accumulate more and more wealth?

Thinking back to Chapter 1 and the central idea of this book that our working definition of social justice is a radical one, it can easily be seen that to adhere to that value position, social workers must understand these ideas and support moves towards a fairer distribution of resources and wealth. In defence of this radical position, let me point out that some of the effects of the individualistic neoliberal policies over the last years have led to the number of people unable to heat their homes adequately doubling between 1983 and 2012 and the proportion of households unable to afford the most basic necessities also rising (Lansley and Mack 2015). As the country gets richer, is that acceptable?

What, then, of the outward signs of lack of poverty as pointed out by some students? The trainers for the kids, the phones, etc? There are three main points that are worthy of consideration when trying to understand what is going on here. The first is the impact of inequality (see later in this chapter). However, suffice it to say at this point in the discussion that there is overwhelming evidence that the psychological impact of inequality includes a pressure for people to *demonstrate* their position on the status hierarchy – which, of course, becomes steeper and more oppressive the more unequal the country is (Wilkinson and Pickett 2010). The urge to 'keep up with the Joneses' or at least to protect yourself and your family from material shaming is extremely powerful – think of the 'pester power' of children, or how parents feel if their children do not have the types of items their friends do, or how powerful advertisers inform us we need to have things if we are successful human beings.

Secondly, neoliberalism has an answer to the tension between feeling the pressure to buy things and the lack of money – credit and the deregulation of banks to allow them to lend money prolifically and make profits on interest (McKaskill 2010). It is well known that household debt has increased over the last decade, and this can be explained somewhat by the facts that unscrupulous lenders are lending to vulnerable people and imposing punitive and expensive sanctions, that there are links between debt and mental ill health, that debt is incurred after family breakdown or because of people moving in and out of low-paid jobs and having benefit payments delayed (JRF 2010). In essence, debt is due to inadequate income rather than over-consumerism (ibid.). So, the focus or 'blame' for borrowing too much should be on inadequacy of income as a priority, with an understanding also of the pressure to buy things in a very unequal and competitive society.

Thirdly, it is worth attending to the other aspect of the students' questions about so-called poor people always having money for their cigarettes and booze. We must keep in mind that these accusations are fuelled and exaggerated by media with a vested interest in keeping neoliberal thinking alive (as it profits huge businesses like many of our media companies), so stories about benefit scroungers, lounging around and smoking and drinking when we are all working hard, abound. These isolated examples are *not* typical of people on benefits (see next section). However, many of the families with whom social workers are involved do, for example, smoke, and it's very easy to think that if only parents were more caring, sensible, and selfless they would spend that cigarette money on their children. Linda Tirado (2014) in her book *Hand to Mouth* helps us understand that. It is tempting from a position of comfort – and most social workers are in that position – to criticise lack of long-term planning or making poor choices. However, Tirado points out that when life is grim and a struggle, poorer people use the same coping strategies as wealthier people and find them just as addictive. She sums up her smoking habit as follows:

> Unless you're prepared to convince me that smoking, and smoking alone, keeps me poor then, please, spare me the lecture. I know it's bad for me. I'm addicted, not addled. There are reasons that I smoke and they're reasonable ones. They keep me awake, they keep me going. Do they poison my lungs and increase my chances of getting cancer? Obviously. Does that stop me? No, because the cost-benefit analysis isn't a simple *I like it* versus *I'll live longer*, it's *I will be able to tolerate more* versus *I will perpetually sort of want to punch someone.*
>
> (Tirado 2014, p 82)

Tirado also notes that it's difficult, when living in poverty, to make healthy sensible plans for the future. Life is hard, so grabbing moments of pleasure or relief when you can seems far more important than planning for a future that holds no joy anyway. Another interesting point to think about is that poor people's coping strategies (smoking and drinking for example) are no different from richer people's strategies. It's just that, as Tirado says, 'Once you take a penny from the government, a morality clause goes into effect where you are not allowed to have anything that you might actually enjoy. It's the hair shirt of welfarism' (ibid., p84). She asks readers to consider the handouts from the government to the banks and the millions lost in tax evasion. Tirado's point is that, once again, neoliberal thinking justifies taking a punitive and moralistic view of the coping strategies of poor people, whilst defending the rights of the property-owning classes to behave in the same ways.

Understanding and empathising with Tirado's point of view is perhaps the first step to understanding some of our service users more and blaming them less.

Work-shy scroungers on benefits

In terms of unemployment and lack of opportunities, 'the communities that suffer the most are the biggest victims of the class war unleashed by Thatcherism' (O. Jones 2011, p195). Jones outlines the decimation of many working-class communities when Margaret Thatcher's government closed heavy industries, destroying whole communities in terms of identity, employment, community, and pride. Jones suggests, however, that this is absolutely downplayed in the rhetoric around what is wrong with Britain. The 'chav' caricature is encouraged to obscure the idea that the destruction of communities and lack of work have clearly had an effect of the social problems within those communities, in favour of an interpretation involving teenagers pushing prams and swearing, feckless unemployed adults, and drug users – *they* need to change their behaviour and take responsibility for the social damage that was done to their communities! The politicians are really asking something that is impossible for people to achieve, and they are blamed when they fail. Again, how fair is that? Also inaccurate is the assumption that people languish on benefits for years (living a life of relative luxury?). It is clear from patterns of claiming that unemployed men and women are much more likely to be moving in and out of poorly paid, insecure work and spending periods of time on benefit between periods of work (O. Jones 2011).

The caricature is further perpetuated by untrue headlines such as: 'Behind the statistics lie households where three generations have never had a job' (former Prime Minister Blair 1997, in R. MacDonald 2015); and 'on some deprived estates...often three generations of the same family have never worked' (Iain Duncan Smith 2009, former minister for work and pensions, in R. MacDonald 2015).

When R. MacDonald investigated these claims, and many more like them, he found no statistics to support them, even although they have become a particularly strong image in today's thinking. Duncan Smith stated that his statements were based on 'personal observations'. MacDonald and his team of researchers were unable to find any families who fitted the 'three generations' label. They also drew on the best secondary statistical evidence available and concluded that 'less than half of one per cent of workless households in the UK might have two generations when no one ever had a job. Households with three generations that have never worked are, logically, going to be far, far fewer in number than even this tiny fraction' (R. MacDonald 2015, np). It seems to be without doubt that this potent caricature, which contributes to hardening attitudes against people on benefits, is completely untrue. Once again, social workers need to be fully vigilant against being influenced by false imagery and ideas.

Also, it is important to realise that more than half the people living in relative poverty have a job, and many people in work are not on a 'living wage' and have their wages topped up by benefits. The scandal of 'the working poor' is, thankfully, one that is beginning to receive attention (O. Jones 2011).

Indisputably, however, the glare of the media attention is turned squarely on individuals who live up to the 'chav' caricature, and this is demonstrated in television programmes such as *Benefits Street*. These individuals are held up as examples of the reality of what people on benefits are like, and punitive and harsh policies receive more and more support:

> Harsh rules to drive the long-term unemployed into work come into force today, which state they will only receive their benefits if they either show up at a jobcentre every day or commit to six months of voluntary work.
>
> Those who fail to comply with the rules, which also offer signing up to a training scheme as a third option, will have their jobseeker's allowance docked for four weeks for the first offence, and 13 weeks for the second.
>
> (*Independent* 2015)

'Driving the long-term unemployed into work', of course, depends on work being available – and, as already shown, the type of part-time, insecure, and temporary jobs that are available is driving more people into poverty and debt as they move in and out of work. Harsh sanctions for those who 'fail to comply' with, for example, turning up, on time, every day at a job centre will also increase poverty as people inevitable slip up. This will deny people even the most basic subsistence.

Junkies and alkies

Through a neoliberal lens, people who are dependent on substances have made poor choices and should be subject to punishments for indulging in, often illegal, harmful behaviour. The notion that substance misuse is so much more prevalent in deprived, poor and depressed areas with high unemployment is explained by the idea that *those* are the kind of people who take drugs. That image fits the stereotype well. The alternative explanation, that grim circumstances, poverty, lack of hope or opportunity, and daily feelings of exclusion and failure encourage people to escape into substance misuse is, again, simply an excuse as per Mr Gove's theory mentioned earlier. As Russell Brand said: 'Drugs and alcohol are not my problem, reality is my problem, drugs and alcohol are my solution' (*Guardian* 2013c). Wilkinson and Pickett (2010) also note that substance misuse is correlated with inequality within countries, so the more unequal a country is, the higher the rate of substance misuse. This is linked to mental health problems and anxiety, which explains Russell Brand's comment above even further. Inequality leads to negative psychological effects, often due to pressure to obtain material goods, to achieve higher and higher status (to climb the steep hierarchy) and then often to failing to be 'successful' as judged by those measures, especially if starting from a position of significant disadvantage. This can then lead to escapist behaviour such as substance misuse.

O. Jones (2011) further explains that many working-class communities, decimated by the closure of heavy industry such as mining, became fertile ground for the spread of drug dealing and use:

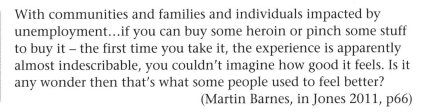

> With communities and families and individuals impacted by unemployment...if you can buy some heroin or pinch some stuff to buy it – the first time you take it, the experience is apparently almost indescribable, you couldn't imagine how good it feels. Is it any wonder then that's what some people used to feel better?
>
> (Martin Barnes, in Jones 2011, p66)

It is important, then, that social workers understand the context of substance misuse and see beyond individual poor behaviour choices.

Refugees and illegals

Refugees have a legal right to be in the country due to the UK being a signatory of the United Nations Convention Relating to the Status of Refugees (UNHCR 2012). This means that if the person is in fear of prosecution in his or her own country because of beliefs or culture or religion, then he or she should be afforded protection by the UK. In contrast, 'asylum seekers' are people who are waiting to be recognised as refugees. In this way, they are people without status or citizenship (Tyler 2013). Asylum seekers, much like other groups already discussed, have also become objects of media manipulation which leads to exaggerated worries and populist media targeting of people. As Tyler points out, the *Sun* had a headline in 2003 stating 'Detain all asylum seekers' (ibid.).

The role of social workers has increasingly become one concerned with enforcement of the legislation concerning asylum seekers and assessing people for eligibility for services. A requirement of social workers in this role is to report anyone they suspect of being 'bogus'. McLaughlin (2008) presents evidence that social workers are not objecting to this aspect of their role. Because it concerns illegality, there appears to be no further investigation of moral or ethical implications. Once again, social workers might be adhering to underpinning neoliberal assumptions, in that they agree with the hype around 'too many immigrants' and right-wing inflammatory thinking around immigration. McLaughlin points out, for example, that social workers who had to check immigration status, and thus contribute to racist internal immigration controls, viewed the activity as simply a bureaucratic annoyance rather than an ethical or moral problem.

This brings us back to social work's concern with social justice and human rights. Social workers need to question whether some policies and legislation might be oppressive in terms of human rights. This would mean that they might begin their work with asylum-seeking families from a position of support for human rights and critical reflection on the tasks asked of them. Even if their hands are tied in carrying out some tasks, those tasks should cause them to experience ethical stress because of the disconnect from the social work values of human rights and social justice, and this should influence how they do those tasks. As Gray and Webb (2013, p12) say, critical practice is often 'a form of critique', and if that is as much as can be achieved in some circumstances, it still must be achieved.

Criminals and rioting thugs

As already mentioned in relation to work with offenders (which sits within social work departments in Scotland), Fenton (2014a) found that when helping and welfare activities were thwarted, this was viewed by social workers as an administrative and practical irritation rather than a moral problem of not being able to carry out work in line with social work values. Workers, as in the example of working with asylum seekers, seemed very clear indeed that their imperatives were about demonstrating management and control of service users, with traditional social work such as helping and relationship-based practice being undertaken only if there was time. This wasn't seen as a significant problem. In common with the above account by McLaughlin, it may once again be that the potential illegality of the service users' behaviour means that further thought, reflection, or critical analysis is simply not required. We just do what the law says, and our part in that is, unquestioningly, good. Once again, these examples are exactly in line with neoliberal thinking – the focus is on individual behaviour and responsibility with no recognition of structural difference, oppression, or disadvantage.

In contrast to the above neoliberal examples of practice, social work practice consistent with social justice would try to help with 'the appalling reality' of service users' lives (Gregory 2010, p2280) and to protect or enforce their rights to decent standards, as discussed earlier. Herein lies the absolute fundamental requirement that social workers explicitly understand their commitment to social justice. If workers see asylum seekers and offenders simply as rational actors who 'should' be making law-abiding and sensible choices, then very narrow, correctional, individualised practice may well ensue, because the rational actor is viewed as a person 'in need of correction, re-moralising and as a neutral receptor of correct, normative information' (Kemshall 2010, p1249). Kemshall further points out that a person is actually a 'social actor...mediating social and personal constraints on their choices, and acting prudently within a situated rationality in which options to act otherwise can be severely limited by structural constraints and lack of power' (ibid., p1249). This, therefore, requires a critical understanding of the service user's life in terms of growing up, opportunities (or lack of), and current context and constraints.

The 2011 riots in the UK, sparked by the shooting dead of a black man, Mark Duggan, by white police, serve as a vivid illustration of the use of a 'moral underclass discourse' (MUD, see Chapter 1) (Levitas 2005) to understand events. Tyler (2013) and Turbett (2014) give very clear accounts of how the rioters were described in the media as 'a more menacing underclass', 'ruined generation', 'the underclass', and 'scum, thugs, feral rats, wolves' (Tyler 2013, p181) and an 'underclass', a symptom of Britain's 'broken' and 'sick' society (Turbett 2014). The message in the media was that these riots were *not* political but were simply the result of the 'underclass' and its lack of morality or normal standards of behaviour. This successfully promoted interpretation led seamlessly to calls for harsher punishments and sentences and, often, the withdrawal of welfare (Tyler 2013). This was a horrendous underclass of subhumans, devoid of any morality and undeserving of anything the state can offer. In reality, 86 per cent of rioters said they were rioting against poverty and only 51 per cent agreed that they felt integrated into British society (compared to 92 per cent of the population as whole) (*Guardian* 2011, cited in Turbett 2014). These riots were undeniably political in nature and cannot simply be reduced to the notion of 'bad' people being greedy. The targets of the riots were businesses and shops stocking status-enhancing goods such as brand labels, mobile devices, televisions, etc. Being aware of the pressure people are under to have goods to display their worth (as discussed earlier) can lead to some understanding of this. The materialistic pressure that results from neoliberal-driven inequality makes us all susceptible to preoccupations with 'things', status symbols, and brand names. For many people taking part in the riots, looting shops for material gain was irresistible. So, the action itself (rioting) *and* the form the rioting took (stealing goods from shops) are both plausibly interpreted as a reaction against neoliberalism's tenets of social inequality and material acquisition. However, the interpretation promoted by politicians and the media was quite simply one of apolitical 'underclass' behaviour.

stop and think

■ Reflect on your own deeply held and secret thoughts. Have you worked with or known anyone who fits into the above stereotypical categories? Think about how you might have felt just knowing *about* them. Did this change when you got to know them as a person? How?

Research Box 3.1

How do young people, stereotyped as 'chavs', speak back to those 'markers of abjection'?

Nayak and Kehily (2014) undertook media analysis and brought together findings from qualitative research with young people in two studies. Their findings suggest that, indeed, representations of young men and women as 'chavs' and other derogatory terms/stereotypes are both widespread and hateful. The researchers found that the young people in the study were very aware of how they were represented and demonstrated 'agency and affiliation' – identifying with differently configured images of these caricatures; the 'chav' idea, for example, often being understood and 'lived' as an affiliation with music or fashion and completely dissociated from violence or anti-social behaviour. This makes it clear that getting to know people beyond the stereotypes opens up a whole new level of understanding. As the authors state, we should not underestimate 'the value of eliciting the perspectives of marginalised youth to reconfigure social norms and hollow out at least some of the markings of stigma' (p1343). (See Chapter 7 for more on the value of relationship-based practice.)

The above account of how people in society can be classified and understood in a punitive, neoliberal way demonstrates how, perhaps, new social workers and students might have come to absorb the ideas quite unquestioningly. It is certainly clear that these ideas *are* powerful and can be seen in hardening attitudes to the poor (JRF 2014) and in the research and motivation underpinning this book (see Chapter 1). This chapter will now go on to explore other influences that serve to strengthen these ideas further.

Inequality

Wilkinson and Pickett (2010) demonstrate how social problems are worse in more unequal countries. They also note that levels of trust decrease with increasing inequality. In essence, this means that we know less about, and trust less, people in a different position on the hierarchy from ourselves. This works in both directions: we may be suspicious of people further up the hierarchy when we are scrambling to get there (Dorling 1998) as well as very wary of those further down the hierarchy – will we be mugged walking through this housing scheme? Of course, in such a steeply hierarchical society, the gap between often middle-class students and social workers and those who are seen in 'underclass' terms is very wide indeed. It may well be that students and social workers don't know anyone from those communities, don't mix with people there, have children who go to very different schools, etc. Buying notions of the 'underclass', then, is much more likely. In a more equal society, people mix more, trust each other more, and social cohesion is far better. This is an extremely important and core idea that we will analyse in greater depth in Chapter 6, when we consider that relationship-based practice, in conditions of inequality, poverty, and lack of trust, becomes both more important and more difficult.

There Is No Alternative (TINA)

I asked a class of MSc social work students if they would describe themselves as 'political', and, except for a few, the students generally replied 'not really'. When we explored this, there were some explanations around not knowing about politics or not being interested, but one student said: 'It feels like all the big battles have been won. We are where we are now, and there really doesn't seem to be another way. The politicians all sound kinda the same.' I think this expresses a view, held by many people, that politics is no longer really relevant. 'We are all middle class now' (*Telegraph* 2010), apart from, of course, that deviant and feckless underclass. Anyone who wants to can work hard and join in with the middle-class ethic. There is an understandable futility in this thinking, with much of it emanating from the famous Thatcher phrase 'there is no alternative [to neoliberalism]' (Furedi 2005). It is important, therefore, that students and social workers do realise there is an alternative; to austerity, to shrinking public services, to individual 'blaming', and to the idea that dependency is necessarily a bad thing. Understanding the historical shifts, economically, politically, and in social work, can aid this understanding as can the link to a radical view of social justice based on a premise of wealth redistribution and increased equality.

The 'Something for Nothing' Culture Must Be Tackled!

> Iain Duncan Smith has said forcing unemployed people to simulate the working day in jobcentres will mark an end to Britain's 'something-for-nothing culture'.
>
> In a speech at the Conservative party conference in Manchester, the work and pensions secretary said some unemployed people would have to spend 35 hours a week looking for work under supervision.
>
> (*Guardian* 2013d)

The 'something for nothing' culture is a phrase we have probably all heard and, because of all the reasons presented in this chapter, we may have uncritically accepted. However, think back to the section on Keynesian economics and the political parallels that culminated in a central idea: the state should make sure that every individual should have the basics, including a home. The implication of this is that if people cannot provide a basic need for themselves, the state will step in and provide it – usually via benefits. This means that pre-neoliberalism, people had a *right* to these basic standards. In a wealthy country like ours, does that feel right on an ethical level? I think most people would agree with that, until politicians and the media invent and exaggerate caricatures of people living in luxury and lounging on benefits. We have, perhaps, seen that this is not the true picture, but the fiction easily persuades people that, whilst they are working hard, others are getting an easy (and quite luxurious) life by doing nothing. Go back to the section on 'work-shy scroungers' to challenge the stereotype.

Individuals as Representative of an Entire Class

This is a technique that is very easy to spot in the media. Stories are written or broadcast about an individual who has fathered however many children and is living in comfort in a huge house, smoking, drinking, swearing, ignorant, and all the while on benefits. For example, the *Daily Mail* (2010) ran a headline as follows: 'Benefits couple with ELEVEN children rake in £30,000 a year and a free five-bedroom home (and now they've got another baby on the way)'. Whilst the story might be true for that one family, it is *used* to exemplify an entire non-working population or 'underclass'. The statistics demonstrating how rare the situation might be and giving the true picture are omitted. To illustrate this further, this section will look in a little more detail at a couple of relatively recent examples, pertinent to social work.

O. Jones (2011) makes the observation that when a person, somewhat fitting the stereotype of a 'chav', does something abhorrent, the media and politicians will hold that person up as a typical example of the 'under-class'. So, for example, he analyses the case of Shannon Matthews, the child who was reported as missing, an event that attracted extensive media coverage and support and action from the community. It was later dis-covered that Karen Matthews, Shannon's mother, had been instrumental in the faked abduction. There was, rightly so, an angry outcry to this finding, but the media interpreted the situation as one that was fitting in 'that kind' of community. Comments were made stating that the situa-tion had helped to 'reveal the existence of an underclass which is a world apart from the lives that most of us lead and the attitudes and social con-ventions that most of us take for granted' (Melanie Phillips, journalist, cited in Jones 2011, p18). Other stereotypes pertaining to the 'underclass' abounded – such as teenage boys who had impregnated maybe four girls – with no evidence whatsoever. The demonisation of the entire community was vociferous.

The reality, however, was that the people in the community had been as fooled by Karen Matthews as the rest of the public. They had spent pre-cious money (many were living in poverty) on leaflets and had given up much of their time in organised searches and campaigns. The true picture was ignored, and the estate was painted as a wasteland of feckless and amoral layabouts.

Another example of the above type of generalisation, used to perpetuate a myth, can be seen in the aftermath of the tragic death of Peter Con-nolly or 'Baby P'. Warner (2015) undertook an analysis of media cover-age of the Baby P story and found that the stories were overwhelmingly concerned with linking the circumstances of Peter Connolly's death to ideas and images of the 'underclass'. For example, Warner (2015, p225) cites an article in the *News of the World* under the headline 'Evil and Idle' as follows: 'When a truly abhorrent crime happens, you can be sure of one thing: it'll have taken place in a welfare ghetto'. This one sentence links abhorrent crime, unemployment, and the 'underclass' in a powerful message to the public. Interestingly when middle-class people commit 'abhorrent crime', for example Harold Shipman or Andreas Lubitz, no one holds them up as typical of the middle-class communities they come from. In conclusion, Warner states, 'Underclass parents were represented as threats to the moral order and as requiring moral regulation through their identification with evil, which the Baby P story facilitated' (ibid., p229).

Hegemony

Hegemony was a concept developed by Gramsci (1971). In essence, hegemony sums up the entirety of this chapter – it encompasses how the ruling government gets consent from people to govern in the way it wants. In order for hegemony to be effective, the major institutions of civic life have to be in agreement about aims, goals, and philosophy, so education, media, law and order, to name a few, must be in agreement. We have seen in this chapter the different methods the government uses to perpetuate neoliberal thinking, and of course social work as part of civic life becomes subject to pressure to adopt the same hegemony. Hence the neoliberal shift in social work.

Sheedy (2013) points out that political disengagement and the idea that 'there is no alternative, so what interest do politics hold?' can be a powerful hegemonic technique, as the prevailing and institutionalised way of thinking becomes separate and out of reach. Sheedy also notes that the focus on the 'something for nothing' culture, the 'underclass', and all the other neoliberal concepts covered in this chapter, *and* the exaggeration of these ideas perpetuated by the media, obscure any alternative interpretation of what is happening in society. So, 'the alternative discourse focusing on tax avoidance and evasion, city bonuses, bank profits and fiscal and monetary inequality is given much less prominence' (Sheedy 2013, p15). In fact, as Crouch (2011) states, 'already we have seen how a crisis caused by appalling behaviour among banks has been redefined as a crisis of public spending. Bankers' bonuses are returning to their pre-crisis level, whilst thousands of public employees are losing their jobs [and further welfare cuts are made]' (Crouch 2011, p179). Hegemony allows this to happen.

Further evidence of neoliberal hegemony and its power can be seen in the *Independent*'s report on a study conducted by the Royal Statistical Society and Kings College London, which, shockingly, included the following findings:

- Benefit fraud: the public think this is 34 times higher than it actually is.
- The public think 31% of the population is made up of recent immigrants, when it is actually 13%.
- Teen pregnancy is judged by the public to be 25 times higher than it actually is!
- 29% of people think that the government spends more on Job Seekers' Allowance than it does on pensions. In truth, the government spends 15 times more on pensions.
- The majority of people think crime is worse than it actually is.

The Executive Director of the Royal Statistical Society said that several things need to happen so that the public understand accurately what is going on in the country: 'First, politicians need to be better at talking about the real state of affairs of the country, rather than spinning the numbers. Secondly, the media has to try and genuinely illuminate issues, rather than use statistics to sensationalise' (*Independent* 2013). Currently, the public's perceptions are completely skewed in favour of neoliberal messages and stereotypes. As a consequence, the public's attitude to people in poverty, which has hardened significantly over the last few decades, remains hardened, even though people are expressing a new awareness of poverty because they can see the evidence such as increasing homelessness and the rise of food banks (JRF 2014). It is interesting that seeing the evidence for themselves is the only way the public are beginning to challenge the skewed messages they receive from the media. It does suggest that those messages are well out of step with reality.

For people who work with those sectors of the public who are being demonised and about whom the myths are being believed, it is even more crucial that they do not buy into the untruths and are able to see the true picture – to avoid 'blaming' and stereotyping and to be more inclined to help and advocate. For social workers it surely is a necessity, if practice such as is illustrated in Practice Example 3.1 is to be challenged and critiqued.

stop and think

■ Start to pay attention to the neoliberal messages perpetuated by the media. Do you now have information to give a counter-argument? Try to discuss these things with others and notice in what ways they, too, have been affected by the hegemony.

We should now be able to understand hegemonic power and influence. It is little wonder that students and newer workers often buy into the neoliberal version of work with service users. If you accept the neoliberal hegemony, that type of practice makes sense. Now let us look at Practice Example 3.1.

3.1 The Smith family

practice example

Meet the Smith family, where the children are being neglected and alcohol use is an issue. School have referred the family, and the referral has come to the local social work team. The social worker attends the family home and sees evidence of neglect, alcohol misuse, and chaos. She introduces herself and clarifies her role as per good practice she remembers from her teaching at university (Trotter 2006). She remembers to be explicit about the authority in her role and starts off by making it clear to Mrs Smith that she needs to comply or there could be serious consequences. She also remembers her learning about active listening and relationship-based practice, but she doesn't have much time, so she listens to Mrs Smith's 'story' whilst also looking for clues and hints about levels of risk and opportunities for concrete suggestions about routines, alcohol use, etc. Finally, the social worker empowers Mrs Smith to contact the school to arrange to go and discuss the children by finding the phone number for her. She will later check that the phone call has been made.

The social worker returns to the office and writes up her case notes, bullet-pointing all of the things she has asked Mrs Smith to do and making it clear that she left her in no doubt as to the consequences if she doesn't make improvements. At the end of the day, the social worker reflects, she must keep focused on the children's welfare as paramount. When her team manager sees her file, he comments that she has done a good piece of work today, with everything 'nice and clear'.

The social worker in this example does not feel ethical stress – she employed her values of respect (she treated Mrs Smith well), non-judgementality (she didn't leap to conclusions, but listened well) and took cognisance of Mrs Smith's right to self-determination – as long as that didn't impact negatively on the children. Her team manager says she has done good work – defensible if anything goes wrong. The social worker feels pleased – there is nothing else she should have done.

Exercise 3.2

What do you think of the above social work practice? Is there anything else the social worker should have or might have done? Make a list of the positive and negative aspects to this piece of practice. Identify the underpinning neoliberal assumptions (see references to Schein 2010 in Chapter 2).

Neoliberal practice in action can be seen in the above example. Therein can be seen the individual-only focus of current practice – the service user in the example needs to hurry up and make changes. Mrs Smith is a person who has made bad choices and needs to stop being selfish and think about her children as a priority (or she shouldn't have had children – right?). She also needs to stop drinking so much and get out and get a job – that can be for future work.

The social worker in the above example ascribes to that type of neoliberal social work practice quite comfortably – and feels it is congruent with social work values. She does not feel there is anything in her practice to reflect on further or critique *and* neither does her team manager.

All is good in the world of neoliberal practice. Or is it? There seems to be something else missing from this scenario, not only attention to wider structural, social justice issues. Even in her individual-level interaction with Mrs Smith the social worker's practice seems to be devoid of something. It could be suggested that the missing 'something' is *care*. The social worker seems uncaring and does not appear to see a place for care. It is that element of practice that the next chapter will explore.

main points

■ Approximately 30 years ago, the economic governance of the UK changed from Keynesian to neoliberal – a conscious change of direction.

■ Ideas of 'underclass' and individual responsibility sit comfortably within that philosophy and are promoted by media attention, stereotyping and political rhetoric.

■ The effects of inequality and poverty, however, cannot be dismissed, such is the evidence.

■ The influence of media, stereotyping, political rhetoric, and hegemony and the perpetuation of ideas such as 'the something for nothing culture' and 'there is no alternative' can be seen in the public's skewed beliefs about 'work-shy scroungers' and the feckless underclass.

taking it further

■ Jones, O. (2011) *Chavs: The Demonization of the Working Class* (London: Verso). Very important reading to help understand just how the public have been encouraged to internalise the unjust picture of working-class people.

■ Wilkinson, R. G., and Pickett, K. (2010) *The Spirit Level: Why Equality Is Better for Everyone* (London: Penguin). Essential reading. This seminal book explains the effects of inequality (a feature of neoliberalism) and its link to social problems. Crucial understanding for social workers and students.

■ Lansley, S., and Mack, J. (2015) *Breadline Britain: The Rise of Poverty* (London: Oneworld). An important text for understanding poverty and its perpetuation.

■ Tirado, L. (2014) *Hand to Mouth: The Truth about Being Poor in a Wealthy World* (London: Virago). This book affords some really valuable insights into the grim reality of life in poverty in America. The ridiculous idea that people can just 'pull themselves' out of poverty is exposed for what it is.

■ Murray, C. (1990) *The Emerging British Underclass* (London: IEA Health and Welfare Unit). This is a good text to read to see an opposing view to the one presented in this book. Can you critique Murray's thesis?

4 Current Ethical Approaches and Care

Overview

This chapter will explore the current ethical approaches used in social work today, namely utilitarianism, deontology, virtue ethics, and the ethics of care. The question of whether social workers can justify and analyse neoliberal, value-poor practice through these ethical frameworks will be posed. An ethics of care approach will be offered as the one most in keeping with value-informed practice, and the idea of keeping care at the heart of practice will be discussed.

Recap of Thinking So Far

So far we have explored the two organising concepts or themes of this book. The first, ethical stress, has been defined, and examples of situations, linked to neoliberalism, that should produce ethical stress in social workers have been discussed. Secondly, social work's dissociation from the core principle of social justice has been analysed, once again in terms of neoliberal hegemony. Readers should, at this point, be able to understand the changing face of social work and the very negative effect this can have on service users. This chapter will further that understanding by exploring how social workers and students *can* justify neoliberal practice by reference to a blunt understanding of existing ethical approaches. To begin that exploration, current ethical approaches will be discussed.

Utilitarianism

Utilitarianism is associated with Jeremy Bentham and John Stuart Mill, nineteenth-century British philosophers and social reformers. The central idea of utilitarianism is that the right action is the one that produces the greatest good over evil for the greatest number of people. This is the principle of *utility* (Banks 2012).

The philosophy, according to Banks, became gradually more and more complicated as philosophers added more nuances to try to cope with all eventualities and ethical situations. So, for example, under 'act' utilitarianism the utility of one individual act should be judged in terms of producing good, whilst 'rule' utilitarianism concerns the utility of the act as a generalisable rule (Reamer 1993). Later thinkers considered themselves to be 'consequentialists', as the philosophy is ultimately concerned with the outcomes of actions rather than the actions themselves.

Although utilitarianism might sound appealing to social workers and students alike, focused as it is on producing the greatest amount of 'good', it is not well developed within social work, where the emphasis is on the personal relationship with service users and the equal worth afforded to all service users regardless of ability or minority status (Banks 2012). Thinking about 'the greatest good for the greatest number of people' can easily be interpreted as a majoritarian idea that excludes the interests of minority groups within society. Why, for example, should scarce resources be spent on making buildings accessible for wheelchair users, when a far greater number could have their happiness enhanced by other alterations to the building. The exclusion of a very small number of building users might, in utilitarian thinking, be a worthwhile price to pay. As Solas (2014, p815) very explicitly states: 'In fact the principle [of utility] *requires* that some individuals should accept lower prospects of life for the gratification of others.'

Notwithstanding those drawbacks, however, the more recent emphasis within social work on measuring outcomes and on risk assessment and management does draw on utilitarian principles – prioritising consequences rather than process or content.

Deontology

Deontology is associated with Immanuel Kant (1724–1804), a German philosopher; and it has as its central idea an emphasis on doing one's *duty*. Deontology is concerned with 'rules' and principles that must be followed. It is based on rational thought – we logically work out what our duty is in any given circumstance (Banks 2012). Under a deontological philosophy, people must never be treated as a means to an end but always as ends in themselves. So, for example, if lying is wrong, it should never be justified as for the 'greater good' (as it might be under utilitarianism). Kant's 'categorical imperative' means that we should only do something if we believe it should be a universal law (Banks 2012). So, in the case of lying, you should only lie if you feel lying should always be seen as a good course of action.

Deontology is the most influential of the ethical approaches within social work (Carey and Green 2013). For example, the fundamental social work principle of 'respect for persons' is a categorical imperative and is embedded in social work values. Codes of practice and ethics are often derived from deontological thinking, for example, promoting self-determination and empowerment and respecting autonomy. Doing one's duty, however, by following rules and procedures might not always be in the best interests of service users and can lead to significant uncertainties if codes and rules are in conflict (Carey and Green 2013). Lorenzetti (2013, p52) considers the concept of empowerment, which, she says is 'ingrained in the social work psyche' as a tool for challenging oppression. However, empowerment *'without a critical lens'* (ibid.) will not challenge oppression, and social work's approach to empowerment has rendered the concept quite empty. Lorenzetti gives the example of a social worker 'empowering' a service user to access a foodbank which does nothing to recognise or address the inequalities that have caused the necessity of foodbanks in the first place. Practising in this way, without a critical understanding of the wider forces and causes of oppression and disadvantage, is neoliberal practice at its worst.

Utilitarianism and deontology can be termed 'principle-based theories' because they are concerned with the principles of action rather than any moral qualities of the actor (Banks and Gallacher 2009, p32) and have formed the 'dominant paradigm' in the study of social work ethics (Banks 2014). Criticisms of principle-based approaches to social work include the idea that they are often too blunt and absolutist to cope with the difficult and nuanced situations social workers encounter on a daily basis; they are based on rational thought and logic and, thus, negate the influence of the 'soft' features of social work such as emotional content (Ingram et al. 2014); and they are reductionist in nature, tending to 'compartmentalise morality or reduce it to specific actions or decisions rather than acknowledge the on-going and integrated nature of moral life' (Banks and Gallacher 2009, p33).

As a social work educator, I read students' work in which they are tasked with analysing their practice through different ethical frameworks. It seems that students can, quite frequently, justify value-poor, neoliberal practice by reference to a basic understanding of utilitarianism and/or deontology. At this point, it would be useful to expose and explore that tendency.

Exercise 4.1

Analysis of neoliberal practice

Read over Practice Example 3.1 once again. Attempt to analyse whether the social worker can justify her practice within both utilitarian and deontological frameworks. Make bullet points of the main points of justification from each ethical approach.

How did you get on with that exercise? See below for some suggestions – did you find the same?

Utilitarianism

- Mrs Smith is a member of the 'underclass' and needs to join in with the acceptable norms of behaviour to allow the 'greatest good for the greatest number' in society (i.e. the nice, law-abiding majority) to flourish.
- To do this, Mrs Smith needs to change her behaviour, and the social worker is helping her do this by giving goals and ultimatums.
- The weight of the law is essential in situations like this, and can be used to make sure behaviour is changed. The social worker is giving Mrs Smith time to change (empathy), but the law is there to protect the majority of people and will be used against Mrs Smith if her behaviour does not change.
- The social worker's resulting emphasis on uncompromising behaviour change is thus justified.
- The social worker is concerned about consequences, so if her work with Mrs Smith means she will drink less alcohol because she is afraid of what might happen, then that's fine. The aim has been achieved as has risk reduction – and that is the priority.

Deontology

- The law is there as a set of rules that the social worker must follow. Therefore, if Mrs Smith does not ensure the welfare of her child, the social worker is obliged to take action. She is a neutral observer who will take action if she deems the situation not to be good enough. That is the law.
- The code of ethics for social work means the social worker must demonstrate 'respect' for Mrs Smith, so she politely called her 'Mrs Smith' during the interview and she acted in a manneredly way, by asking permission to sit down and smiling.
- The social worker is also obliged to communicate in an honest way, which she does by being very clear about her role and the consequences to Mrs Smith if she does not make changes. A social worker could keep those potential consequences hidden, but that would be poor practice. Honesty is important.
- The social worker also followed the procedure to the letter and made sure she documented all of this clearly – doing her duty and following all of the rules.
- The codes of practice are clear – the social work task is to support or coerce Mrs Smith into taking her own action to sort the situation out. The social worker is explicitly supporting her self-determination and autonomy.
- The social worker is pleased that she has enacted the principles of empowerment and self-determination by not doing things *for* Mrs Smith (for example, not making the phone call to the school for her).

Hopefully, it will be easy to see from the above exercise that neoliberal and managerial social work can indeed be rationalised within principle-based approaches to ethical practice. The social worker is a good example of one who is concerned with 'doing things right' rather than 'doing the right things' (Munro 2011, p6). Banks (2014, p15) illuminates this phenomenon further with her account of how approaches to ethics can indeed support managerialism, or New Public Management (NPM), via four key interpretations of 'ethics':

- 'Developing more regulatory codes of ethics'. Banks states that codes of practice/ethics are getting longer and are used increasingly frequently as regulatory and disciplinary tools. She views this as a way of micro-managing social workers' practice and, thus, reducing autonomy. As noted in Chapter 1, Reamer and Shardlow (2009) concur with this view, describing the codes as narrow managerial tools used for the regulation of social work practice. Herein, then, lies the very clear link to deontology and 'rule following' as exemplified in the social work practice in Practice Example 3.1.
- 'Highlighting the responsibilities of social workers and service users ('responsibilisation').' Because there is a strong focus on the agency and choice of the service user (see Chapter 1 for an analysis of the codes in terms of social work's main aim defined as supporting the service user's own, individual endeavour), Banks suggests that the tendency is to define social problems in terms of individual service users' behaviour rather than structural problems. It is also interesting to refer to I. Ferguson's (2008) point, mentioned in Chapter 2, that many service users do not have the personal and social resources to exert agency and influence and are then vilified for dependency. Banks also notes that 'responsibilisation' can also apply to individual social workers who bear the brunt of blame for 'wrong' decisions. Attention is often drawn to the behaviour/decisions of individual social workers as opposed to the employing agency or wider issues such as understaffing and governmental policy decisions.
- 'Placing the focus of attention on the relationship between the individual social worker and service user or family.' Although further chapters in this book will highlight and promote relationship-based practice, Banks's point is that to focus *solely* on that individual level of relational work is dangerously neoliberal if wider political and societal influences are neglected. She suggests that the way ethical issues are interpreted in social work can lead to the individual level being the only site for reflection. The interpretation is that social workers make decisions in difficult circumstances – often exemplified in social work education by 'short, decontextualized cases' (ibid., p16). This leads to the question of what the social worker should do – supporting the notion that ethical decisions are problems of individual practice.

- 'De-personalising and de-politicising of ethics.' Banks suggests that social work, in a managerial context, is about a 'contract' between the parties involved. It is a predetermined conformity to rules and standards rather than a 'real' relationship based on mutual trust. The rules and standards are applied in the same way to everyone – a practice concerned with impartiality, objectivity, and equity as opposed to one concerned with empathy, good outcomes for society, and meeting the needs of oppressed people (aiming for equality). As Banks sums up: 'It [NPM] encourages a narrow vision of the role of social work divorced from people with personalities and from political debates about what counts as fairness or equality' (ibid., p16).

The above comprehensive critique can be supplemented by an overarching concern with utilitarianism, which fits neatly with neoliberal thinking. Marginalised people, that is the group that falls outside the 'we are all middle class now' framing of society (*Telegraph* 2010), are legitimately relegated to the margins and legitimately left with the very poorest of services (threadbare welfare and charitable endeavours) due the 'greatest number' in society enjoying the 'greatest good' or happiness. Utilitarianism can absorb the small group of the very wealthiest as long as a large 'middle-class' group can also be seen to be thriving. This can lead to a dangerous justification for not attending to the needs of the poorest and most vulnerable people.

Virtue ethics

In contrast to principle-based approaches to social work ethics, virtue ethics is concerned with the qualities of the person taking the action rather than the intrinsic 'rightness' of the act itself. According to Carey and Green (2013, p9), virtue ethics emphasises the virtues of 'integrity, honesty, loyalty, wisdom and kindness'. Banks and Gallacher (2009) list professional wisdom, care, respectfulness, trustworthiness, justice, courage, and integrity as their chosen virtues – with a rationale and analysis for each.

There is not much to disagree with in the idea that social workers should be virtuous in their dealings with people, and it is a refreshing alternative to the requirement to follow lists of principles and rules. However, the difficulty comes when virtues conflict or when, once again, interpretation of virtues remains at the level of individual practice. Clifford (2013) suggests that the limitations of virtue ethics centre on their emphasis on the individuals and their 'will', perhaps to the exclusion of the forces around them that often shape behaviour. As Preston-Shoot (2003) pointed out, social workers are often at the mercy of very managerial and oppressive contexts where acting virtuously might be difficult. He explains consequences of these types of oppressive cultures, which include: secret-keeping, for example, when workers do not discuss the gap between the theory and the reality of resource restrictions (lack of the virtue of honesty); making no requests or demands for entitlements such as supervision, due to a lack of belief in their needs being met (lack of the virtues of courage and justice); a feeling that there is no point in making requests or taking action on behalf of service users (lack of the virtues of trustworthiness, courage, care, integrity); and an expressed belief in the espoused reality of social work when in the full knowledge that the image is at odds with the reality (lack of the virtues of honesty and integrity). This is not to suggest that the workers themselves lacked virtuousness, just that the influence of the dominant culture was such that it left workers unable to express themselves virtuously. Another way to encapsulate this idea is, of course, that workers experience ethical stress when they are unable to express their virtues in practice.

Clifford (2013) also elaborates on further limitations around the idea that society itself, beyond the social work context, is deeply divided and unjust, and that virtues themselves are defined within the dominant narrative. This means that they are skewed in favour of the privileged. He also makes the point that oppression has significant effects on people's moral character – a more generalised version of Preston-Shoot's idea above. Sometimes the surrounding context does not allow for virtuousness, and virtues and context cannot be considered separately, and yet, according to Clifford (2013, p9) virtue ethics 'does not take oppression seriously'.

Clifford points out two further concerns with virtue ethics in social work. The first is a tendency to 'self-absorption'. By this he means that the subject is ultimately interested in the development of his or her own moral character, to the detriment, again, of recognition of other forces and the contextualised nature of virtues. Secondly, he considers the idea of 'flourishing' which, again, is about putting one's own 'flourishing' and wellbeing at the heart of practice, without acknowledging that the service user should be the central focus. There is also a lack of acknowledgement that 'flourishing' for the privileged might mean something very different from 'flourishing' for the oppressed. Overall, Clifford urges caution when considering virtue ethics because of their seemingly comfortable connection with dominant values and narrative. For the purposes of this book, promoting a model of practice grounded in a radical framework, we must also exercise caution in our appraisal of virtue ethics. If Clifford is correct, then the neoliberal practice from Practice Example 3.1 might also be justifiable through a virtue ethics lens.

> **Exercise 4.2**
>
> Repeat exercise 4.1, but this time use a virtue ethics approach. Could a social worker rationalise his or her practice this way?

Virtue ethics

Using Carey and Green (2013) to define the virtues:

- Integrity: the social worker feels she has done everything correctly and has acted with integrity – there was nothing dishonest or sneaky about her practice and her motivation was all good (welfare of the child).
- Honesty: definitely! The social worker prides herself on this, as she said the 'difficult things' to Mrs Smith in terms of consequences of non-compliance and how some of her behaviour was unacceptable. It was difficult to do this, but the social worker knew she had to be honest and is proud of being able to do it.
- Loyalty: the social worker feels very loyal to the social work profession and to her agency. She would never do anything to bring criticism to the door of her agency, and her practice would pass anyone's inspection.
- Wisdom: she feels she consciously applied knowledge (for example, Trotter (2006) and knowledge of child development). She also drew on her own practice wisdom – getting the balance right between appearing friendly yet being firm, for example.
- Kindness: the social worker feels there is always a place to act in a kind way, so she was as warm as was appropriate and understanding about giving Mrs Smith time to make the changes. There wasn't much else to be 'kind' about.

Looking at Banks and Gallacher's (2009) extra virtues, you can probably justify trustworthiness, justice, and courage. What about care? Is that more difficult? Sander-Staudt (2006) remarks that several thinkers have tried to subsume 'care' into virtue ethics but makes the point that care is more than a virtue – it is not enough to be a 'caring' person; we must, instead, express that within the context of relationships. A point worth thinking about as you read on.

It is now becoming clear that there is value in virtue ethics as one kind of ethics – but as contributory rather than *the* one (Banks and Gallacher 2009). Banks's (2014) analysis of four types of ethics might help make sense of the complex ethical picture and identify where virtue ethics might indeed contribute: conduct, character, relationships, and the good society. Ito (2014) further delineates these types as follows: conduct and the good society are social justice ethics, whilst character (virtue ethics) and relationships are care ethics. In this analysis, Ito absorbs virtue ethics into an ethics of care – thus illustrating the contributory nature of virtue ethics. At this point, then, it is important to understand and get to grips with what we mean by an 'ethics of care'.

Ethics of care

The development of an ethics of care approach owes much to C. Gilligan (1982) and her research into how people approach ethical dilemmas. In her seminal work *In a Different Voice,* she identifies two quite different 'voices': a justice voice (concerned with principles and rules) and a care voice (concerned with relationships, connectedness, and care). Researching from a feminist perspective, she differentiates these voices into masculine/justice and feminine/care. In essence, the ethics of care is about the person in the context of their relatedness to others – their loved ones, families, support system, friends, and with the social worker and other professionals.

The ethics of care was developed further by several writers, but the one most useful to this exploration is Tronto (1993). In contrast to others who have developed thinking around the ethics of care, for example Noddings (1984, cited in Banks 2012) who analysed care within education, Tronto makes a firm link between the ethics of care and the wider political context – a 'political ethics of care' (Tronto 1993, p155). Whereas Noddings's ideas might be vulnerable to the same criticisms levelled at virtue ethics – that the focus is dislocated from context – Tronto very much situates her thinking within a social justice framework. To understand the ethics of care further, Tronto's (1993 pp127–136) five elements of care will be explored:

- 'Attentiveness' – actively finding out the person's point of view and needs. Making a concerted effort to find out *from him or her* what the problems are and what's important to him or her. In social work practice, this would mean really hearing the services user's voice and actively listening to *his or her* definition of the situation and what's going on. I have read practice essays from students where I come to the end of an ethical analysis of a situation and still have to ask 'but what did Mrs X think about it all?'
- 'Responsibility' – taking responsibility for care – being interested enough in the person to shoulder that. Not out of a duty, but because

it is the right thing to do in the situation. In practice, not saying or thinking 'that's not my job' but taking responsibility to try to find a way to meet needs – by one's own practice or by mobilising resources/ other agencies. Stepping up to being responsible because you *care*.

- 'Competence' – actually doing the caring. In social care this is more obvious – helping with personal care for example. In social work too, however, this is about taking action to meet needs. Once responsibility is assumed – then what do you need to do to meet those needs? This might mean arguing with your manager about resources or going beyond the call of duty to make links to other agencies.
- 'Responsiveness' – staying attuned to the reactions of the service user. Being alert to overbearing or intrusive practice, picking up cues and adjusting practice as required.
- 'Integrity of care' – this means understanding how the four elements above fit together. More than that, however, it is about understanding the social and political context within which the caring is taking place. This encompasses the social work culture (which might be hostile to care-based practice) as well as the wider societal culture (which, as we know, is neoliberal and more comfortable with controlling and punitive measures). To actually be explicit in the practice of caring with, for example, involuntary service users in criminal justice or child protection contexts might well elicit disapproval or derision. Calls of 'you're too soft, naïve, or "nice"' (disparagingly) might well ensue...

So, to briefly exemplify the ethics of care in action, imagine the situation of a Scottish criminal justice worker writing a court report. A situation more likely to excuse neoliberal managerial practice would be hard to find. How would an ethics of care approach look in this setting? First of all, the worker would approach the person and get to know him or her, clearly caring about *his or her* story, *his or her* situation, and how *he or she* sees it. This would mean eliciting his or her story and using skills to get the full picture of how he or she understands things. Listening, reflecting back and all those good old social work skills would be in play. Sympathetic understanding (Manning 1998) would be felt and conveyed. This is Tronto's 'attentiveness'. In terms of 'responsibility' the worker could legitimately feel no responsibility for the service user's needs – they are simply there to report on them. However, adopting an ethics of care approach would mean that the worker should work to meet expressed needs: liaising with other agencies, attempting to secure resources, asking the service user to return, or doing a home visit having followed things up would all demonstrate both caring and taking responsibility. This would include the 'competence' to actually do these things, beyond identifying them and taking responsibility. Staying attuned to the service user's response, and being sensitive to clues about how he or she was feeling, and acknowledging that, would demonstrate 'responsiveness'. Understanding, for example, an anxiety about going to court and inviting the service user to return to read the report or accompanying him or her to court would be practical demonstrations of this element of care. Finally, understanding that all of these pieces fit together in an ethics of care framework, and so have coherence, is important. Also, and vitally for the approach taken in this book, the worker would realise that the interaction was taking place within a managerial, procedural, and punitive context, where an ethics of care approach might well be derided. The worker would also understand that the interaction was taking place in a wider social context where inequality and poverty were making things increasingly difficult for people and hopelessness, despair, anxiety, substance misuse, and crime were all flourishing as symptoms of an unhealthy and unequal society. As well as having broken the law, the service user is understood as a victim of that society. The other element in an ethics of care approach is, of course, the focus on the service user's relationships. The worker would encourage an exploration of the person's system of support and relationships – how the person is connected to others. Where there were gaps or paucity in those relationships, the worker would attempt to address that in any way he or she could (initiating connections or contacting family if the person wanted that) (Manning 1998).

Exercise 4.3

Think about the five elements of an ethics of care approach and see if the social worker in Practice Example 3.1 could rationalise or justify her work by reference to them. It might very well be that this is the approach that makes neoliberal practice very difficult to justify, but try it before reading the bullet points below.

Ethics of care

- Attentiveness: the social worker simply did not ask Mrs Smith at all what her understanding of the situation was. What is life like for Mrs Smith? What are her difficulties? What are her needs?
- Responsibility: the worker only took responsibility for reporting on the situation and getting Mrs Smith to make changes. No responsibility was taken for trying to help her or to address her (unidentified) needs.
- Competence: actually taking action to meet needs? No. No needs identified or met.
- Responsiveness: the social worker seemed unconcerned about how Mrs Smith reacted; her reaction mattered only in her being malleable enough for the social worker to get her tasks done.

- Integrity of care: no care was shown towards Mrs Smith what-soever. Unsurprisingly, the social work context did not need to be challenged, and the social worker's view of Mrs Smith was a million miles away from seeing her in any way as a victim of an unfair and oppressive society.

Think about the relationship element also – did the social worker do anything to explore or enhance Mrs Smith's network of relationships?

Tronto (2010, pp163–165) identifies seven warning signs that care is poor. If we assume that we want social work agencies to be caring, which is part of the explicit premise of this book, then the warning signs should be useful when attempting to assess the care emphasis within those agencies. Thinking about the kind of agency/practice in Practice Example 3.1, we can explore whether the warning signs do indeed apply. The first sign is that 'misfortune causes the need for care'. Dependency is bad, and people should be independent agents, managing their own lives without help. This is clearly underpinned by neoliberal thinking, and we can see it within the case study. Mrs Smith needs to sort herself out, and the social worker will check on that. Secondly, 'needs are taken as given within the organisation' and Tronto states: 'any agency…that presumes needs are fixed is likely to be mistaken and to inflict harm'. This is definitely the case for Mrs Smith. The social worker has no idea what her needs are and, as a consequence, has no idea how these relate to what her child needs. This lack of identification means that needs are assumed; what people 'like her' simply need to do. Thirdly, 'care is considered a commodity, not a process'. Tronto suggests that if we think of care or social work practice as a commodity, we think in financial terms of scarcity and that care is best distributed and managed by the market. In the case study, and in many practice agencies, the shortage of resources for home visits and caring or 'real social work' is seen as a practical problem only, not an ethical one (Fenton 2014a), perhaps a symptom of the commodification and market principles accepted within social work. Surely, lack of care should be defined as an ethical problem of extreme importance? Next, 'care receivers are excluded from making judgements because they lack expertise'. This is very clear in the case study, where Mrs Smith is considered not to have anything of worth to say, thus, the social worker does not seek her opinion or view. Sign five is 'Care is narrowed to care giving, rather than understanding the full process of care which includes attentiveness to needs and responsibility', a weakness very clear in the case study when the social worker does not consider that identifying needs from Mrs Smith's point of view is important, never mind taking responsibility for trying to help with them. Number six is 'care givers see organisational requirements as hindrances to, rather than support for, care'. This is a very interesting point in terms of this book's premise, because its expression would depend on a worker who was *trying* to approach the work from a care ethics basis. So, imagine another, caring worker visiting Mrs Smith. Any care work about helping with needs, really listening to Mrs Smith's views, and taking responsibility and action would very likely not go down well within the agency. In this case the agency requirements and managerial nature would definitely be seen as getting in the way of value-based practice. The social worker in this case would almost certainly experience ethical stress. This particular warning sign, then, could be expressed as 'the experience of ethical stress'. The final warning sign is that 'care work is distributed along lines of class, caste, gender, race'. Care work is usually poorly paid and undertaken in almost its entirety by women. The low status it is afforded might well be because it is seen simply as a 'natural' and easy thing for women to do. The real picture of the difficult and complex work of caring for sometimes fragile and confused older people, for example, is seriously underestimated. Social work, as in the case study, has lost status over the last few decades (though it still carries a higher status than care work), and it is often vilified. It is also heavily gendered, with over 75 per cent of social workers being women (*Guardian* 2014).

It is clear then, that Tronto's warning signs about the lack of care apply completely to the neoliberal practice in the case study. This is yet more evidence for promoting an ethics of care and its attendant concepts, such as warning signs and the production of ethical stress when care is thwarted, as useful countermeasures to neoliberal practice.

In conclusion to this section, then, the case has been made to keep an ethics of care at the heart of our approach to social work. In a context where neoliberal managerial practice can be justified by recourse to traditional approaches to social work ethics, it is *essential* that an alternative approach is promoted where neoliberal practice simply cannot be rationalised. The adoption of such an approach in a more explicit and comprehensive way would make some progress towards allowing a return to value-based practice and would counteract the derision and labels of 'soft' often given to social work colleagues who, quite simply, care about the people they work with.

Care and Compassion

Lorenzetti (2013, p55) states that part of social work's primary aspiration should be 'the development of an authentic and motivating compassion for others'. Also, the BASW (2012, p11) *Code of Ethics* states that social workers 'should act with integrity and treat people with compassion, empathy and care'. It has already been demonstrated that a very useful way to ensure that this happens is the explicit adoption of an ethics of care approach. So far then, we have the first iteration of a new model of practice:

Figure 4.1 Practice Model Iteration 1

Although the above hardly constitutes a diagram, it is the first, very important step in constructing a new model of social work ethical practice, and so it deserves recognition!

The Ethics of Care in Practice

Horner and Kelly (2007) give an example of the ethics of care applied to Mrs Jones, an 81-year-old woman living in a residential home. Mrs Jones has two adult daughters who visit daily and care very much about their mother. They have told staff that all her life Mrs Jones has avoided facing up to problems and has liked other people to deal with things and make decisions for her. During a routine medical examination, two lumps were found in Mrs Jones's breast, which were likely to be cancerous. The daughters have asked the care staff not to tell their mother and stated that they do not want their mother to have any more tests or treatment, as they know she would rather deny anything was wrong with her and would prefer to live out her last few years without having to worry about her health. The staff feel they should tell Mrs Jones, but they do not want to go against the daughters' wishes.

Applying a principle-based approach and considering honesty, self-determination, and empowerment, the 'right thing' to do in rational terms and in terms of duty would be to tell Mrs Jones. However, applying an ethics of care approach allows the following to also be considered: Mrs Jones in the context of her relationships with her daughters and staff; the *relevance* of her daughters and their knowledge of their mother, which is far deeper than that of the staff; the fact that Mrs Jones has never mentioned the lumps, even though they are quite obvious; and the fact that she has always liked others to make decisions for her. The consideration of these factors allows other possible solutions to emerge. The one suggested by Horner and Kelly is that staff, in the daily ritual of washing, mention the lumps to Mrs Jones and ask her if she wants the doctor to look at them. This should give an indication of whether she wants to have knowledge about the lumps or not. This solution allows for the relational element of the approach to guide it and also allows for attentiveness, responsibility, competence, responsivity, and integrity of care. Responsivity is probably the element of care primarily highlighted by this case study – the further, caring, actions of the daughters and staff are guided by how Mrs Jones responds.

Tronto (2010, p158) discusses the ethics of care within institutions and poses the question 'how do we know which institutions provide good care?' She explores how care in a loving family can teach us something about what kind of care we should be providing in our institutions. So, for example, she states that good family care comprises three elements: purpose (to help family members flourish), power (which is clearly understood, for example, parent to child), and particularity (understanding the individual peculiarities of the person and the family). So, these are the qualities that, if we want to provide them, we need to recognise and explicitly encourage within institutional care. Purpose, that is, flourishing rather than maintenance (so often the mediocre aim of institutional care), recognition and discussion of power, within the institution and within society, and particularity, insofar as really finding out what the individual wants in terms of needs and care. For Mrs Jones, above, all of the elements can be seen very clearly in the proposed solution – a solution that could only be reached because an explicit ethics of care, rather than a principle-based, approach was taken. Once again, the person, embedded in her network of relationships, is at the centre of the care, rather than institutional systems, procedures, rules, and a disconnected and distant notion of duty.

Personalisation was discussed in Chapter 2, and Lloyd (2010) looks at the concept through an ethics of care framework. In essence, Lloyd shares the concerns expressed in Chapter 2 regarding the financing of the personalisation agenda and the resources required to make choice real. Lloyd makes direct reference to the 'responsiveness' element of care that necessitates proper choice. Lloyd also points out that the emphasis on independence is unhelpful and not in keeping with an ethics of care; for example, residential care and not remaining at home might be a positive choice for a person and yet be antithetical to policy direction. An ethics of care can help in a further critical understanding of personalisation by highlighting dependency as a normal part of the human condition. Throughout the life course people are interdependent – at various times and in varying degrees. This means that the stigma attached to 'the growing older population' and the identification of that population as 'burdensome' is socially and financially constructed. As part of the neoliberal hegemony, however, it translates into an on-going quest to maintain independence at all costs.

As an example, Lloyd discusses the use of telecare, a service that remotely monitors older people's movements and triggers an alarm if unusual activity takes place. Lloyd suggests that the emphasis on maintaining people in their own homes has driven the development of telecare. From the perspective of an ethics of care, telecare should supplement the maintenance or development of a support network of care and not supplant it (which is what happens). In its current use it will undoubtedly worsen the experience of loneliness and isolation amongst older people. Once again, adopting an explicit ethics of care approach allows the identification of the hidden dangers of technological and procedural developments such as telecare. The underpinning basic assumptions (Schein 2010; see Chapter 2), in this case, that dependency is bad and relationships are unimportant are exposed as flawed and highlighted for critique.

In residential care with children and young people, the issue of touch, for example hugging, is often considered as an ethical dilemma. This is especially acute for male members of staff and young female residents. As Green and Day (2013) note, managerial practice concerned with the protection of the agency (and staff from allegations) can lead to 'no touch' policies. Approaching this from an ethics of care perspective means that such cold and bureaucratic policies would immediately be subject to questioning – what about the relatedness of the young people, with touch as part of caring relationships with staff? What about attentiveness – required to ascertain the young person's needs? Those needs may well be related to the need for physical touch and warmth. Capability to meet those needs must be facilitated by a supportive and caring environment where touch is accepted as normal and healthy. Of crucial importance are responsiveness and sensitivity to whether touch is meeting the young person's needs and is wanted (and by whom in what circumstances). Also, the integrity of care element would mean that social workers had to explicitly recognise the risk-averse social work context as well as the oppressive wider society where children in care are so disadvantaged and often damaged by the experience. The idea that an ethics of care can help us navigate this difficult issue is not to downplay the complexity of it for both young people and staff, as Green and Day (2013) recognise. They point out that no amount of evidence-based practice or research will address this very individual, person- and context-specific issue. Neither would rules, duty, or virtues assist in guiding workers. An ethics of care approach, however, opens up the discussion and the possibilities for tailored and 'particular' practice (Tronto 2010).

There are other practice instances where, at first glance, an ethics of care may seem less useful, for example dealing with service users involved in the criminal justice or child protection systems. Such service users may very well have done terrible things and may feel extremely resistant to engaging with a social worker and also resistant to being on the receiving end of professional 'care'! There may be hostility and aggression in their interactions with social workers, and the situation and encounter might seem very distant and different from applying an ethics of care approach to a vulnerable older person in a residential establishment, for example. These less comfortable examples and an exploration of how an ethics of care can still be useful will be covered in the next chapter where the individual level of practice is further analysed.

In conclusion, this chapter has introduced an ethics of care as the heart of the model that will unfold in subsequent chapters. It has been demonstrated that value-poor neoliberal practice as exemplified in Practice Example 3.1 cannot be justified by reference to an ethics of care, which gives a rationale for its promotion in this book and inclusion in the model. Also, there is a direct connection between an ethics of care approach and social justice via the integrity element of the approach (Tronto 1993), which is also necessary – as will be become clear as the model builds. Finally, in promoting the idea of care at the heart of social work practice, the neoliberal, hegemonic ideas about the 'underclass' and resultant punitive and controlling practice are undermined completely. To care for another human is to define him or her as worthy of respect, compassion, attention, and help.

main points

- Utilitarian and deontological approaches are principle-based approaches and, as such, have some limitations. Neoliberal practice can be justified within their frameworks.

- Virtue ethics is a useful approach to social work practice, but caution must be exercised due to the approach's easy alignment with dominant societal values.

- An ethics of care approach, with an explicit connection to wider political and social justice thinking, appears to be antithetical to neoliberal practice and is, therefore, promoted as the most useful starting point for a new model of practice.

taking it further

- Banks, S. (2012) *Ethics and Values in Social Work* (4th Ed) (Basingstoke: Palgrave Macmillan). An essential text for any scholar of social work values. Covers all the key elements.
- Banks, S. (Ed.) (2014) *Ethics* (Bristol: Policy Press). This collection of essays from renowned writers takes a radical stance in relation to social work ethics. Ultimately, is the interest in social work ethics part of a managerialist agenda to control and regulate behaviour, as in codes of practice?

- Lloyd, R. E. (2010) 'The individual in social care: The ethics of care and the personalisation agenda in services for older people in England', *Ethics and Social Welfare* 4 (2) 188–200. An excellent critique of personalisation through an ethics of care lens.
- Tronto, J. (2010) 'Creating caring institutions: Politics, plurality, and purpose', *Ethics and Social Welfare,* 4 (2) 158–171. Food for thought about how we construct institutional care as 'good' or 'bad'. Lessons from this article can be applied to care more widely.

5 Connecting an Ethics of Care with Ethical Stress: As Easy As It Sounds?

chapter

Overview

This chapter will tackle the reality of the conscious implementation of an ethics of care approach in the current social work context. It will also introduce ways of coping with (healthy) ontological anxiety and ways to act on the experience of ethical stress, which is a sign that practice is not value-congruent. (See Chapter 8 for further development of these ideas.) Finally, the chapter will consider situations where taking an ethics of care approach is less straightforward.

At this point in the book it has been suggested that an ethics of care approach can resist managerial procedural practice. However, taking an ethics of care approach to your own practice may not be as easy as it sounds in the current context, where managerialism and risk aversion abounds, time is short, colleagues are not all like-minded, and some of the people we work with have done terrible things and simply do not want to engage with social workers. The choice for many social workers is between following the party line, on one hand, and making sure the bureaucratic imperatives are top priority; or, on the other hand, prioritising the relationship with services users and prioritising their needs in order to care. Those who choose the latter might well feel out on a limb and experience a certain amount of what Taylor (2007) calls ontological anxiety. Taylor defines ontological anxiety as anxiety arising from the actions a social worker takes *in good faith* but that still produce worries and uncertainty for the worker.

Deepening this analysis, Taylor explores decision-making through an existential framework, using key concepts such as 'becoming' (Taylor 2007, p92). Becoming is a continual process in which human beings must be engaged to avoid stagnation: 'In order to always be "becoming" and not have stagnated, the person must continue to act authentically and avoid bad faith actions' (ibid., p92). Authenticity equates to congruence or genuineness as made central to social work by Carl Rogers (1966). In order to be authentic, people take responsibility for their decisions, are clear that they are acting in accordance with inner guidance, that is, their actions are congruent with their inner voice (conscience or value beliefs) and that the decision is taken in good faith (congruent with an ethics of care approach). The point is, however, that good-faith decisions still produce anxiety and uncertainty. In fact, good-faith decisions may produce more anxiety and uncertainty than decisions that are simply rule bound and unreflective.

Bad-faith decisions occur when a worker makes a decision that does not feel right, due to risk-averse procedures, punitive methods, or instructions from management. That worker will, according to Taylor, experience ontological guilt which equates to ethical stress (see Chapter 1). Taylor states that individuals who continually choose bad-faith actions over authentic responses stop progressing as 'becoming' human beings (Taylor 2007, p93).

At this point, then, we can see the potential for two types of decision-making. One type is good-faith decision-making, in line with values and conscience and part of a responsive, individually tailored approach to the work. This is congruent with authenticity and genuineness, and a worker who can make such decisions would be, according to Taylor, in the healthy process of becoming. The other type of decision is where the worker feels that the action is wrong and yet acquiesces to its execution due to other pressures. This leads to action characterised by the opposite of authenticity in that conscience and actions are in conflict. Avoiding taking responsibility for decision-making is another feature of this way of acting ('the supervisor told me to do it'). Taylor links the first type of decision to the existential concept of ontological anxiety and the second to ontological guilt and sums up the difference very usefully as follows: 'Quite simply, ontological anxiety is the price of living authentically. By contrast, choosing the more comfortable, non-anxiety-provoking course of action will, in the short term, result in feeling safer but in the long term lead to the more malignant state of ontological guilt' (Taylor 2007, p94). Long-term ontological guilt can cause regret, shame, and a feeling of stagnation. Taylor paints a picture of ontological guilt (or ethical stress) as extremely corrosive. Ontological anxiety, on the other hand, produced as a result of good-faith decisions, is, according to Taylor, a healthy by-product of being responsive and using discretion.

So, it is clear that doing the right thing is absolutely not without anxiety. And this is made far worse when actions are taken in a restrictive, managerial, risk-averse, and procedural context where values and care may mean very little. The key point here, however, is that the social worker recognises the anxiety as a healthy by-product of acting in good faith. The worker must be able to distinguish between the feeling of ontological anxiety and the far more corrosive state of feeling ontological guilt or ethical stress. In essence:

- I have done what I feel is the right thing here, but I feel very anxious about it (ontological anxiety). I will seek support to contain and work through those feelings. OR
- I know that was the wrong thing to do, but I did it because my senior told me to and I didn't feel confident enough to argue the point. I now feel really bad about it. Ok, I must speak to my senior about the decision and let him know I want to do something different (ontological guilt/ethical stress leading to ethical action).

It can be seen, then, that in distinguishing the different feelings experienced, the social worker can work out what needs to happen next. The recognition of ethical stress can lead to ethical action when practice has been value-poor, risk averse, or overly procedural. This is a key point, and it is *why* ethical stress can be extremely useful. Explicitly recognising it as a real thing can help workers take the required action to reconnect their practice to social work values. As discussed in Chapter 1, when I have shared the concept of ethical stress with social work students, I am invariably met with nods of recognition and relief resulting from the identification, naming, and discussion of the concept.

Banks and Williams (2005) give an example of the interplay between these concepts. They interviewed a social worker who felt real anxiety about leaving an older man, who wanted to be left alone, without intervention, despite his excessive drinking problem. The man was able to make his own decisions and was clear about what he wanted. The right thing to do was to respect his wishes (after talking through services available and using skills to involve him – to no avail). This right decision, however, led to real anxiety about something 'bad' happening and the possibility of the worker being blamed. Alternatively, the risk-averse actions here might have been to involve other agencies, exaggerate his level of need, or refer him without his consent, *simply* as a back-covering exercise. The man might have been subjected to unwanted and illegitimate interference from the state had this happened. Also, a worker following that path might well have suffered ethical stress due to the knowledge that he or she had done the wrong thing primarily for his or her own safety rather than the good of the service user. Such is the level of anxiety in those situations that when the man died, the worker commented *'fortunately* not falling down the stairs' (Banks and Williams 2005, p1015). This starkly illustrates the difficulty of doing the right thing and then living with the resultant ontological anxiety in the existing managerial and blame culture. The implication is that had the man fallen down the stairs when inebriated, the worker would have been blamed for his or her non-intervention decision.

practice example

5.1 Ontological anxiety versus ontological guilt/ethical stress

An approved social worker (or mental health officer, MHO, in Scotland) is working with a very mentally disordered, but not dangerous, person. Taking everything into consideration, the worker agrees to a compulsory detention. He feels it is the right thing, but he loses sleep that night over the enormity of taking away the freedom of a person (with whom he has a good, trusting relationship). He experiences (healthy) ontological anxiety.

The same social worker wants to uphold the right of a person he is working with to stop taking his medication due to the horrendous side effects. However, his team manager insists that he take further action to compel the service user to take the medication – there have been a great number of stories in the media recently about people with mental health problems doing awful things. The social worker complies but feels it is the wrong thing to do. He experiences ontological guilt and ethical stress.

In the light of the reality of contemporary social work, it would take a very motivated, committed, brave, un-risk-averse, and anxiety-tolerant social worker to behave in the way he or she thinks is right and, as in the practice illustration, resist the instructions of the team leader. Given the finding that newer workers object much less to the restrictions of the managerial, risk-averse, and controlling nature of contemporary social work, is it likely they will opt to be guided by their feelings of ethical stress and to take matters further? Is it not more likely they will take the easiest route and follow the instructions or rules? Preston-Shoot (2011, p187) suggests that 'technical rationality, expressed through expert knowledge, regulations and established bureaucratic procedures, can promote a sense of legitimacy and routine without the need to engage with social or ethical concerns'. In other words, social workers might respond to service users by following employer instructions when faced with conflicting ethical principles rather than resolve them by ethical consideration. One method of recognising and challenging that simple type of managerial or rule-following-only practice is, as stated, the explicit identification of ethical stress as a useful element of practice.

So, leading on from Practice Example 5.1, the following two sections will look at practical ways to 1) employ an ethics of care approach and deal with the resultant ontological anxiety and 2) identify and act on the experience of ethical stress.

Ethics of Care and Ontological Anxiety

Applying the ethics of care elements

The elements of an ethics of care approach (see Chapter 4) can be applied to the first case in Practice Example 5.1 above. The worker demonstrated attentiveness, by getting to know the service user and building the best possible relationship he or she could. He or she did this by really listening and understanding the service user's point of view – and empathising with his or her situation. How must it feel for the service user? Unashamedly, compassion is brought to the worker's thoughts, feelings, and actions. It is crucial that the worker knows this is not 'soft' but is actually essential (BASW 2012). In the practice example, and this is a very important point, the worker explores the service user's view as the central and priority element in the decision-making process *but* does not agree. Really listening and empathising does not mean automatic agreement – but disagreement does not validate non-listening and imperious practice. An ethics of care requires listening, understanding, empathising, explanation, and discussion – carried out with care and compassion.

The worker then has to take responsibility for the care of the service user and the decision. This would involve taking seriously all of the service user's concerns and worries – for example sorting out domestic arrangements. The social worker would not revert to 'that's someone else's job' but would make sure that things are carried out as promised (by liaison with other agencies but *not* by abdicating responsibility to them). Doing the work competently is the third element – again this might mean going beyond the call of duty to make sure things happen properly. Staying attuned to the needs and feelings of the service user and remaining responsive is the next element. In the practice example, this might be an extremely important element as the service user might become, understandably, very distressed. Being able to anticipate, staying tuned in, and knowing how to deal with very heightened emotion would be a crucial part of the work in this instance – very much linked to competence. Keeping things de-escalated so that the situation does not become worse for the service user would be crucial. Finally, understanding how this situation links to the wider political and social context is an essential element. Understanding how and why our society stigmatises people with mental health issues, making sure that the resultant risk aversion and fear-of-blame culture has *not* influenced the social worker's decision must be at the heart of the social worker's reflection-in-action (Schon 1983).

The ethics of care approach, of course, is centrally concerned with the service user's relationship with the worker and with the people in his or her life. The worker must discuss this with the service user to find out the extent of involvement of family and friends and whom the service user considers the important people in his or her life (not assuming). The social worker needs to do everything possible to maximise the involvement of people whom the service user wants to be involved.

It is clear that an ethics of care approach would not apply to the actions of the social worker in the second example. The worker there has listened to the service user and has empathised, understood, and actually agreed, but then he or she fails to take responsibility to act on that understanding and agreement. The worker does not include the elements of 'responsibility' (taking charge of the care and formulating a case for the desired course of action); 'competence' (using logic, the concept of defensible decision-making, and social work knowledge – see later in the chapter – to form a persuasive argument to the team manager *and* to competently formulate an alternative plan to the team manager's preferred option); and 'integrity of care' (not acting on critical reflection that would help the worker understand and expose the team manager's risk-averse thinking). It may also have been that the worker did not think about the care of the service user in the context of his or her existing supports or relationships.

It is apparent that it would not have been easy for the social worker in the second example to employ an ethics of care, but perhaps being explicitly conscious of trying to do so, and being sure of the rightness of doing so, would have afforded some conviction to his or her preferred course of action. It might also have given the worker a clear framework within which to operate, for example, seeing it as his or her responsibility to make an argument to the team manager and to have a well-developed and logical alternative plan, rather than to acquiesce without even realising that responsibility. An essential element of that type of thinking (rather than the abdication of responsibility that comes with ontological guilt/ ethical stress) is understanding how to make defensible decisions (Kemshall 2002) in your own right – understanding it is your responsibility to do this, argue for it, and not just follow instructions.

Defensible decision-making and ontological anxiety

Defensible decision-making must, at the outset, be differentiated from defensi*ve* decision-making. Defensible decision-making is ethical, reasoned, and considers all factors, whilst defensive decision-making is risk averse and made with 'in case something goes wrong' thinking central. So, saying 'no' to all travel requests from people who are on supervision from the court or parole board and who are actuarially assessed as high risk, 'just in case something goes wrong and we are in the newspaper/sacked', is an example of a defensive rule of thumb that might apply in a probation office.

When it comes to practice involving risk assessment, the temptation to operate in a defensive manner may become even more acute. Littlechild (2010) points out that agencies, for example, use actuarial tools and processes to avoid mistakes and to assist workers to make defensible decisions or, perhaps more accurately, to be able to demonstrate due diligence and defend their practice should something go wrong. The faith invested in these tools and procedures means that if there is a bad outcome to a decision, then the assumption is that it *must* be the social workers fault: 'if only they had used the tool properly'. This in turn can lead to the idea that social workers are not competent to use the tool properly, and so the tool itself needs to be more detailed and controlling to avoid further mistakes. In other words, where there is a bad outcome to a decision and a resultant media outcry, the government will respond with 'managerialism...which consists of a controlling approach to micro-practice' (Littlechild 2010, p665).

Research Box 5.1

Managerialism in children's services

In 2009, UNISON conducted a survey of children and families social workers for the second Lord Laming report and found that workers were still in a very difficult situation with heavy caseloads and serious absence levels in teams. In terms of increased managerialism, 43 per cent of respondents agreed that procedures had improved (demonstrating that there is a place for procedure and guidelines), but there was widespread criticism of the new bureaucratic computerised information system, which was seen as doing nothing to help protect children. Instead, it increased the burden of administration for workers – a common consequence of managerialism, which leaves less time for face-to-face work with families.

The above managerial response leads to less autonomy for social workers to make decisions and more rules, procedures, and checklists for them to follow, a situation that Littlechild condemns as he suggests that social workers engage with untidy and complex situations that require them to be autonomous and supported in order to respond individually and properly. This chimes with Taylor's idea that social workers (and agencies) must be supported to help them live with the ontological anxiety produced by having autonomy, acting in good faith, taking responsibility and, ultimately, caring.

Clearly, in the contemporary context this might well lead to a situation where workers are consumed with anxiety that the (good-faith) decisions they have made will end in bad outcomes and they will be blamed and vilified. Phillips (2009) suggests that social workers feel this anxiety more strongly than any other. He describes it as the lying-awake, nightmarish scenario of 'what if something goes wrong, and I will be blamed/sacked/vilified'. This leads to an emphasis on defensive decision-making, although even this might not be a protective strategy because, as Philips points out, in hindsight any decision can seem indefensible. How much will this anxiety be exacerbated by the government's plans to charge social workers with wilful neglect for 'failing to protect children' (Community Care 2015)? Social workers could face up to five years in prison if found guilty. If we could think of the most likely way to increase risk-averse, defensive practice, this is surely it. Social workers will live with ontological anxiety as well as actual fear of criminal charges – caring, autonomous, and responsive practice looks like an unimportant consideration in the face of that reality...

This seems like an irresolvable and desperate situation. Who would want to be a social worker? How can a worker resist the dominant managerial culture, employ an ethics of care, argue for an ethical course of action, then live with the resultant (healthy) anxiety? How is this possible, when we have just acknowledged that the culture surrounding social work is one that vilifies workers for poor outcomes, when media responses are damning, and when there are such significant consequences for ourselves in terms of losing our jobs, being reviled, or being arrested? Surely it is much easier to ignore ethical stress and just follow risk-averse instructions: 'I will make sure *I* am safe, as the absolute priority.' That may be true, but the literature and research suggests that down this path lies ethical stress, ontological guilt, corrosive and toxic regret, and, most importantly, a very poor and uncaring service for service users.

What is to be done? Again, the concept of defensible decision-making emerges as useful when implementing an ethics of care approach and trying to contain resultant ontological anxiety. The first step in understanding this concept is to think through the idea that decisions and outcomes are not clearly causally linked. In fact, there is a body of literature to suggest that decisions should be uncoupled from outcomes when it comes to evaluating them. O'Sullivan (1999) in his exploration of how decisions should be evaluated, states that evaluation needs to be based on what the average skilled practitioner would have done, given what was known and what could reasonably be expected to have been known at the time, *without the benefit of hindsight* (O'Sullivan 1999, p155, emphasis added). In other words, a good decision, based on good, defensible reasons, should be evaluated as it stands, detached from information that might come to light after a bad outcome has been investigated. Was the decision a good one at the time, considering what was known then? This is a very important point and quite a departure for the common-sense view that a decision's worth should be measured by its outcome. For example, if a child dies, the decision to leave the child at home with the parent who killed her or him was clearly wrong and the evaluation should start from that assumption. How can it be otherwise? How can the decision to leave the child at home ever be considered a good one?

Banks (2012, p208) helps us advance our thinking about this by discussing the complex reality of decision-making in social work and defines a social work decision as often more akin to a dilemma, that is, 'a choice between two equally unwelcome alternatives'. Banks (2012, p33) also suggests that these types of decisions have no clearly right and clearly wrong choices; rather, the social worker must choose the 'lesser of two evils'. Whatever the choice, it might still be an evil. Within every evil is the potential for a poor outcome, even if the social worker has chosen the path most likely for success. G. MacDonald (1990a) was involved in a very interesting exchange with Hollis and Howe (1990) about decision-making and blame in social work. She draws attention to the Report of the Panel of Inquiry into the death of Jasmine Beckford as follows: 'In assessing whether a reasonable person would have known or seen an event, *we are entitled to have regard to what actually happened*' (G. MacDonald 1990a, p526, emphasis added). MacDonald debates this statement, arguing that the social worker's course of action might have been the right one, despite the bad outcome. The assumption that a bad outcome equates to a bad decision is, she suggests, the starting point for most enquiries. Thus, guilt of the worker is already established by the fact of the bad outcome, exacerbated further by hindsight-informed investigations to find support for this assumption. In summing up her criticism of this practice, MacDonald proposes that the 'criteria for assessment [of social work practice] should not be the outcomes, but the appropriateness of the *decisions* given the information available at the time' (G. MacDonald 1990a, p527, emphasis added). In the ensuing argument between MacDonald and Hollis and Howe (G. MacDonald 1990a; Hollis and Howe 1990; and MacDonald 1990b), Hollis and Howe are quite clear in their view that outcomes are the best measure of practice competence (or otherwise): 'the test of sound judgement verges on success' (Hollis and Howe 1990, p549). The authors suggest that if a person has accepted the role of a social worker, then he or she has accepted the risks that go with that. MacDonald, on the other hand, states quite simply that we cannot always predict whether a bad outcome will happen and living with this uncertainty is inevitable. This equates to Taylor's and Littlechild's ideas about living with ontological anxiety generated by uncertainty and to Banks's idea that sometimes a course of action is chosen that is the lesser of two evils but that can still go badly wrong. MacDonald sums up by stating that social workers always have a responsibility to make the best possible decision, but 'if the best possible decision is made, then even if a bad outcome occurs, it is morally correct' (G. MacDonald 1990a, p543).

This may be a new way of thinking about decisions for social work students who may feel overwhelmed by the difficulty of 'getting things right'. Further weight is added to MacDonald's view by MacDonald and MacDonald (2010) who introduce the idea of 'uncertainty'. A risk is when the person taking the risk has an awareness of the odds or likelihood, whereas in an uncertain situation even the likelihood is unknown. The authors suggest that child protection work is fraught with uncertainty and subject to huge, unexpected turns of event and unpredictable twists. They also note that there can be, as a result, a very limited link between effort, competent practice, progress, and outcomes. They suggest, as MacDonald (1990) did, that this has implications for how practice is evaluated – the decisions should be scrutinised, uncoupled from the outcome. In her review of child protection Munro also draws attention to uncertainty:

> The second stage at which uncertainty arises is when making predictions about children's future safety. The big problem for society (and consequently for professionals) is establishing a real-istic expectation of professionals' ability to predict the future and manage risk of harm to children and young people. Even when it is ascertained that abuse or neglect has occurred, there are dif-ficult decisions to make about whether the parents can be helped to keep children safe from harm or whether the child needs to be removed. Such decisions involve making predictions about likely future harm and so are fallible. It may be judged highly unlikely that the child will be re-abused but low probability events happen. *This does not in itself indicate flaws in the professional reasoning.* The ideal would be if risk management could eradicate risk but this is not possible; it can only try to reduce the probability of harm.
>
> (Munro 2011, p18, emphasis added)

> It is important to be aware how much hindsight distorts our judg-ment about the predictability of an adverse outcome. Once we know that the outcome was tragic, we look backwards from it and it seems clear which assessments or actions were critical in leading to that outcome. It is then easy to say in amazement how could they not have seen X? Or how could they not have realised that X would lead to Y? Even when we know the evidence on the hindsight bias, it is difficult to shift it; we still look back and over-estimate how visible the signs of danger were. The hindsight bias

oversimplifies or trivialises the situation confronting the practitioners and masks the processes affecting practitioner behaviour before-the-fact. Hindsight bias blocks our ability to see the
deeper story of systematic factors that predictably shape human
performance.

(ibid.)

In fact, one of Munro's (2011, p43) principles for risk-sensible practice is
as follows:

> Principle 4: Harm can never be totally prevented. Risk decisions
> should, therefore, be judged by the quality of the decision-making,
> not by the outcome.

Exercise 5.1 — Decision versus outcome

Think about any recent stories of social work decisions that led
to tragedies, covered by the media. Can you detect the poor
outcome = poor practice assumption in the coverage? Pick
one such example and write down bullet points about how
you would argue with somebody who said 'how could a social
worker let that happen?' Would you be able to explain that the
outcome does not mean the decision was necessarily wrong?
Practise thinking it through.

It seems we have agreement for an approach to investigating tragedies
and scrutinising practitioner decision-making that focuses on the decision made at the time and does not ascribe to the 'poor outcome = poor
decision' school of thought. Actual investigations may have not quite
embraced this approach, but there seems to be movement in that direction, and it is a way of thinking that social workers and students can
apply to their own practice: 'I will be absolutely accountable for making
good decisions, but poor outcomes may still ensue, and I understand
that and the limits of my responsibility.' This may lessen the anxiety
burden a little. The next step, then, is to consider how an ethical, defensible decision is made within an overarching ethics of care approach.

Elements of defensible decision-making

According to Carson (1996), a defensible decision is one that a body of co-
professionals would have made in the same circumstances. This concept
is still well and truly alive in current social work thinking, and another of
Munro's (2011, p44) risk principles deals with exactly that:

> Principle 6: The standard expected and required of those working in child protection is that their risk decisions should be consistent with those that would have been made in the same circumstances by professionals of similar specialism or experience.

The standard is therefore reasonably clear. That does not help, however, with the elements that should be considered when making a defensible decision. According to Kemshall (2002), workers' decisions should be:

- made by taking all reasonable steps
- made by using reliable assessment methods (if appropriate)
- made once all information, that can be collected, is collected (and missing information sought out) and thoroughly evaluated
- correct in terms of policy and procedure
- made after communication with others.

So, some elements such as following procedures and using tools are subject to the critiques of managerialism outlined earlier. The point is that if social workers must use tools/procedures, then they must do so, but *critically*. Deviation or a decision that a procedure/tool is not appropriate should be well documented, otherwise it looks like shoddy practice. A conscious decision to not use a tool is very different from simply not bothering. Information-gathering is also an important element of defensible practice – it is not defensible to not gather available information. Missing information should also be sought rather than just tolerated (and efforts made should be recorded). This practice is starting to sound a little like back-covering, but good practice should be explicit and recorded and knowledge of what decision elements would be scrutinised in the event of a bad outcome is not a bad thing. Poor practice emerges when this awareness of scrutiny supplants the other elements of practice, for example, caring. This leads into Kemshall's point that the decision must be made by taking *all reasonable steps* or for *good, explicit reasons*, and herein lies the opportunity for explicit ethics of care practice. Being explicit about values-related reasons is essential here. So, thinking through and documenting that you considered the relationships in the person's life, that you listened attentively to what he or she wanted and why – and tried to understand his or her point of view – and that you let all of that influence and guide your practice should be explicit. Recourse to BASW and IFSW definitions and statements of values, the Professional Capabilities Framework (PCF; College of Social Work 2012) and, to a more limited degree, the Codes of Practice (see Chapter 1) should all be drawn on explicitly and linked to your decision. Although every detail of the sources of your decisions might not be documented, there should be a clear line of sight from your documented actions to underpinning values, and you need to *know* that explicitly. Interpretation of legislation and policy are also reasons for decisions, and often the rhetoric in government policy will support caring and responsive practice and might be a good source of evidence. In essence, it is incumbent on the worker, as an expert in that area of practice, to find the sources – procedures (or explicit critique of same), codes of values/ ethics, policy, research evidence, and legislation – that promote caring practice. The worker should then draw on these sources, keep the service user's voice and relationships central, and seek out all relevant information. The recording of all of that should, in turn, lead to a defensible and robust decision with an ethics of care approach at its heart. The worker should be able to rest more easily that such a decision should stand up to scrutiny, even in the event of a bad outcome.

Exercise 5.2 — Decision-making

Think of a decision you or a colleague made recently or one that you were part of (a case conference, for example). Was it defensible? List the good reasons for which the decision was made and try to emphasise the service user's voice and care and compassion, even if the decision was not what the service user wanted. Check the practice against the other defensible decision elements. Ultimately, was this a defensible or a defensive decision?

Supervision and ontological anxiety

Supervision is widely understood as a meeting between social worker and manager where support for the emotional demands of the work, guidance, and oversight of the actual work being done is provided by the manager. Supervision is not without tensions, however, and depending on the supervisor, can be very technical and managerial, for example checking that all appointments have been done and that paperwork is up to date, or very supportive, with space for exploration of emotions, feelings, and concerns. Fenton (2014a) found that supervision was a good indicator of the type of ethical climate in the agency. Managerial supervision reflected a managerial ethical climate. In turn, this was significantly correlated with increased ethical stress, thus providing evidence for the importance of value-rich and supportive supervision to social workers' wellbeing.

Beddoe (2010) conducted a study interviewing six experienced supervisors about their experiences of supervising staff. The author looked at whether practice had become 'ruled by technicist approaches in which risk assessment systems and checklists are put in place to minimise the risk of practitioners missing something important' (Beddoe 2010, p1281) and had resulted in supervision coming to 'focus attention on micro-management and surveillance' (ibid., p1280). She found that the supervisors she interviewed still had a commitment to the various purposes of supervision, whilst they acknowledged that the emphasis on risk management could make this difficult. A clear theme emerged from the study that supervision must recognise the possibility of change and retain a commitment to care; that is, discussions about care, helping, and change must be explicitly recognised. This means that social workers must be helped, in supervision, to live with uncertainty and anxiety. Beddoe quotes Parton (1998, p23) who stated that 'social work needed the rehabilitation of the idea of uncertainty, and the permission to talk about indeterminacy rather than greater proceduralism' (Beddoe 2010, p1288). This reinforces a key message of the chapter that uncertainty will produce ontological anxiety and social workers can be helped to contain and live with that anxiety via supervision. Beddoe also found that her study did expose the possibility of a risk-averse ethical climate reducing and undermining the quality of supervision. In summary, Beddoe's study demonstrates that the six supervisors interviewed were able to retain a holistic approach to supervision and were balancing the different requirements of the task, but the author acknowledges that further research is required to better understand how good supervision can be implemented within the context of current social work practice. One way to reconcile the tensions between space for critical reflection and discussion of values and case work and managerial requirements is suggested by a model developed by Jindal-Snape and Ingram (2013) and adapted for the particular social work context in Ingram et al. (2014). The SuReCom (Supervision Remit Compatibility) model facilitates discussion of the competing tensions, negotiation, and reconciliation:

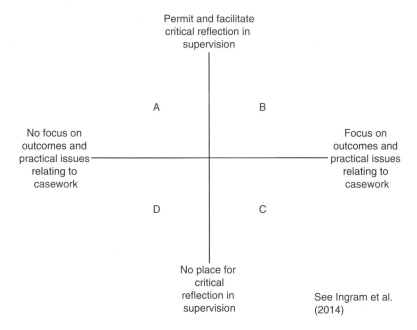

Figure 5.1 The SuReCom model

The model allows the participants to identify an agreed, collaborative method of supervision. The authors suggest plotting the aspirational locus of supervision and say that this should be done separately. So, for example, quadrant B allows for consideration of both essential elements, although workers may require a different locus for each supervision – depending on what is going on for them at the time. A mis-match in aspirations between supervisor and worker will lead to discussion and negotiation. The value of the model lies in making the tensions explicit and thus available for discussion, rather than the social worker feeling he or she has to initiate the request for a different type of supervision. In terms of attempting to take an ethics of care approach to social work practice and to doing it within a potentially hostile context, beginning with an aspirational identification of supervision as allowing critical reflection is a starting point for creating a useful space for discussion of anxiety. Of course much of this depends on the supervisor, who might be party to the perpetuation of a managerial culture, but at least the model opens up the discussion and explicitly talking about values allows for debate (and persuasion?).

Colleague support

Seeking opportunities for peer support is something that most social workers would recognise, whether it be meeting for a coffee, having lunch, or just mulling something over in the office with a trusted colleague. Ingram (2015a) found in his study of local authority social workers that informal peer support was the most valued type of support identified by the workers. Ingram shows that the reasons for this include: knowing that others have had similar experiences to one's own; the support is not recorded and, therefore, provides a safe space to be really honest; availability and immediacy of this support; and the opportunity for the worker to 'think through' or reflect with another person, perhaps in preparation for a further discussion when the argument needs to be well prepared.

It would seem that another element in informal peer support is that workers will seek out like-minded colleagues to provide it and will probably offer it in return to the same people. Although there is the danger of collusion, due to the absence of an alternative point of view or ethos, there is also the opportunity to share sources of evidence for utilising a care approach, for explicit discussion of values, and simply to recharge the batteries if the worker feels somewhat ground down by an increasing pressure to just do the task and 'manage' service users. Wider sources of peer support are also available in the form of seminars run at local universities, articles in journals such as *Critical and Radical Social Work*

(Policy Press), and the Social Work Action Network (SWAN), an explicitly radical, anti-managerial UK-wide organisation which arranges conferences and events. There may be a local branch near you, and it will be one environment where an approach to practice based on care will be most welcome!

In summary, ontological anxiety is *not* ethical stress and is, in fact, a healthy consequence of acting in good faith, in line with your values and going beyond the 'task' to employ an ethics of care. The social worker's challenge in relation to ontological anxiety is to learn how to contain it and work through it (see Chapter 8 for further thinking on this topic). On the other hand, the challenge when one experiences ethical stress is to recognise it as such and *act on it*; in other words, to use it as impetus for ethical action.

Identify and Act on Ethical Stress

Identifying ethical stress is relatively easy once you understand the concept. It can begin with disquiet, creeping guilt, and an unsettled feeling that you have done, or colluded with, something that was not 'right'. The next step is to, very honestly, reflect on why you feel like that. If, as in the first scenario in Practice Example 5.1, it is because you really believe you did the 'right' thing and yet feel the enormity of your decision – in this case, taking away a person's freedom – then you are experiencing ontological anxiety. How to work with that is the subsequent question. However, if, on reflection, you come to the conclusion that you have not acted in the 'right' way, then you need to act to remedy or tackle the 'wrong'. Virtue ethics would suggest that a worker needs courage in this situation to do what's required, and an ethics of care approach would include this in taking responsibility for the care of the person you are working with. Taking on the problem competently (the next element of an ethics of care) includes being able to analyse what went wrong and to formulate a solid, value-based, knowledgeable, and caring alternative solution. This is very important, because if you want to change the existing response/decision, you must be persuasive. Competently formulating your argument will also guard against accusations of just being 'soft' or 'naïve', although, realistically these barbs will always come your way from some quarters.

O'Donnell et al. (2008) and Fenton (2014a) found that the experience of ethical stress was very much influenced by the ethical climate within the agency. O'Donnell et al. also found that ethical action, that is, taking action based on the experience of ethical stress to put things right, was more likely to happen if the organisational climate was conducive to this and if ethics resources were available (supervision, support, and discussion of ethical issues, for example). In an overly managerial culture, where ethical stress may abound and ethical action is required to a greater degree, action might be much more difficult. Intuitively, it seems obvious that a managerial, neoliberal, and risk-averse culture might well be hostile to challenge or argument for a different way of doing things. Once again, we can see the difficulty in taking an ethics of care approach and taking action based on ethical stress as an indicator of things not being ethically sound. It is unsurprising, then, that social workers who attempt to challenge and to take ethical action are rare (Fine and Teram 2012).

Fine and Teram (2012, p1313) conducted a study in Canada, analysing the views of social workers on ethical issues in their practice. The investigation into what motivates workers to 'stand up' to moral injustices and to take moral or ethical action to address them is illustrated by the following quote from a participant:

> I think it's very important to know what you consider to be right and very important to speak up when you think something is not right and to explore it and to be willing to sort of be one of the few voices and not just go with the flow because everyone else is comfortable with it...

The key point embedded in this quote is: 'know what you consider to be right'. This brings us back to the finding that newer workers and students are more accepting of a neoliberal, managerial type of social work and so might not see that there is anything wrong in risk-averse practice centrally concerned with managing the behaviour of deviant people. Once again, the importance of challenging and exposing the hegemony in an overtly radical way is crucial to helping students come to a world view, based on social justice, about what is 'right'. Clearly, the identification of ethical stress and resultant ethical action will never happen without that. (See Chapter 3 for more detail on how the contemporary hegemony operates.)

In essence, Fine and Teram found that all respondents who could take ethical action had 'a very robust sense of knowing what ought to be done' and 'the welfare of the client' in common. That is not to say that taking ethical action was painless or without anxiety, but the researchers found that workers almost felt there was no alternative. Another way to look at this is that, with a very well-developed sense of social justice and care, living with ethical stress is almost intolerable and ethical action is seen as a necessity. Inevitably, we return to the importance of encouraging this type of social justice- and care-informed thinking and developing courage in students. In relation to an ethics of care approach, these concepts sit within the 'responsibility', 'competence', and 'integrity of care' elements.

Emphatically adding weight to this idea, Stanford (2011, p1520) found, from a study of Australian social workers, that personal moral codes were the deciding factor in whether a worker would 'advocate for and protect' a service user, or 'control and dismiss' him or her. Likewise, compassion and empathy were very important elements in the 'advocating' group and absent in the 'controlling and dismissing' group. In fact, the 'controlling and dismissing' group used justification by reference to ethics, as described in Chapter 3:

> I think, at the end of the day, morally and ethically I would have done the right thing and I feel very settled and secure in that because I used client self-determination. I can say, 'You still provided a certain amount but it has been up to the family and up to the young person to take that and do what they want with it.'

(Stanford 2011, p1521)

Stanford feels that there was a lack of compassion and empathy in this worker's response and that recourse to blunt understanding of social work ethical principles was used to justify that. Also, a belief in the possibility of change and a practice framework drawn from understanding of oppression and social justice were features unique to the 'advocate and protect' group. This is a very important point as it adds weight yet again to social workers having a clear understanding of what is right in terms of social justice. If this is part of their practice framework, they are much more likely to 'know what's right' and to take action. Finally, echoing O'Donnell et al.'s findings, Sanford found that it was easier for workers to 'advocate and protect' when the organisational culture facilitated that.

The conclusion to this section, then, is very clear indeed. Workers will experience ethical stress and feel inclined, or driven, to act on that and to put things right only if they have a well-developed value base: a belief in, and understanding of, social justice and anti-oppression; care, compassion, and empathy; a sense that the service user's wellbeing comes first; and, to a lesser extent, a supportive agency ethical climate.

Figure 5.2 Practice Model Iteration 2

Covert moral or ethical action

Weinberg and Taylor (2014) reported on findings from a large-scale Canadian study, carried out over three years. The study looked at the effect of the proliferation of rules in contemporary, managerial social work. The researchers found that rules, due to over-complexity or not being in the best interests of the service user, were often bent or relaxed by individual social workers. On a cautionary note, this covert moral action might be considered to impede structural or organisation change for the better, as the rules were simply worked around (with individual workers taking the risk). Although not explicitly stated, it was clear from the study that the workers who bent the rules did so at times of ethical stress and, although covert action is maybe not as useful as overt action, the underlying feature that the rule-bending workers had in common was that it was done for the good of the service user.

Further Difficulty with Ethics of Care Implementation

This section of the chapter will look at situations where implementing an ethics of care approach is even more difficult. Beyond organisational and political impediments, what about when situations and service users themselves cause the application of care to be more difficult, for example, when service users have done terrible things? H. Ferguson (2005) notes that when workers are left in a situation where empathy, care, and unconditional positive regard are difficult to apply, they are left without a reference point. He also points out that social workers in hostile situations often feel as if they are hostages, trapped in the situation. This can lead to appeasement, turning a blind eye so as to stay on the 'side' of the service users. It is at this point that the social worker might resort to either unwarranted approbatory or, at the other extreme, controlling and managerial behaviour. Gregory (2010) suggests that an alternative, value-based response is still possible; dealing properly with risks and protection whilst still promoting relationship building, care, and understanding of that person's situation. Gregory's study demonstrates that experienced probation officers knew, beyond any doubt, that although they were working with people who had done some extremely bad things, they still had to work to build a genuine relationship with the service users and to care about them – an ethics of care approach in action:

> 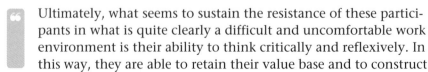 Ultimately, what seems to sustain the resistance of these participants in what is quite clearly a difficult and uncomfortable work environment is their ability to think critically and reflexively. In this way, they are able to retain their value base and to construct

for themselves a form of subjectivity in which they continue to see themselves as social workers. As they reflect upon practice encounters, the value base that the participants continue to deploy, in the face of working practices that do not facilitate or support it, is essentially an ethic of care.

(Gregory 2010, p2281)

So, in practical terms *how* can social workers do this given Ferguson's assertion that they have been left without a reference point? The practitioners in Gregory's study were very experienced, had real belief in their values (that theme again), and had accumulated significant practice wisdom.

Tallant, Sambrook, and Green (2008) suggest that the starting point for working with resistant or hostile service users is finding out from their perspective what the reality of the situation is. This might be a view about how useless all social workers are or how unfairly they have been treated, but the task of the worker is to really listen to that and try to understand and empathise with the service user's view. This is entirely congruent with the first element of an ethics of care approach, 'attentiveness', and should be applied to any service user with whom we work. Being listened to properly, rather than being listened to defensively, is a starting point. H. H. Ferguson (2005) also states that being clear about the authority in the role of the social worker is very important. Being up front and honest about this, but conveying it in a skilled and unauthoritarian way, is crucial to allowing social workers to ask future difficult questions. So, for example, 'remember when I said I had to check...' is much easier than suddenly announcing that you want to check, which transmits mistrust and disbelief.

Having engaged in a manner that is completely congruent with the ethics of care elements of 'attentiveness' and 'responsibility', which is no different from the engagement with any service user, how do we then go on to work with someone where we are being, of necessity, controlling and enforcing? Held (2010, p116) tackles that very question by asking 'can the ethics of care handle violence?' Held is including child abuse, violence against women, and terrorism in her concept of 'violence' and says:

Scepticism is certainly in order if it is suggested that we can deal with violence simply by caring. Violence seems to call for the harsh arm of the law and enforcement, not the soft touch of care. I will argue, nevertheless, that the ethics of care is a comprehensive morality that can offer guidance for problems of violence as it can for other problems.

(ibid.)

To guide our understanding of this, Held uses a game of tennis between two friends as an analogy. During the match, the friends try to win at all costs and play by the fair and definite rules of the game. If this approach was generalised to the remainder of their relationship, they would no longer be friends, but it does not have to do that, nor should it. It is only suitable for limited and defined interactions. In the same way, social workers should, as a default, employ an ethics of care approach, allowing the rules of hard justice to prevail when they are required. This does not negate care, compassion, or kindness; it simply recognises that rules and control sometimes become the priority in specific interactions. So, for example, in working with a family where there is domestic violence, if evidence and research show that programmes of cognitive-behavioural work reduce the recidivism of male abusers, then an ethics of care can accommodate that. Rules of justice and hard evidence are brought to bear to make that happen, for the limited time required, and to ensure that everyone in the situation is cared for. Being 'competent' to organise the care and to understand why it is necessary is an important element of the ethics of care – never more so than in situations such as this. Alternatively, if corporate responses to something like domestic abuse mean that individual women's voices are lost and caring is not as it should be, the competent and caring practitioner would take a critical stance, hopefully leading to ethical action (such as arguing in an evidence-informed way against such responses).

Although implementing the rules and enforcing requirements should be used only when necessary, a study by ADT Fourth World, the Family Rights Group, and academics demonstrates that social workers often use authoritarian practice as a matter of course, including: demonstrating a lack of respect; blaming families for their poverty; treating people as liars; making assumptions about wrongdoing; not listening in case conferences; and writing reports that families do not understand or agree with (Gupta 2015). Essentially, many workers were 'othering' the families, as described in Chapter 3. Conversely, families also reported practice that mirrored an ethics of care in action, including: being respectful; getting to know the families properly and spending time with them; not adopting a 'tick box' style; adopting a mutual learning approach; being open with information and transparent about process; and making expectations manageable. Therein, we can see the 'attentiveness' element of an ethics of care approach as well as 'responsiveness' and 'competence'. The authors conclude that, in contrast to practice that stigmatises and 'others', 'social work can be experienced differently through practice that recognises the complex interactions between personal problems and structural inequality, and challenges the dominant discourse individualising risk and blaming families for their poverty' (Gupta 2015, p138).

The above section demonstrates and gives an outline for an ethics of care approach with involuntary service users. It is clear, however, that this practice needs to be underpinned by a robust understanding of social justice. In Kosny and Eakin's (2008) study, the workers viewed the service users as victims of an unfair and unjust society and this facilitated feelings of compassion and care. This is echoed by Gupta's findings that families experienced the best, non-stigmatising practice when workers understood the effects of structural inequality. For social workers starting out, it is very important that they understand how increasing inequality, poverty, and austerity increase the incidence of child abuse, violence, and stress (Ferguson and Lavalette 2009; see Chapter 6) and thus understand that the 'blame' does not sit solely with the individuals involved. This is the topic of the next chapter.

main points

- Implementing an ethics of care approach is not always easy.

- Ontological anxiety is a healthy consequence of doing so, and can be ameliorated by defensible decision-making, supervision, and peer support.

- Ethical stress should be an impetus for taking ethical action BUT workers need a very well-developed sense of values and social justice in order to take action.

- An ethics of care approach is appropriate for all interactions with service users, even those where control is a necessary element.

taking it further

- Taylor, M. (2007) 'Professional dissonance: A promising concept for clinical social work', *Smith College Studies in Social Work* 77, 89–99. An important article for understanding the usefulness of ontological anxiety.
- Munro, E. (2011) *The Munro Review of Child Protection: Final Report* (London: TSO). Very important to understand the recommendations made by Munro in terms of uncertainty and autonomy. They are congruent with the messages in this chapter.
- Ingram, R., Fenton, J., Hodson, A., and Jindal-Snape, D. (2014) *Reflective Social Work Practice* (Basingstoke: Palgrave Macmillan). An accessible text that contains useful sections on decision-making and supervision, among others.

chapter 6 Social Justice

Overview

This chapter will get to grips with *how* social workers can keep a robust connection to social justice in all of their practice. No matter what the setting, social workers should be able to practise in a socially just manner. Ideas from radical and critical social work and anti-oppressive and human rights-based practice will inform and underpin the practicalities of practising in this way.

So far we have acquired some knowledge about social justice. As explained in Chapter 1, we are adopting a radical interpretation of social justice that is redistributive in nature, that is, a belief in increased equality of condition as well as opportunity. We have also taken a position that neoliberalism is antithetical to social justice since its consequences include increased inequality and poverty for those on the lowest rungs of the social status and economic ladder. Chapter 3 explored neoliberal hegemonic efforts to justify and perpetuate increased inequality by blaming individuals and their behaviour for poverty, unemployment, and other social problems. In contrast to this, a social justice-informed view would be that structural inequalities are primarily to blame for social problems. As poverty, inequality, pressure, and stress increase, so do problems of family violence, crime, and substance misuse (Ferguson and Lavalette 2009; Wilkinson and Pickett 2010).

It is useful to remember at this point that BASW's elements of a social justice approach are congruent with a radical or social democratic interpretation: challenging discrimination, recognising diversity, distributing resources, challenging unjust policies and practices, and working in solidarity (BASW 2012, p9). The code of ethics goes further to state that social workers must challenge unfair distribution of resources and social conditions that contribute to exclusion. This is an important point in the book, because when notions of social justice are applied, for example to the Smith family featured in Chapter 3, the situation cannot be reduced to a simplistic and neoliberal view that the family members have access to education, health care, etc., like everyone else but have simply not made use of the opportunities available due to their own failings. BASW has made it clear that unfair distribution of resources and poor social conditions *have an effect*. (Another way to understand and approach the Smith family and their situation will be explored later in Chapter 8.) Marston (2013, p130) summarises:

> If poverty were understood as a personal or moral failing then social workers would most likely seek out information to confirm this bias. They would understand any form of state dependency as a moral failing, while, at the same time, encouraging market-based dependency as a sign of independence. Politicians and mass-media reports of 'welfare fraud', unemployed 'scroungers' or 'dole bludgers' are social identities that symbolize this dominant social policy discourse. Reframing self sufficiency and moral deficiency requires that social workers take apart the value assumptions and policy logic that lie behind these sentiments and the silence in the text about connected responsibility.

So, as social workers, we need to understand and believe that these injustices have had an impact on how someone has come to be in his or her current circumstances. We must understand that there are other factors beyond bad choices and must lift our practice from individual eye level to consider the wider context and the idea that social work intervenes at the points where people interact with their environments. In other words, we are now taking our practice beyond an ethics of care to integrate understanding and knowledge about the impact of structural oppression. How do we do that?

Several approaches to social work that are centred on social justice can assist our practice here. These are: radical social work, critical social work, anti-oppressive practice, and a positive human rights framework. In my experience of teaching social work students, the struggle with these models concerns knowing *how* to use them. Students might understand the underpinning thinking and theory but are then unsure how to apply that understanding in their daily practice. Woodward and MacKay's (2012) study found that even when social work students understood models of social justice, they struggled to apply them. Unlike the exploration of ethical approaches in Chapter 4, when the ethics of care was identified as *the* approach for use in our new Practice Model, this chapter will recommend using elements of all the models. Because *using* them in practice is the difficulty for students, the wider the choice of social justice-based responses available, the better.

Radical Social Work

Radical social work is based on the Marxist premise that societal problems stem from class difference. The ruling class, in Marxist thinking, perpetuates the status quo, including vast structural inequality, as this serves its interests and keeps its members in a privileged position. Marx lived in the nineteenth century, the time of the Industrial Revolution and crushing inner-city poverty and terrible living conditions. This set the scene for workers and poor people to demand changes and to listen to an alternative ideology in the form of socialism (see Chapter 2). It is very easy to see the worth of Marx's ideas during that era but less easy to situate them in our contemporary society, where we have almost eradicated absolute poverty and have free health care, education, and welfare. In discussing Marx with students, it is clear that many of them feel the ideas are outdated and do not apply to contemporary society. And so, the first step in introducing radical practice is to ensure that the audience understands fundamentals such as hegemony, strategies used to perpetuate the current structure, and the difficulties people have in taking (often sub-standard) opportunities due to the physical and psychological effects of poverty and inequality. (Re-read Chapters 2, 3, and 4 if necessary.) Also students and social workers need to step back from individual-level practice, think structurally, and understand how privilege and disadvantage are perpetuated.

stop and think

An individualist, neoliberal way of thinking is derived from so-called Social Darwinist ideas of meritocracy, that is, everyone can achieve success if they are talented/intelligent/hardworking enough (in other words, a misapplication of the principle of natural selection to human social hierarchy). Radical thinking, on the other hand, asserts that the class you are born into is the main predictor of prosperity.

Think about individuals in government. Is it coincidence that they were educated at private schools and went to Oxford University, like so many of their colleagues? Think about other people in positions of power who come from the most privileged echelons of society and, again, question whether that is coincidence or the result of merit and intelligence or whether they were set on a clear trajectory from school to university to power. Reflect on this issue and re-read O. Jones's (2011) quote in Chapter 1.

Hopefully, by understanding the above concept of the effect of structural disadvantage, social workers can become 'suitably equipped' to 'see through capitalism's trickery' and expose for themselves the neoliberal hegemony (Turbett 2014, p3).

So, to return to radical social work, the 1970s, the heyday of radical social work, saw the formation of the Case Con Collective, a grouping of social workers and academics who were disillusioned with social work agencies' failure to tackle poverty and hardship and its emphasis on casework (including psychoanalysis) (Turbett 2014). The Case Con movement led to the seminal text *Radical Social Work* (Bailey and Brake 1975) in which the authors describe radical social work as follows:

> Radical work, we feel, is essentially understanding the position of the oppressed in the context of the social and economic structure they live in. A socialist perspective is, for us, the most human approach for social workers. Our aim is not, for example, to eliminate casework but to eliminate casework that supports ruling-class hegemony.
>
> (Bailey and Brake 1975, p9)

There is nothing in the above quote that does not apply to social work today. If we understand the hegemony and want to work in a radical way that takes account of class difference, we need to undertake casework *in that way*. The question is *how* to do that?

To interact with service users in any way that goes beyond procedure and management of behaviour, social workers need to be able to respond in individually tailored ways, especially if taking an ethics of care approach as recommended in Chapter 4 and/or attempting to embrace radical ideas within a social work response. This requires a certain amount of discretion and autonomy, and the question arises as to whether social workers have any discretion in the contemporary context. Evans and Harris (2004) comprehensively analyse two opposing views on this subject. The 'continuation' (of discretion) literature is of the opinion that there is discretion for workers in their unobserved practice with service users in how they *interpret* policy and legislation and, therefore, there is autonomy in how they choose to work with people. The 'curtailment' (of discretion) literature, on the other hand, is quite clear that the only arenas left for social workers in which to exercise autonomy are whether to respond when they are the only resource available, for example with ad hoc and on the spot counselling, and the *style* in which they carry out their work. This is an important point because we have already seen that an ethics of care as the main approach to work could be interpreted as a *style* to a degree. Such an approach does go further in demanding autonomy to allow responsivity and choice in what the social worker decides to do. According to 'curtailment' writers, however, autonomy is in short supply.

Evans and Harris reconcile this debate by, firstly, teasing out what is meant by discretion: it is the space allowed in a decision-making context. Using the analogy of a hole in a doughnut, the idea is that discretion is non-existent unless it is surrounded by an area of decision-making rules and restriction. Evans and Harris further identify where discretion can happen as follows: actually doing the job, for example deciding which piece of legislation to use or whether someone has reached a threshold of need sufficient to qualify for assistance; what style to use as previously discussed – the authors say that the power of style should not be down-played; when policy is nebulous and sometimes confused and contradictory, social workers are left to interpret the rules in actual daily practice (allowing blame if anything goes wrong to rest with the interpreter, that is the grass-roots worker); and bending of the rules or covert ethical action (see Research Box 5.2). The authors also acknowledge, however, that there may be increasing denial of autonomy as workers choose to *deny* discretion due to fear of being blamed if something goes wrong.

In essence, then, there may still be discretion and autonomy for workers, albeit reduced significantly by procedures and hierarchical decision-making. Fenton (2014b) found that younger social workers did not want more discretion and autonomy, which fits well with Evans and Harris's idea that workers deny discretion in order to abide by the rules and stay safe. This will be explored further later in this chapter.

What does all of this mean for radical practice? It would seem that in terms of creating spaces to do radical practice, there may still be cause for some optimism. However, social workers have to *want* to do it, to *want* the discretion and to see why it's important. Only then is there any hope of non-risk-averse, responsive, discretionary practice. However, although there may be spaces to undertake radical practice, that does not help answer the question of *what* to do.

One way that radical thinkers suggest their ideas can be put into daily practice involves 'deviant' practice and 'quiet challenges'. Rogowski (2012), for example, gives examples of social workers massaging information to acquire resources for social workers, delaying information flow to manipulate timelines, bending and interpreting rules, and going beyond the call of duty. Rogowski also asserts that because the neoliberal 'common sense' version of social work is actually about processing people bureaucratically (as opposed to really helping and making a difference), it fails to capture the messy reality of actual social work and, thus, throws up contradictions and is fraught with tensions. This, in turn, has given impetus to a resurgence in radical practice. For example, the tension between the humanistic value base of social work and the privatisation of services (profit based) has led to resistance and opposition in the form of, for example, the Social Work Action Network (SWAN) and trade union action. In the wake of the Baby P tragedy, Ofsted, as the regulator, came in for criticism due to previous positive ratings of Haringay Council – in other words, the paperwork had been good, but clearly this was not

enough. According to Rogowski, this led to a more sensible consideration of child protection, for example in the *Munro Review of Child Protection* (Munro 2011), which criticised the overly managerial and prescribed
nature of child protection as a whole. As a consequence, the public have
become more aware of the reality of child protection in terms of high
staff turnover, huge caseloads, use of agency staff, and low morale caused
by unrealistic expectations. Anti-capitalist, service-user, trade union, and
social work movements have all embraced this better understanding. All
of this allows *informed* social workers to draw on other knowledge and
anti-neoliberal thought to back up or reinforce actions they want to take.
Explicit reference to the Munro report with its emphasis on prevention
might be very useful to argue for a radical, helping, advocacy response to
a family, for example.

Another practical way of implementing radical ideas is to think not
just about risk but also about needs of service users. Revisit Chapter 2
to remind yourself of neoliberal social work's preoccupation with risk.
Stanford (2010, p1068) sums the situation up when she says that 'the
mentalities of the neoliberal risk society have undermined social work's
capacity to meaningfully, purposively and creatively respond to these
[welfare] dilemmas'; she gives mandatory reporting (for example, in
criminal justice social work or probation) as an instance of a social work
response that does nothing to alleviate hardship or deal with welfare
issues. She considers how 'ideas of risk are constituted and integrated into
social workers' interventions' (ibid., p1069) and investigates this research
area by analysing discussion groups of social workers in Tasmania. The
main finding was that definitions of risk were attached to individual
service users. Risk was always a negative concept and was considered an
'intensely moral' (ibid., p1071) construct, therefore 'risky' clients were
also 'bad'.

A further complication was that the workers in Stanford's study often
identified clients as being 'at risk' *as well* as 'a risk'. Stanford suggests that
this leads to a similar definition of 'need' *and* 'risk' presenting in the same
client (which is, of course, the accurate picture). Workers are then torn as
to which of these polarisations takes priority, which Stanford's workers
experienced as moral dilemmas. In Fenton's (2014a) study, however,
workers were clear: risk and public protection take priority, welfare and
need come later if there is time, *and* this was viewed only as a practical,
not an ethical problem.

Preston-Shoot (2011, p184) states that 'institutional patterns of conduct
and organisational compliance, rather than professional norms, domi-
nate responses to genuine cases for help and distance practitioners from
people's needs'. It appears, then, that it has become acceptable to only
focus on 'risk' and neglect 'need' (Stanford 2010). The official language
and pseudo-scientific jargon of technical tools and procedures can also

'distance officials from the people "served" and...promote a sense of legitimacy and routine without the need to engage with social or ethical concerns' (Preston-Shoot 2011, p187). This also illuminates further Gregory's
finding that the 'appalling reality of offenders' lives is being ignored with
the abandonment of a social work approach to the work (Gregory 2010,
p2280).

In terms of 'doing' radical practice, then, resisting the tendency for
risk-priority work is a practical course of action. If a social worker has
a radical understanding of the circumstances the service user is in and
is able to avoid 'blaming' him or her and individualising the problem,
then he or she is more inclined to attempt to meet the user's needs as
well as manage the risks. Of course, this depends on a critical awareness
and understanding of why social work is preoccupied with risk and an
ability to deconstruct that preoccupation and argue for an alternative
frame of reference (a radical one). Ingram et al. (2014, p92) offer an
illustrative example of this in the section 'engaging with risk and need'.
The social worker in the example makes an argument for a sex offender,
subject to MAPPA procedures (multi-agency public protection arrangements), to attend a church at his request, because his needs include
social contact and spiritual wellbeing. MAPPA meetings, in my experience, can be an environment that is hostile to discussion of needs and
one in which social workers tend to avoid this type of advocacy for
fear of being seen as 'soft' and 'overly social worky'. A group of social
workers told me that they felt their managers were 'embarrassed' if they
brought up anything to do with needs in MAPPA meetings, mainly,
they surmised, because the police were equal partners in the meetings
and, again, social work managers did not want to be considered 'soft'.
Speaking out in this, and similar, environments and explicitly discussing needs as well as risks would be a good example of taking 'ethical
action' and, again, will depend on the social worker's underpinning
value system (see Chapter 5).

Advocacy, as touched on above, and empowerment are, according
to Turbett (2014), connected concepts. Empowerment, the idea that
oppressed people, robbed of power, can be helped to take back some of
that power and gain control over their own lives, often depends on access
to information that can be privileged. Advocacy can help give voice to
people to gain access to information or to be heard in fora where the
service user's voice is disallowed, for example, arguing with a panel for a
community care resource. Cree (2013), however, exposes the potential of
'empowerment' to be an 'individualistic, consumerist and conservative'
practice. Examples of students and social workers who write about not
helping a disempowered service user and justifying this as 'empowering'
the person to take his or her own action are commonplace. As Cree (2013,
p155) says, in relation to social workers:

> They also demonstrate a capacity to care for others, and this may mean being prepared to do things for service users, such as making a phone call or accompanying someone on a visit, rather than showing them how to do this themselves (a typical example of a so-called 'empowering' approach).

This quote nicely links an ethics of care approach with notions of empowerment and advocacy. In attempting to take a radical approach, social workers need to be alert to any tendency to use 'empowerment' as a excuse to *not* take action, when the caring and socially just thing to do is to take ethical action themselves and, often, to *advocate*. Once again, an understanding of the psychological and social effects of oppression and poverty must be present to allow this process of thought and, ultimately, action to happen.

Turbett (2014) also draws on ideas from deviant and anarchistic practice to suggest some other ideas around putting radical ideas into practice. For example, Turbett discusses 'power shedding' (p52) and 'minimisation of professional distance' (p78), which probably relate to the 'style' that workers can choose to adopt and that, according to Evans and Harris (2004), can be very powerful. The idea of professional distance can be seen in the way the social worker dresses, the language used, whether appointments are all office based, drawing up to a house in a disadvantaged area in an expensive car, refusing to sit down or accept a cup of tea (rejecting care from service users), showing no emotion, and, ultimately, using a style that emphasises perceived superiority and 'professional' and bureaucratic distance and coldness. 'Shedding' these trappings of status or imperious ways of behaving is another way of authentically attempting to embrace radical ideas. Beresford, Croft, and Ashead (2008, p1403), in their study of service users' opinions about their social workers, reinforce this idea with the finding that 'one of the characteristics of practice that emerged from what service users said was the lack of professional trappings that accompanied the social work role. Service users, in our study, welcomed this and saw it as a real strength.'

Resisting the economic and managerial argument for certain courses of action is also very important. Choosing to run a group, of, for example, young boys in a community where crime and antisocial behaviour is rife – over and above the traditional casework, risk management approach – has resource implications in terms of space, staff time, and budgetary requirements for refreshments. Such a group might facilitate the discussion of radical ideas about oppression and structural difference and the effect of this on young people in the community. As stated in Chapter 5, it is the responsibility of the social worker, in terms of ethics of care, to step up and make a cogent argument for the group, drawing on theory, evidence, and values. However, it is also important that the social workers understand that they are up against a powerful neoliberal hegemony that will prove quite resistant to spending money on what could be construed as collective action (including managers, budget holders, and even colleagues). This understanding might then lead to communication and collaboration with other bodies who have influence and carry weight with decision-makers, in this case, the police. To advocate for the boys, to get the police 'on side', and to make a case for this sort of work, is skilled radical practice in action.

Finally, all the writers on radical practice agree on a fundamental requirement – building a relationship with the people we are working with. Without a starting point which involves getting to know the person, hearing from him or her and understanding his or her world view, we cannot hope to implement anything other than neoliberal, managerial, and conveyer belt–type people processing. Referring back to an ethics of care approach, it is within the realm of relationship-based practice that we see the crossover between care and social justice. I. Ferguson (2013, p201) states:

> One view, then, is that value-based work prioritizing a worker-client relationship, once regarded as *traditional – mainstream – practice,* has now become radical in contemporary, managerial environments.

The above features of radical practice are also crucial to the approaches to social justice-based practice we are about to examine, namely critical practice, anti-oppressive practice, and human rights-based practice. As we shall see, however, each also has its own unique features worthy of exploration.

Critical Social Work

This approach shares the idea with radical social work that service users are not to blame for their predicaments. What differentiates it is the emphasis on the multiple forms of oppression that any individual can experience (gender, ethnicity, disability, sexual orientation, for example), rather than solely class, and it includes the idea that people can participate in their own oppression by not recognising the forces at play. As a result, raising consciousness is very important.

Using critical ideas in practice is exemplified by Rogowski's (2012) discussion of the situation of a teenage girl who continually absconds from home and sometimes stays out for days at a time. She associates with other girls and they 'hang around', often targeted by teenaged and older men who make friends with them, win them over, then sexually exploit them. The girls describe these men as 'their boyfriends'. Rogowski suggests an alternative response to the standard focus on the girls' parents and their inadequacy in protecting or controlling their behaviour – in effect blaming the parents who are often trying their hardest in very challenging circumstances. A progressive social work response would be to advocate for a community-based groupwork method, where the girl and her friends would be involved in discussing their situation in an empowering way (Mullender and Ward 1991, quoted in Rogowski 2012). Groupwork would focus explicitly on the issues and concerns *but* with the emphasis on the young women learning from each others' views and experiences. Rogowski suggests linking this to a critical understanding of society, in this case the dominance of men and critical feminist responses.

Another important feature is challenging dominant notions of knowledge: positivist theory and hard knowledge are challenged by practical wisdom and service users' knowledge of the situation (Fook 2012; Ingram et al. 2014). Fook (2000, quoted in Fook 2012) undertook a study that found that social workers viewed themselves as quite powerless in terms of feeling at the mercy of, for example, managers, procedures, bureaucracy, and supervisors. This lack of power might also equate to lack of autonomy, and it needs to be considered in terms of finding spaces for autonomy or power and *wanting* them (see previously in this chapter). Critical social work would hold that the sorts of power under discussion are formal, hierarchical, and traditional notions, aligned to the status given to different types of knowledge. So, traditional role knowledge, scientific, hard, evidence-based, and 'expert' knowledge would all be considered more worthy and the holders of those types of knowledge more powerful. The task of critical social work is to upset those dominant notions of expert knowledge and power and to do so in the interests of service users. What does this mean? It means that social workers must give equal worth to alternative sources of knowledge, for example of the service user's point of view (which they will have gained as part of an ethics of care/social justice-informed approach and which they can highlight by making it possible for the service user to speak or by advocating on his or her behalf); the knowledge they have from their relationship with the service user; family and important others' views and feelings; 'soft' knowledge gained from emotional content; and explicit reference to values. Encouraging the service user to believe that his or her point of view is as worthy as, for example, the consultant's view is an intrinsic part of this approach.

A theme that runs through critical social work is that it is concerned with how 'structures of oppression are reproduced in the everyday lived reality of people' (Dalrymple and Burke 2006, p18). To consider this in day-to-day practice, social workers need two things: an understanding of 'structures of oppression'; and a relationship with the service user that is conducive to understanding, from him or her, what his or her 'lived reality' is really like.

Anti-oppressive Practice

This is a way of practising that is based on challenging stereotyping, bias, and injustice. It is underpinned by a strong belief that people should *not* be treated unfairly due to any of those factors (and requires practitioners to uncover their own biases, prejudices, assumptions, and stereotypes). AOP also reaches above the level of individual practice to consider an awareness of how structural discrimination can affect service users and, thus, it is closely linked to the promotion of social justice (Okitikpi and Aymer 2010). Social workers who buy into 'underclass' thinking and accept terms such as 'chavs' and 'junkies' perpetuate discriminatory and oppressive thinking by holding onto an underpinning assumption (Schein 2010) that these groups of people *do* deserve to be treated differently.

Thompson's seminal work on anti-discriminatory practice can help us understand this thinking further. Anti-discriminatory practice (ADP) differs from but is linked to AOP in that, because discrimination leads to oppression, we need to tackle discrimination in order to tackle oppression. Thompson's (2001, p22) 'PCS' model asks us to consider discrimination on three levels: personal (individual-level thoughts, feelings, prejudices); cultural ('common sense' level of shared prejudices and beliefs – in whose perpetuation humour is a powerful tool); and structural (the level of structural divisions within society).

stop and think

Think about the 'P' level of anti-discriminatory practice. You have most influence over this level, the first step of which is to uncover your own prejudices and stereotypes. Think carefully about this and choose one particular stereotype that you have not been able to shake off. Reflect on how it is embedded in, and perpetuated by, both the C and S levels. Endeavour to argue against your own stereotype – find literature and knowledge that challenge your thinking.

Anti-oppressive practice can be illustrated by the ideas presented by Rogowski (2014), drawn from his work with young offenders. Young people and children in our society are considered in a systemic way as part of their families and wider contexts, the underpinning assumption being that these contexts are crucial to understanding the child's behaviour. However, Rogowski (2014, p12) discusses the 'adulteration' of young offenders, where family and social circumstances are ignored and they are treated *differently* from other young people by being held exclusively responsible for their actions. In actuality, to work in an anti-oppressive way with these young people workers need: to understand and take real account of their homes and surrounding circumstances; a real belief that the young people are capable of change (rather than just managing their risk). The workers need to feel hopeful about the possibility of change and also really need to understand the young people's point of view and outlook on their own world. This can only be achieved by recognition of their young age and by really getting to know them via a relationship. Workers also need to understand the effects of inequality on young people in terms of status, 'saving face', substance misuse, and violence (Wilkinson and Pickett 2010). Applying anti-discriminatory ideas to this kind of work would require a fierce challenge to the P, C, and S levels – so we can see just how important it is that social workers are equipped with the knowledge, facts, values, understanding, and commitment to mount such a challenge.

Human Rights-Based Practice

Hudson (2001, p110) discusses a 'positive human rights framework' in her work on probation, and it is a concept that can usefully apply to social work in a wider sense when thinking about social justice. A positive human rights framework entails making sure that the human rights of the people we work with are maximised, and this must go well beyond an agency compliance with human rights legislation. In terms of risk decisions, Hudson talks about making sure there is fair attention to both risks and rights to avoid slipping into a controlling-risk response that erodes human rights. Social workers adopting a positive human rights approach need to understand the rights enshrined in the Universal Declaration of Human Rights, agreed in 1948 by the United Nations. This led to the European Convention of Human Rights (adopted in the UK in 1965) and the Human Rights Act (1997). If social workers have a working knowledge of the ECHR and the articles that apply to social work in particular, and have a commitment to maximising people's human rights, they will be basically equipped to identify a human rights response to situations. The articles that are particularly relevant to social work are: Article 5 'Right to liberty and security'; Article 6 'Right to a fair trial'; Article 8 'Right to respect for privacy and family life'; and Articles 9 and 10 'Freedom of thought, conscience, and religion' and 'Right to freedom of expression'.

6.1 Curtailing human rights

Although these seem the most obvious rights for social work to be concerned about, workers also need to be familiar with the other articles. So, for example, I worked in an agency where groups for sex offenders were run. Attendees were given instructions not to socialise with other attendees outside of group meetings. One group member who was out of prison on a licence was recalled to prison for breaking that particular rule and, thus, lost his liberty. During the subsequent hearing, the social worker was asked why he had given the instruction to the group member, to which the social worker replied, 'that's just what we do.' This horrendous practice might have been avoided had the social worker realised the enormity of that instruction: curtailing the person's human rights in terms of right to a private life, *and* Article 11 'Freedom of assembly and association'. An explicit awareness of trying to maximise people's human rights leads to the curtailment of said rights being conscious, serious, absolutely justifiable, and thought through.

Staunton (2009, p53) also argues that human rights legislation can assist in the pursuit of more resources for children's services: 'Advocating children's rights underpins the demand for more resources, for planning for and prioritising the future generation over the current.' Once again, going beyond mere compliance with HR legislation (and the requirement to protect children from overt abuse), a positive human rights approach can lead to action for the maximisation of those rights.

An Eclectic Social Justice Approach

This section will draw out the themes covered by the different social justice-based approaches discussed previously. This should allow for an eclectic understanding of how to put social justice principles into action.

Political action

Gray and Webb (2013) make the point that social workers often do not have the time or energy to take part in collective social action. However, doing so when one can and looking into joining a trade union or the Social Work Action Network enables workers to keep up to date with developments and be aware of opportunities when they arise (conferences, for example). Thinking politically, trying to foster an interest in politics and social justice and, as Sheedy (2013, p5) recommends, developing a 'world view' is a great starting point and may be as much as is manageable for some busy workers. *Not* doing this, on the other hand, very often leads to the kind of hegemony-perpetuating, managerial practice that this book is trying hard to argue against – so do what you can to work through how the ideas in this book link to your political beliefs and *get interested.* The importance of doing so is further explained under 'ethical action'.

Quiet challenges (covert or overt?)

All of the above approaches include quiet challenges (to mainstream managerial practice) and small actions. It is worth reflecting on the spaces for discretion that you already have and where you might make more space. Once again, it is up to the worker to look for sources of support for social justice-informed practice – found most obviously in codes of ethics but also in the rhetoric of governmental policy and espoused aspirations and in research evidence. Once you can explicitly draw on these sources of support, then you can feel justified in deviating from 'rules of thumb' or in arguing with managers and colleagues for another type of social work response. Turbett (2014) and other authors remind us that covert action might well have its place but can also mask the troubling practice and perpetuate it by *not* exposing it and directly challenging it. Overt resistance and challenge is therefore preferable where possible.

Advocacy

Again, all of the social justice approaches require social workers to act as advocates. Identifying that *it is your job* to try to make lives a bit better for the people you work with can lead to advocacy for services, for input from other agencies, for a second chance, for financial aid, or for understanding. Relating this to an ethics of care approach, the 'responsibility' requirement would mean that workers extend their influence to 'helping' the people they work with. Advocacy is a central part of that endeavour (see Chapter 4).

Understanding leading to Ethical Action

In my opinion, this is the most important element in a social justice-informed practice approach. Linking all of the above themes, from political nous to quiet, small acts of resistance through to explicit advocacy, is the understanding and belief system of the social worker. In Chapter 1, Banks's (2012, p7) definition of 'values' was discussed, that is, 'values can be regarded as particular types of belief that people hold about what is worthy or valuable...the use of the term "belief" reflects the status that values have as stronger than mere opinions or preferences'. It seems from this chapter so far that the underpinning value base or belief system of the social worker is the most important feature of his or her professional self in leading to social justice-informed ethical action such as political action, quiet challenges, and advocacy. Without that value base, social workers do not want discretion, are not inclined to take ethical action and, in fact, are quite happy with neoliberal managerial practice.

This extremely significant point then leads us to the question of how this kind of value base can be engendered in workers, especially new workers, and students. The challenge here is that students and new workers need to be exposed to the knowledge, hard facts, and frames of reference that challenge the 'common sense' of neoliberal, hegemonic thinking; otherwise we, as educators, will fail in our endeavour to help students grow a social justice-informed value base (Fenton 2014b). Thus, new social workers will tend not to take ethical action because the belief system required to drive said action is not there. This is indeed what seems to be happening, as can be seen from the evidence explored in Chapter 1 that new workers and students are more uncritically accepting of neoliberal practices. This would also explain why workers might deny or avoid discretion: the 'risk' of responsive, radical practice is simply not worth it if the passion for what is believed to be 'right' is absent.

Exercise 6.1

Reader as educator

Recently, I undertook a session with newly qualified social workers. As part of the discussion, we were exploring risk-averse, defensive practice. One new worker started from a position of supporting risk-averse procedural practice and was very happy with a managerial framework that was about managing people, setting goals, and keeping records. She was not perturbed by the idea that defensive practice prioritises the job safety of the worker and not the service user, and she did not feel that relationship building, responsive practice, or 'helping' were at all important features of practice. When I spoke about social justice, disadvantage, poverty, and inequality, it seemed that she was thinking 'Why are those things important to what I have to do?' Depressingly, I feel that I failed to make any impact on that worker and that my session seemed to her to be left-wing woolly nonsense that had no place in the real world of dealing with difficult service users.

Imagine yourself as the facilitator in that session. What would be the main messages you would want that worker to 'get'? How would you go about trying to convey them? Could you convince her?

The social worker in the above example will not see ethical action as a feature of her practice, because the basis from which ethical action can develop is missing.

So far, then, we have see what we can do, on a daily basis, to make sure our practice is informed by social justice ideas. It is time to illustrate that by a further iteration of our Practice Model:

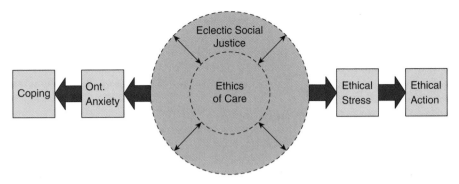

Figure 6.1 Practice Model Iteration 3

Research Box 6.1

Social justice practice in Ireland

Ashley and Garrett (2015) interviewed Irish social workers in regard to their experiences of the Habitual Residence Condition that restricts access to welfare and other 'safety net' services for those who cannot prove their connection to the Republic of Ireland. Whilst the social workers generally saw the condition as being contrary to human rights and social work values, their actions were, in the main, limited to individualised acts of 'deviance' and resistance. Several did not want to jeopardise their positions by being overly combative and outspoken (there is a personal cost to this), and a few felt that the policy itself was quite reasonable: 'You can only get out of the system what you put into it' (p42). When faced with the reality of people's circumstances, however, and in getting to know the people affected, they did want to resist and advocate on their behalf. The authors suggest that collective action (for example, SWAN) was missing from what the workers felt they could or should do.

Relationships

As well as understanding, beliefs, and values leading to ethical action, the other completely crucial element, common across all social justice approaches, is the importance of relationship-based practice. To understand the people we are working with, to engage with care, compassion, and empathy, as well as to feel motivated to strive for social justice, are impossible without building a relationship with them. Although this seems obvious, I. Ferguson (2013) reminded us above that relationship building, once a mainstream practice, has in the current climate become radical practice. Fenton (2014a) also found in her study that the lack of time to build relationships was only viewed as a practical, rather than an ethical problem. It was not overly concerning, especially to younger and newer workers. Relationship-based practice is the subject of the next chapter, such is its importance.

The final section of this chapter will look at a practice example concerning Mrs Lenska. An eclectic social justice approach will be applied to the situation.

6.2 Working with Mrs Lenska

A social worker is working with an older woman, Mrs Lenska, who wants to return home from hospital but for whom the health professionals are suggesting residential care due to a diagnosis of dementia and some unsafe behaviour (leaving the cooker on, drying clothes over an electric heater, etc.). Mrs Lenska was admitted to hospital after a fall. She has been assessed as having capacity, but she is amenable to persuasion and has faith in professionals knowing 'what's for the best'. She has said, however, that she wants to return to her home and has been independent all of her life.

An eclectic social justice approach to this situation would begin by requiring that the social worker stand back from the individual level of practice (ethics of care, which is not the subject here) and view it from a knowledge base about societal divisions and oppression. The social worker would consider how older adults are deprioritised as recipients of good services due to their not being financially viable units of productivity and thus of less worth. In an unequal and hierarchical society, older people are clustered around the bottom of the hierarchy and current hegemony perpetuates this. The social worker will understand this context of practice and will be alert for signs of these structural inequalities in play, for example, less access to services (will fight for those), less willingness to let Mrs Lenska take her own risks (will employ risk minimisation techniques rather than a controlling form of risk eradication), and he or she will seek to redress the balance of power between carer and cared-for by, perhaps, introducing the idea of personalisation of services and self-directed support to allow Mrs Lenska to return home as she wishes. A radical understanding of the neoliberal use of self-directed support will allow the social worker to ameliorate the drawbacks by advocating for resources, helping Mrs Lenska with the bureaucracy, and not trying to *persuade* her to be independent in this way if she finds it too difficult. He or she would work on income maximisation in the belief that poverty contributes to stress, struggle, and anxiety.

If appropriate, the social worker would help Mrs Lenska to understand that she is being oppressed by a health service that might well have its own agendas. In other words, the social worker would help Mrs Lenska to state her needs and would advocate for her. The worker would understand the multiple oppressions at play in this situation – gender, age, and disability – and would reflect on whether he or she him- or herself was bringing any of these pre-judgements to bear. In case conferences or meetings, the social worker would attempt to effect change by not accepting the prioritisation of the dominant discourse in terms of knowledge (in this case perhaps the consultant with the medical knowledge) and would feel empowered to speak about softer sources of knowledge with the belief that these are equally valid, for example, Mrs Lenska's expressed desires and concerns and the social worker's knowledge of Mrs Lenska gained through his or her relationship with her. Also, the social worker would want to find out about Mrs Lenska's ethnic origin (Polish) and what this means for her. Has she been discriminated against because of her ethnicity? What is important to her in regard to her culture? The worker would make sure that this was a significant factor in any planning. Mrs Lenska has the right to a private home life, and the worker would be very comfortable with the human rights basis of his or her work with Mrs Lenska. This is not to say that his or her practice stops at 'she has a right to choose' and thus justifies not doing anything, but after employing skills and giving choices, the social worker ultimately knows that Mrs Lenska is in charge.

In terms of style, the worker is friendly, does not use jargon, and does not exaggerate economic or status differences. He or she feels his or her loyalty is to Mrs Lenska, rather than managerial imperatives, and is happy to argue and advocate for her. Because he or she understands the competing tensions of social justice and neoliberalism; because he or she has a well-developed knowledge base about progression of dementia and what can exacerbate its progression; because he or she understands the legislation and policy and maximises her discretion; and because he or she is very comfortable with, and passionate about, his or her value base, he or she has no trouble in seeing ethical action as his or her job.

main points

- Taking a radical social justice position is important because social structures and inequality have an effect on people.
- An eclectic social justice approach comprises ideas from radical and critical social work, anti-oppressive practice, and human rights-informed practice, and the endeavour to do this must be maximised.
- Doing (ethical action) depends on deep, critical understanding and a robust and prioritised value base.
- Relationship-based practice lies at the heart of *how* to do it.

- Social Work Action Network (SWAN) at http://socialworkfuture.org/. This is the website for social workers, academics, students, service users, and carers who are 'united by our concern that social work practice is being undermined by managerialism and marketisation, by the stigmatisation of service users and by welfare cuts and restrictions'. You can join SWAN via the website and take the first step in joining with others to uphold social justice-informed social work.
- Ferguson, I. (2008) *Reclaiming Social Work: Challenging Neo-liberalism and Promoting Social Justice* (London: Sage). A really informative exploration of the 'neoliberalisation' of social work.
- Rogowski, S. (2015) 'Margaret Thatcher's legacy for social work with children and families: Critical possibilities?' *Critical and Radical Social Work* 3 (1) 53–65. An article about how critical social work is still possible in a neoliberal, punitive context. The lessons from the article apply to an eclectic social justice approach to social work.
- Gray, M., and Webb, S. A. (2013) *The New Politics of Social Work* (Basingstoke: Palgrave Macmillan). A collection of chapters from radical and critical perspectives, including some new ways to think about things.

7 Relationship-Based Practice

chapter

Overview

This chapter considers relationship-based practice as the main tenet in employing an ethics of care and an eclectic social justice approach. Relationship-based practice is, in fact, the glue that holds the suggested Practice Model together. What relationship practice is, is explored and the links between it and the other aspects of the model are analysed. The chapter then considers some possible limitations on relationship-based practice and suggests possible countermeasures.

Relationships are central to being human, and social work is undertaken within a myriad of different kinds of relationships. This aspect of social work is often what attracts people to the profession – potential students may give examples of how their friends approach them for advice, how they are good at developing relationships (especially in situations where it has been quite difficult to do so), and how they enjoy human interaction rather than more distant or detached types of work.

It is difficult to overstate the importance of relationships to human beings and, more specifically, to social work. Hennessey (2011, p31), for example, sums up a key foundational belief of relationship-based social work which is: 'Who we are is a construction of how others have related to us.' In other words, we are *formed* by the relationships that we have experienced throughout our lives, and we need to understand this in relation to ourselves and to those we work with. The other aspect to this core belief is that we can also be damaged by the relationships we experience – something that relationship-based practitioners have no difficulty in adopting as an intrinsic value of their approach to the people they work with. So, social workers should be able to separate the essential personhood from the behaviour of people they work with and to understand that people have been shaped, sometimes negatively, by the relationships they have experienced, very often in their own childhoods. Hold on to this idea as we will look at it in more detail in this chapter.

Another basic tenet of relationship-based practice is that the social worker is willing, again as a core element of the approach, to offer him- or herself as a 'relational and, possibly, reparative, resource for their client' (Hennessey 2011, p43). This means that the social worker, in order to 'do' relationship-based practice, must start from the position that he or she is willing and motivated to make the best efforts to build a relationship. The social worker must *want* to do this.

What is relationship-based social work?

Trevithick (2012) states that in the past, the worker–service user relationship was accepted as being at the heart of social work and essential to good practice. However, I. Ferguson (2013) suggests that relationship-based practice, once mainstream practice, is now considered radical. Having traced the development of social work in Chapter 2 and having understood the current context of managerialism, individualism, participationism, and privatisation, it is not a surprise that relationship-based practice is viewed by some practitioners as somewhat outdated and niche.

So, what *is* the essential nature of relationship-based practice that is so contentious in the current context? Put simply, Trevithick (2012, p13) states that the 'quality of the interaction and the trust and understanding that are held within the relationship can act as a vital thread'. Hennessey identifies a key component of relationship-based practices as *tuning into* the service user, using emotional intelligence and empathy. A key point he makes is that much of contemporary social work is concerned with the service user's 'outer world', characterised by observable behaviour and *doing* the tasks as required by the social worker or agency (compliance). There is little attention to the service user's 'inner world', that is his or her emotions, feelings, thoughts, views, and opinions (Hennessey 2011, p87). Hennessey makes the point that, of course, both of the service user's worlds are important in social work, but attention to the outer world is simply not enough on its own: what is required is 'empathy with the inner world, attention to the outer world' (ibid). The importance of empathy in relationship-based practice should not be underestimated, and we will now look at that in some more detail.

Empathy

It is impossible to discuss empathy without locating the concept within Carl Rogers's core conditions of the counselling relationship, namely empathy, unconditional positive regard/warmth, and genuineness

(Rogers 1966). Rogerian theory is now a well-established part of the social work knowledge and skill base, and it is central to an ethics of care and a relationship-based approach. Of course, those skills do not always apply completely and in their purest form to every social work encounter, and some qualifications are discussed later in the chapter with reference to Murphy, Duggan, and Joseph (2013). Notwithstanding those further nuances, it is fair to say that empathy is at the centre of good, skilled relationship-based practice. So, what is it? Howe (2013, p9) states:

> It was the psychologist Edward Titchener who, in 1909, was the first to use the term *empathy* as the English translation of the German word *Einfühlung*. Its etymology is from the Greek word *empatheia*, meaning to enter feelings from the outside, or to be with a person's feelings, passions or suffering.

So, we can see that empathy is about understanding another person's feelings from outside their 'inner world'. Hennessey (2011) contrasts this with *sym*pathy, which means feeling *with* another person, and warns that sympathising can indicate an over-immersion in another's feeling. It is worth dwelling on this point, however, because there may be times when sympathy is a healthy emotional reaction, even though it may be unfashionable to acknowledge this. So, if a service user is extremely upset by, for example, a bereavement and is crying, would it be the worst thing in the world for the social worker to shed a tear also?

stop and think

An example from my own practice comes from a time when I was a social worker with a fostering and adoption team. A temporary foster carer had the care of a three-year-old girl for approximately one year and was facilitating the move to permanent carers. The child had had a terrible past and had taken a good while to settle into the carer's home and life. However, she did manage to do so, and the carer and child forged a strong and mutually loving bond – it was a fantastic placement. When it came to the move, the carer was upset for a myriad reasons and cried. I also felt moved and put my hand on her arm. A few tears crawled their way down my cheek too.

Was this wrong? I definitely felt more than empathy – I felt sympathy. I was feeling *with* the carer. Think about this, and keep it in mind when you read Research Box 7.1.

The next point about empathy is that it requires an effort on the part of the listener. There are links here with caring, as discussed in Chapter 4, in that it requires an active expression of feeling. Just as it is not enough to be a caring person, it is not enough just to feel empathy; it requires expression. Howe (2013) suggests that this may be about tentatively expressing in words that you are trying to understand the other person, or might be about body language, concentration, touch, and expression. Active and accurate listening, observing, and attending are all required before verbal or nonverbal communication of empathy can take place. Howe cautions against an automatic echoing of people's words, however, which is an ungenuine attempt at 'doing' empathy.

> **Exercise 7.1**
>
> Try this with a partner. Take turns to tell each other something that has an emotional element (this does not have to be something too emotive – make sure you are happy to share it properly). The listener must try to tune in and really understand how the other person is feeling. Ask open questions and try to reflect a genuine empathy to the other person. Discuss afterwards how/what you did and how the teller felt about it.

As well as feelings and emotions, part of a person's 'inner world' is how he or she sees things – the logic he or she applies to whatever the situation is. It is really important, then, to be able to hear from a service user his or her own interpretation of the situation he or she may be in. This is very much where a limited 'outer world' focus can lead to punitive behaviour-control interventions that might not get to the heart of the problem at all and thus be ineffective as well as oppressive. The foundational understanding of relationship-based practice is also very relevant to the ability to empathise; that is, understanding the importance of the person's past and present relationships. Hearing from him or her how the situation has arisen and why he or she thinks about the situation in the way he or she does might well lead to some revealing information about past relationships. The social worker needs to be alert to and understanding of such disclosure. This understanding should be a practice principle, and therein lies the relationship-based practitioner's reaction to the media's portrayal of 'evil' wrongdoers: 'I wonder what their own lives have been like?' There is crystal clarity about the separation of the 'person' from the behaviour, and the belief that the person has been damaged by relationships rather than 'born bad' is evident.

7.1

A young man is being monitored by a youth offending team for brawling drunkenly in the street, usually at the times the pubs are closing. The social worker has visited and asked him how much he is drinking and where and when he drinks and has pointed out the consequences of his continued behaviour. She has referred him for alcohol counselling (although, realistically, she does not think he will go, which she attributes simply to a lack of motivation – he doesn't want to change). She leaves, having given him a list of targets for their next session.

The above is an example of engagement with the young man's outer world only. How is he feeling? What is he thinking? What are his hopes and aspirations? What does he see as a problem in his life? AND what sense does *he* make of why he is drinking? He may find that hard to articulate, but skilled, open questioning and really listening and 'tuning in' could lead the social worker to be able to empathise with a young person who might be lonely, bored, feeling little hope, trying to save face and gain status in his peer group, or whatever. That might lead to knowing him, to an emotional reaction that drives a helping impetus, to intervening at the root cause (so with a better chance of success), and to expressing care in words, actions, and practical help.

Emotional Intelligence

Emotional intelligence is an idea that has become extremely popular in everyday parlance and in any work involving people, such as social work, health, management, etc. People know generally what the term means in that it is something to do with getting along well with people and being aware of how others feel. More precisely, Morrison (2007) defines the four components of emotional intelligence as self-awareness, other awareness, self-management, and relationship management. These components make up the two foundations of emotional intelligence: the ability to recognise our own emotional reactions to stimuli and to contain those emotions to the extent that they do not overwhelm our ability to think and function; and the ability to recognise and understand emotions in others. Morrison also notes that social work students who do very well tend to demonstrate emotional intelligence in an intuitive way, in contrast to their competent but less excelling students who often fail to sufficiently consider service users' or colleagues' feelings or wishes. This chimes very well with my own experience of social work students, and I have come to realise that the failure is in both the recognition of the other person's feelings and in the recognition that it is *important*. It is often those students who are most comfortable with the neoliberal or rational-technical direction of contemporary social work who lack emotional intelligence. This is concerning as Morrison reviews a body of literature and research that quite clearly demonstrates how emotional intelligence (and empathy, or tuning in to the service user) impacts in a significant way on the change process for service users and on each stage of the social work process. Summing up, Morrison states: 'It seems ironical in a profession so steeped in relationship-based theories that such arguments need to be re-stated. But the place of relationships and emotion in social work is in danger of becoming increasingly marginalized' (p259). Ingram (2013) echoes this point in his example of statutory intervention when a child is failing to attend school. The social worker must write a statutory report on the child, and this becomes the priority, and most visible, task. However, relationship skills, emotional intelligence, and empathy are all required to get to know the child and family and to *really understand* what is going on. The danger is that these less visible aspects are supplanted and deprioritised in a climate increasingly concerned with accountability, targets, and efficiency. I would add to this that, in the current context, a social worker could undertake the report and do the task without engaging in any relationship building at all and would not be criticised for this. The boxes would be ticked and the agency would be safe from the risk of blame. If no change is affected, that's the service users' responsibility and they must face the consequences.

In summary, it is essential that emotional intelligence and empathy are re-emphasised as core features in the central social work task of relationship building. Only by asserting that this should be the explicit heart of social work practice can the technical, managerial, and neoliberal direction be resisted. Finally, this section does not discuss in any depth the skills of communication and engagement required to convey empathy and to act on emotional intelligence, so see 'Taking It Further' for a recommended text on skills.

Relationship-based practice, emotions, and ethical action

Ingram (2015b, p61) provides an easy way to think about the connection between relationships and emotions. He suggests thinking about the relationships one has with close family and, using a simple word-association technique, listing the words that are generated. He suggests, for example, 'love, happiness, pride, fear, safety, and belonging'. He suggests that this then leads to a series of behaviour including 'motivation to be in regular contact; an urge to protect them from harm; a willingness to forgive; and a tendency to prioritize their needs over others'. This is a very important link between emotions and behaviour and parallels the connection between value base and ethical action explored in the previous chapter. It was suggested that ethical action can only happen when a social worker has a well-developed sense of social justice and care which then leads to the desire to take action and do the 'right thing' (or ethical stress results – which should lead to a revisiting of the situation). Ingram has enhanced this understanding by introducing an emotional element. When the social worker recognises social injustice or lack of opportunity or care, he or she will, as a result, experience a range of emotions.

It is likely that the first example in the exercise generated emotion words or feelings such as anger and frustration (at the service user), moral outrage about lack of work ethic, and, quite possibly, dislike. This in turn might lead to behaviours such as control, punishment, restriction, cold and distant procedural work, and 'laying down the law'. In contrast, the other example might have generated feelings of sympathy, despair, warmth, care, and anger (at the college) which might lead to caring behaviour, advocacy, spending time with the young man, going 'the extra mile' on his behalf, sustained relationship building, etc.

The difference in these examples is that the second one exemplifies more accurately how the service user might present – a mixture of good and less good qualities, like all of us. The social worker, because he or she *got to know him*, has uncovered his good qualities, his life story, his loyalty, his aspirations, and his personality. In other words, the social worker has engaged with the service user's 'inner world' (Hennessey 2011, p87). The social worker also understands how much of the service user's behaviour has been shaped by his early (and possibly current) relationships *and*, of course, how societal factors impact on him in a negative way. In the first example, the social worker has bought into the stereotype of young, unemployed scroungers and has learned nothing further about the young person (see Chapter 3). We can see that, in emotional and behavioural terms, the resulting practice is neoliberal and akin to Practice Example 3.1 (Smith family).

Links between relationship-based practice and social justice

Doel (2012) gives an example that is very important to our understanding of the link between relationship-based practice and social justice. The unlikely setting is a benefit fraud investigation unit in 2010 when the government employed 200 extra benefit fraud investigators as a result of a campaign to really clamp down on fraudsters. Interestingly, Doel also points out that at the time hostility towards the benefit system echoed similar complaints against the Poor Laws of the nineteenth century, that is, it encourages laziness, forces up wages, and receiving it indicates moral inadequacy. This moral tone strengthened the climate within which benefit claimants and, even worse, benefit 'cheats' were viewed. As such, the fraud investigators might have been expected to be condemnatory and punitive in their attitudes to those that were being fraudulent, but instead they became more understanding as closeness to the individuals led them to understand their situations. This is a key point that is of utmost importance to social work and to the understanding of the importance of relationship building, because 'It is easier to condemn a group of people from a safe distance, but social workers get close to the people and situations they work with, in contrast to a political plutocracy that is distance from the people whom they condemn' (Doel 2012, p30). This is an excellent case in point that illustrates that distance encourages stereotype-reliance, emotional response, and resultant action. 'Distance' in this context does not mean physical distance but emotional and psychological distance, and it is counteracted by the worker endeavouring to build a relationship and getting to know the other party. How different was it for the fraud investigators once they got to know the people they were dealing with – know them as people, their hopes, their views on the situation – and to hear from them *why* they behaved in the way they did; understand their 'inner worlds', in other words. Emotional response changed from condemnation and disapproval to understanding and a desire to help. Very different behaviour is determined by each response. In social work terms, add to this a robust social work value base of care, compassion, respect, and understanding of social justice, and the impetus to 'help' burgeons. O. Jones (2015), writing in the *Guardian* about the country's emotional and resultant practical response to the thousands of migrants fleeing wars and attempting to find safety in Europe, illustrates the point as follows:

> Other than a tiny proportion of sociopaths, our species is naturally empathetic. It is only when we strip the humanity from people – when we stop imagining them as being quite human like us – that our empathetic nature is eroded. That allows us to either accept the misery of others, or even to inflict it on them. Right-wing newspapers hunt down extreme and unsympathetic stories of refugees and we fight back with statistics. Instead we need to show the reality of refugees: their names, their faces, their ambitions and their fear, their loves, what they fled.

Once again, look back to Chapter 3 and notice how the various stereotypes de-humanise people and how, as a consequence, our empathy towards them is eroded. This should help us to forge the link between social justice and relationship-based practice. Without relationship-based practice, it is much more difficult to hang on to our empathy and much easier to demonise people and 'buy into' the stereotypes.

practice example

7.2

Working with students who are about to go out into new practice learning opportunities (PLOs), I see many reactions that can be understood as 'condemning (or being afraid of or seeing as somehow "other") a group from afar'. So, the students might be afraid of working with drug misusers or offenders; they might be disappointed that they are working with 'old folk' because the work will be dull and mundane; they might feel judgemental about parents who are neglecting their children; or whatever. Invariably, those students return from PLO energised, enthusiastic and with the stereotype simply blasted apart. Instead, they know Johnny, Mary, Diane, and all the other service users they have met. Good students have built relationships, got to know people, listened, empathised, and cared. The experience is often transformative for students.

Trevithick (2012) reminds us that, building on the idea that everyone, including the people we work with, has been shaped and often damaged by previous relationships, *how* we act within a relationship with a service user is very important. She suggests that we really need to guard against practice that will add to the often significant number of negative relational experiences the service user has already had, such as broken promises, let downs, and abuse of trust. We must therefore be extremely mindful of the power of respectful behaviour, punctuality (or apology and explanation), not promising what we cannot deliver, and being reliable, for example. All of these features of how we practise are important and resonate with the 'power-shedding' concept discussed in Chapter 6.

stop and think

Use of power and what it signifies

A former social worker colleague of mine in criminal justice services social work used to keep service users waiting without a second thought and some-times even as what appeared to be a matter of principle. Of course, he also did not apologise for his lateness. His behaviour went unchallenged because we worked with people who had committed crime and had 'done wrong'. To challenge him was viewed as 'soft' (and yet to not do so produced ethical stress for a good number of people).

Analysing this now, I would have a much more cogent argument to put to him than 'that just doesn't seem right'. What he was doing was adding to the service user's history of negative relational experience by conveying notions of worthlessness, power, relative status, and complete lack of respect. In the context of relationship-based practice, he actually should have been affording the service user a different experience from those that he might have been used to and thereby helping to repair (Hennessey 2011) or mend (Trevithick 2012) the user's capacity to relate.

Links between relationship-based practice and an ethics of care

Empathy and 'tuning in' to service users is very much related to an ethics of care approach. Consider the stages of attentiveness, responsibility, competence, and responsiveness (see Chapter 4). These stages of practice are impossible without empathy and emotional intelligence. Trying to build a relationship – to get to know the service user and tune into his or her 'inner world' – is also enhanced by the ethics of care stages. An ethics of care approach and relationship-based practice are interdependent and symbiotic. Hennessey (2011, p13) states that 'it is of crucial importance that the educational process also keeps alive the impulsive and untrained prompting to "help others" that first gave emotional impetus to students' career decisions'. Trevithick (2012, p13) states that in order to build a relationship, social workers need 'the capacity to communicate a genuine feeling of warmth, compassion and concern towards another human being'. Both of these quotes about helping and compassion are, of course, also central to an ethics of care.

Relationship-based practice, in congruence with an ethics of care, identifies care as something that must happen within a relationship. In Chapter 4, when considering care as a virtue, the point was made that it is not enough to be a 'caring' person but that the feeling or virtue needs to be acted upon. Relationship-based practice helps further with this because knowing the service user and tuning into him or her should encourage an emotional reaction, which in turn sets the scene for helping or caring behaviour (see the point made by Ingram (2015b) in the introduction to this chapter).

The connection between relationship-based practice and an ethics of care is further promoted in relation to implementing the Munro report in social work with children and young people, as follows:

> First social work education needs to be reconfigured by adopting a more relationship-based approach to practice....This means focusing on the experience of helping, devoting time to the emotional context of young people's lives, using skills that are 'emotionally' and 'relationship' centred rather than procedural...and an emphasis on the ethics of care in social work.
>
> (Higgins, Goodyer, and Whittaker 2015, p336)

Final iteration of model

Such is the centrality of relationship-based practice that it forms the centre ring in our new model. From the above sections, teasing out the connections to the inner and outer rings of the model, it has become apparent that neither an ethics of care approach nor an eclectic social justice approach can be realised without relationship-based practice defining the starting point for a social work encounter and persisting throughout the entirety of the interaction. Relationship-based practice and an ethics of care/social justice are interdependent.

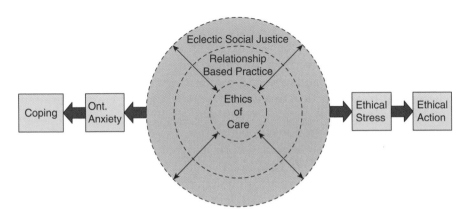

Figure 7.1 Final Practice Model Iteration

Research Box 7.1

What service users say about relationships with social workers

Beresford, Croft, and Ashead (2008) conducted a qualitative study asking service users of specialist palliative care social work what they valued most from their social workers. The relationships they made with the workers were the most valuable aspect to the service, as were the qualities of the social workers associated with empathy, warmth, listening, and caring. They associated those terms with notions of 'friendship', which appeared to be characterised by two qualities: *'reciprocity* and *flexible professional relationships'* (p1394). Participants also highlighted practical qualities such as being accessible, reliable, knowledgeable, and delivering on promises.

One service user said: 'They may have the skill but they have to bond as well, there has to be that trust and that relationship...' (white UK male patient, aged 50 years) (p1394).

Beresford, Croft, and Ashead note that remarkably similar findings have arisen from studies of service users in a variety of settings and, thus, the findings of this study appear to apply to social work much more widely.

Exercise 7.3

Beresford, Croft, and Ashead (2008) above make an important point about social workers being seen as 'friends'. They contrast this with notions of 'professionalism' and 'professional boundaries'. Explore the interface between these ideas, ideally in a discussion with a friend. Consider the qualities of a good counselling relationship: empathy, genuineness, and unconditional positive regard (Rogers 1966). Do these qualities help with the analysis?

When it's not so easy

It was discussed in Chapter 4 how an ethics of care can remain the approach to practice, even when dealing with difficult, risky situations and the need for rules and instructions. Relating the discussion further to relationship-based practice, this kind of work would come into the 'attention to the outer world' category (Hennessey 2011 p87). Sometimes behaviour management, restrictions on behaviour, and clear rules *are* required, and this is a crucial part of social work. The point is, however, that this shouldn't become all there is to practice, and we must guard against it supplanting the need for empathising with the service user's inner world. This means that when working with somebody who has done something you find abhorrent – cruelty, sexual abuse, or whatever – you must still endeavour to apply the model. So, trying to get to know a person, hearing his or her story and his or her understanding of what he or she has done, learning about him or her and *all* his or her qualities, learning about his or her relationships up until this point, and trying to build a healthy and caring relationship with him or her are as important as attending thoroughly to his or her 'outer world' behaviour and resultant rules and restrictions. Think about the social worker who deliberately kept service users waiting (second Stop and Think box above) – how far away from the model was his practice? And yet, he was able to choose to be that type of worker, just as you are free to choose to be a different sort of worker. See Chapter 5 and the section on 'When an ethics of care is less easy...' for a discussion about dealing with resistant and hostile service users.

Murphy, Duggan, and Joseph (2013) highlight another potential difficulty with relationship-based practice. The authors tease out the place of Rogerian person-centred therapy within relationship-based practice and call into question the possibility of fully realised relationship-based practice by suggesting that the current climate is not conducive to the self-actualising aim of person-centred therapy. To create the climate to allow the service user to flourish is actually not what happens in a social work encounter because there is usually an aim or purpose to the encounter: the relationship is *instrumental* and not an end in itself. There would seem to be agreement that relationship building for its own sake is neither possible nor indeed desirable, and in fact Trevithick (2012, p15) states that 'forming and maintaining good relationships, or relationship-building, should not be seen in social work as an end in itself, but as a way of working that provides a foundation on which to build future work'.

However, the point that self-actualisation lies at the heart of true person-centred practice but is unlikely in social work is also true. Person-centred *therapy* is not what goes on in a 'normal' social work interaction and, thus, *pure* person-centred practice does not happen. That is not to deny that principles of human flourishing, a belief that this can happen if the circumstances and context are conducive to it, empathy, genuineness, and unconditional positive regard (for the person as opposed to the behaviour) are all very possible. These Rogerian principles are, I would argue, essential to good social work practice (Rogers 1966).

Murphy, Duggan, and Joseph (2013, p709) go on to give a practice example that illustrates the point that 'real' social work is quite far away from person-centred principles:

A social worker is called to visit a mother because her seven-year-old child might be at risk from the mother, who is potentially suicidal. The social worker, as described by the authors, 'begins by developing and building rapport and then asks the mother about her current suicidal intent and the mother states her intent is low though her ideation is high' (p709). The authors describe the mother as feeling ashamed, looking away, etc., while the social worker 'presses' on with questions about whether she has the means to commit suicide. The worker also gives the mother a risk assessment score sheet to fill in, which she does. The social worker is satisfied that the mother is not suicidal but is probably depressed. The authors describe the social worker as 'sensitive'.

Murphy, Duggan, and Joseph are correct that the above practice is light years away from person-centred principles. However, it is also light years away from the kind of practice advocated in this book, characterised by care, relationship building, and social justice. The worker *could have* actually spent more time with the mother, finding out about her and what she felt was really going on. Why is she depressed? What is her life like? What are her hopes, struggles, worries? What are her days like? What is she feeling – about life, her daughter, in general? The social worker might have demonstrated care for her. She might also have understood that mental health is affected by poverty, circumstances, pressures of inequality, isolation, and many other factors – and might have understood that as a single mother, she might well be subject to disadvantage and structural oppression. None of this would have supplanted a good risk assessment, but the service user's inner world would have been given equal attention. The worker might have also spoken to the child in question and shown the same interest, empathy and relationship-building skills. This type of engagement might have led the worker to advocate for services, to help the family, and to all manner of tasks that did not even enter into the discourse in its current form. Basically, in Murphy, Duggan, and Joseph's paper, they showcase an excellent example of the kind of neoliberal practice to which a social worker *could* reduce his or her practice – but he or she does not *have to*. The example is very similar to the neoliberal practice example given in Practice Example 3.1. Murphy, Duggan, and Joseph make the point that this kind of practice will persist while services define the task, but the point is that a social worker has enough autonomy to define the task *beyond* the narrow requirements of a neoliberal statutory agency.

In her review of child protection, Munro makes it very clear that social workers do indeed need to go beyond the restrictive confines of heavily proceduralised and document-driven practice, to resurrect the central requirement for relationship-based practice. For example:

> [R]ecords of work have acquired a new dominance. The approach to management has assumed that the process can be divided into a series of tasks that can be sequentially completed and recorded. Hence, in child protection work, flowcharts now map out the

ideal management of a case. However, such an approach provides an incomplete account of the intricacies of working with children and families for the many professions involved in child protection. It undervalues the fact that the work is done *in a relationship* with children and family members so that the importance of continuity in human relationships is overlooked, causing considerable distress to children and parents. The assumption that records provide an adequate account of a helping profession has led to a distortion of the priorities of practice. The emotional dimensions and intellectual nuances of reasoning are undervalued in comparison with simple data about service processes such as time to complete a form.

(Munro 2011, p20)

The Munro report is very much advocating a resistance to the kind of practice exemplified by Murphy, Duggan, and Joseph's example. The social worker *should have* adopted a relationship-based approach and, if that had taken longer or come in for criticism from a manager for any reason, the social worker could have called on the principles of the Munro report to argue for his or her methods. Once again, we can see the primary importance of social workers having the knowledge, skill, and desire to facilitate and argue for real relationship-based work.

Featherstone, Broadhurst, and Holt (2012) explore the difficulties of relationship-based practice, or in this article 'partnership working', in some more depth. They consider developments in social work that are not conducive to relationship-based practice, as did Murphy, Duggan, and Joseph, but they also unpick the political assumptions about parenthood that underpin those developments. The child-centred nature of child protection and the child/adult services split, for example, move the focus from the family to the individual child *within* the family. Thus, parents' own needs, which might be quite significant in hard, austere times of great inequality, are less easy to justifiably address. It becomes a case of giving the parents time-limited targets to meet – or else! This is exacerbated by the adoption of evidence-based practice and manualised parenting programmes – long-term help or dependency are eschewed. For parents, these measures do not support improved caring or parenting and, in fact, are very much less than helpful. As Featherstone, Broadhurst, and Holt (2012, p625) state: 'Often, the most valued form of support may indeed be the price of a loaf of bread or a lift to the hospital to see a sick child rather than a parenting programme!' They also point out the increasing distance between social workers and service users. The idea that social workers spend far too much time on computers and not enough with families has already been recognised by the Munro report, as above, but Featherstone, Broadhurst, and Holt (2012, p627) suggest that this is, in fact, a symptom of a much more insidious distancing and of 'objectifying practices' being adopted by social work. A network of professionals share information about a service user or family via e-communication, with often limited actual contact with the family. This in turn leads to less trust (on all sides), less getting to know people, and a perpetuation of stereotyping and 'othering'. This is an important point, discussed previously in terms of psychological distance between service users and social workers. In essence, Featherstone, Broadhurst, and Holt welcome the suggestions in the Munro report in terms of promoting relationship-based practice *but* recognise that the trajectory of the profession is not conducive to their implementation. This means it is even more important for social workers to be critically aware of the politics and neoliberal contemporary context and to be well informed and value-based enough to want to stand against the tide.

In summary, then, it would seem that there is agreement that relationship-based practice is challenging in today's social work context and agreement that relationship building *for its own sake* is not desirable. However, relationship-based social work practice in the form of a helping, compassionate, caring form of practice, which is about helping people to make things better and supporting a process of change, is possible. It is incumbent, of course, on social workers to be clear about purpose, not to be disingenuous about why the encounter is taking place, and to be critically aware of organisational and policy restrictions.

Purposeful Relationship-Based Practice

The relationship-based practice advocated by our model could be described as 'purposeful'. It does not ascribe to relationship building for its own sake and does not exclude models of intervention or work that might be done within the social work relationship. The characteristics of purposeful relationship-based practice in our model are as follows:

- Hearing the service user's voice, getting to know him or her and his or her views and feelings, demonstrating empathy for his or her 'inner world'.
- Providing care in manner and actions.
- Promoting social justice.
- *Intervening*: Models of social work, risk assessments, practical help, etc.
- *Applying rules and restrictions*: as an exception and only for as long as and to the extent required (see Chapter 4): attention to 'outer world'.

It seems obvious that there are significant elements of purposeful relationship-based practice missing from the social worker's practice in Murphy, Duggan, and Joseph's example. It is suggested that better practice *can* happen even in the least conducive situations, despite the concerns raised by Featherstone, Broadhurst, and Holt. The key element, of course, is that the social worker has a sufficiently well-developed value base and understanding of social justice to want to practise in this way. Also the social worker would, via relationship-based practice, break down any stereotypical ideas he or she held about service users 'like that' by getting to know, hearing, and understanding. Once again, this allows the possibility of a different emotional reaction to the service user, which in turn can lead to different behaviour.

main points

- Relationships are central to human functioning and have shaped who we are.

- Relationship-based practice is fundamentally about engaging with a service user's feelings, thoughts, emotions, desires, and logic – whilst not abandoning attention to his or her behaviour.

- Empathy and emotional intelligence are central to relationship building.

- The emotional content of social work interactions can be enhanced and *changed* via relationship-based practice – leading to different responses.

- There are clear links between relationship-based practice and both an ethics of care and an eclectic social justice approach.

- The difficult context within which relationship-based practice must take place is acknowledged, but the suggestion is that it need not *overwhelm* good partnership practice. The social worker, however, must be aware of the political underpinnings of managerial frameworks.

- A final iteration of the Practice Model is suggested.

taking it further

- Ingram, R. (2015b) *Understanding Emotions in Social Work* (Maidenhead: McGraw-Hill). A comprehensive exploration of the role of emotions in social work, with a firm focus on relationship building.
- Trevithick, P. (2012) *Social Work Skills and Knowledge: A Practice Handbook* (Maidenhead: OU Press). For further reading on the skills needed to take a relationship-based approach.
- Hennessey, R. (2011) *Relationship Skills in Social Work* (London: Sage). A readable and accessible text that provides an excellent grounding in relationship-based practice.

8 Ethical Stress, Anxiety, and Professional Practice

Overview

Chapter 8 takes as its focus a further interrogation of the horizontal features of the Practice Model. It analyses the relationship between ethical stress and ethical action and considers the features that enhance that connection. The chapter then looks at ontological anxiety and strategies for coping. Finally, the chapter explores the impact of notions of professionalism on ethical stress and/or anxiety and identifies a form of professionalism that is congruent with the Practice Model.

> With social work, we face the bigger challenge of convincing the uncommitted – and we assume there are many – that there is something worthwhile to be had in taking a political stance and engaging in a radical project. We are persuaded, often by ourselves, that radical politics is futile. So we tend towards compromise, resignation and indifference.
>
> (McKendrick and Webb 2014)

The above quote succinctly captures the feeling of many social work students with whom I have contact, and, I would suggest, many younger workers as per the evidence provided in Chapter 1. It is the younger generation of social workers who appear to be more accepting of neoliberal principles, resigned to things being the way they are, and indifferent to any alternative world view. In order to reshape our values into a form congruent with social justice and the resistance to the neoliberal hegemony, centred on care and relationship-based practice, we need to direct sustained efforts towards clear and achievable goals:

1. Social work education needs to educate students to have a critical understanding of the neoliberal hegemony, how it affects daily social work practice, and how they can understand and resist its influence (knowledge).

2. Social work education also needs to inspire and encourage social workers to feel outrage at social *injustice* in order that the emotional reaction combined with a robust value base and an understanding of neoliberal hegemony will combine to produce an impetus to ethical action (values and ethical action).
3. We need to take an explicitly radical stance to social work and social work education, clearly positioning our approach against neoliberal thinking. To do this we need to face anxieties about being accused of being too political or too leftist. Criticism in this form will surely come (clarity of value position) (Fenton 2014b).
4. We should promote the Practice Model in this book as a practical way of approaching practice that includes the elements above (actual practice).

A further question is, do we persuade ourselves, as in the quote above, that there is no point in taking a radical stance; or is it more accurate to suggest that we are so brainwashed by the neoliberal hegemony that we are unsure what that 'stance' would look like (Fenton 2014b)? Have a significant number of social workers and social work students uncritically absorbed the 'neoliberalist assumptions that people are able to compete unfettered on an even playing field of opportunity with equal access to resources [which] engender the construction "welfare dependence" as an addiction, lifestyle choice or simply the result of individual failure' (Morley and Macfarlane 2014). It seems that this might be the case from some of the evidence on younger workers and students. I taught a new first-year class this week and once again was faced with student social workers who *did* believe that society is benign and that people *do* have equal opportunities. I presented evidence and thinking to challenge this view, but it was an uphill task.

Another point raised by Morley and Macfarlane is that the neoliberal and managerialist constructions of service users as customers/consumers, efficiency as paramount and defined by the aim of reducing costs, and social workers as staff are paralleled by similar constructs within higher education. Academics become customer service providers or marketing consultants, students become customers/consumers, and social work becomes a commodity. I would also add that efficiency, cost cutting and the production of profit have become considerations that are viewed as equal in importance to quality education. Within this context, critical philosophical analysis is 'a brand, at best, and an impediment to economic reform, at worst' (Morley and Macfarlane 2014, p339). Many social work programmes have 'radical social work' or 'critical social work' as a discrete module, course, or topic – a brand rather than an underpinning philosophy. The effect of these developments has been, of course, that the neoliberal hegemony is even less easy to recognise as it contextualises work within the academy as well as outside in the world of social work practice.

Looking into this a little further, it is clear that if students and social workers can be inspired to base their practice on the Practice Model, they will come up against many barriers and challenges. If those students and social workers have embraced the model in its true spirit, they will have an underpinning strongly held value base, including a real desire to promote social justice and a real belief in radical principles. Consequently, ethical stress arising from practice requirements might well be a significant feature of practice, and turning that into the impetus for ethical action is where we now focus our analysis.

Ethical Stress – Ethical Action

Williams and Briskman (2015, p3) state:

> Admonitions to revive the moral and political dimensions of social work are ever present in social work debate, framed around the core value of seeking social justice. Indeed these assertions have been put forward with increasing fervour in recent times, given a growing sense of unease within the profession at its inability to reconcile its social justice ambitions with the realities of practice.

Although this quote appears to encapsulate the impetus for this book, the authors go beyond simply 'blaming' the neoliberal project (although they do recognise that it is of overriding importance) to consider other factors or 'potent sources of malaise' (p4), including the tension between theory and practice, personal inclination, awareness of self-risk, and the push towards professionalism (discussed later). This leads to the realisation that 'the obstacles to action are many' (p5). The authors suggest that one contribution to the discourse about overcoming these obstacles is collective moral outrage. Outrage can be sparked by social workers' close proximity to the site of people's distress and to the effects of injustice, which enables them to empathise and feel with the people they are working with. Outrage in this context can be understood as an intense example of ethical stress, when workers are asked to carry out agency imperatives and yet witness the real struggle, hardship, and injustice suffered by the people they are working with. For example, the authors draw on instances when social workers employ an ethics of care approach, as in our Practice Model, thus sparking emotional reaction, which in turn leads to a desire to take action. These ideas were explored in Chapter 7, which also considered the idea that social workers get close to the people they are working with and react in an emotional way to their distress. However, Williams and Briskman take this further to consider collective motivation in dealing with the big issues of current times such as asylum, war, and global injustice. I would also add austerity, poverty, and inequality as legitimate targets for collective action. The authors draw on literature to suggest that feelings of collective moral outrage combined with a feeling of efficacy (we can *do* something) is a powerful motivator in taking action.

One of the reasons that the above article is important is that it considers a single social worker feeling outrage at injustice and *joining forces* with others who feel the same to create a powerful voice in working for change. In terms of the model, the worker may be arguing with the agency, refusing to implement oppressive policies, or simply stating views that are contrary to the liberal mainstream discourse (taking ethical action) because of feelings of ethical stress. The power involved in finding like-minded others mean that action – individual or collective – is much more likely. So, for example, the Social Work Action Network (SWAN) in the UK would be a resource to help workers to take action and do something to change things. SWAN has had recent demonstrations in opposition to the detention of asylum seekers and has been very active in providing assistance to displaced people who are seeking safety, for example. Workers who do not want to demonstrate can still benefit from finding like-minded 'outraged' voices by accessing the SWAN website, conferences, and journals such as *Critical and Radical Social Work* to increase feelings of outrage/ethical stress and to feel supported and part of a growing body of social workers who feel similarly. This should make individual ethical action also more possible for workers.

Research Box 8.1

Can critical reflection serve as an impetus for ethical action?

Morley and Macfarlane (2014) studied 80 students who completed a Critical Social Work Practice programme and found out from them how their thinking and practice had been affected by their learning. The authors suggest that the programme did indeed have an impact on students, as the quotes below demonstrate:

> Linking critical theory to practice has been the most important learning for me.... Practising social work from a critical perspective in the future gives me the ability to locate all these points of resistance; to challenge the dominant discourses...   *(p344)*

> I have been able not only to assist clients but also to challenge unhelpful dominant discourses within my own organisation...   *(p349)*

The authors conclude that the students demonstrated, among other characteristics, an increased sense of agency to take action and work towards social justice and a willingness to challenge social injustices. These hopeful findings mean that increased capacity and ability to work in the way proposed by the Practice Model are enhanced by the experience of critical social work education.

Do a critical incident analysis

Write down a description of a piece of practice that left you with a feeling of ethical stress. If you witnessed practice that left you feeling like that, you can use that instead of an example of your own practice.

Really think about why you felt ethical stress and see if you can trace it back to political, neoliberal, managerial, and agency priorities. What were the underpinning beliefs that drove the practice and made you feel uncomfortable? Then ask yourself if you can apply some of the thinking from previous chapters to what was actually going on in the piece of practice. Finally, is there anything you should have done or could have done that you didn't?

The findings above mean that the link between ethical stress (even the unconscious experience of this feeling without a real understanding of why) and ethical action can be enhanced by undertaking critical analysis of the situation or incident. If, as we are advocating in this book, social workers must stand up to injustice and *not* simply give in to neoliberal rational-technical practice, then this is surely an extremely important finding. As noted in Chapter 5, there is a body of literature that demonstrates a theme of social workers feeling that they can, and want to, take action, if their value base is strongly held. Critical analysis appears to be one way of enhancing that value base, enhancing social justice understanding, and thus promoting ethical action taking. As Morley and Macfarlane put it, the students developed 'moral courage' (p346).

The link between ethical stress and ethical action might be depicted as follows:

So, what might ethical action be? We have already considered overt/covert action (see Chapter 5), which can be small acts of resistance or 'rule-bending' for the best interests of the service user. We can now add collective action, such as trade union action or action taken by organisations such as SWAN, which might help grow our sense of moral outrage and help us feel supported and not alone in the challenges we face. To these strategies, we might add the following:

Arguing/challenging

Social workers must be brave. Brave to be able to challenge colleagues, managers, and policy-makers. Feeling ethical stress and allowing that to drive us to knock on the manager's door and put a case for different action with a particular service user or family is essential in ethical practice. Living with the ethical stress, and allowing that to corrosively wear away our integrity and ultimately do a real disservice to the people we work with, is the alternative. So, 'reflection-for-action' (Thompson and Thompson 2008) before approaching the discussion is crucial if we are to be effective in our challenge and not perpetuate a reaction such as 'oh no, here comes, X, ranting as usual. I need to get rid of her...'

As mentioned previously, Ingram et al. (2014, p93) describe a situation where a social worker, Erika, is planning for attendance at a multi-agency public protection meeting (MAPPA) at which she wants to advocate for the service user, assessed as a 'dangerous offender', to join a church. The authors draw on the idea of 'reflection-for-action' to explain that Erika would think about the priorities of the meeting, understanding that the members' overriding preoccupation is risk management. Erika would therefore 'plan what (she was) going to say in the light of this. Rather than simply laying out her argument in terms of anti-neoliberalism, promotion of human rights, thinking about the service user as a person for whom she cares and whose needs she would like to try to meet, Erika would frame her initial argument in terms of risk reduction'.

Decision-making

Can decision-making be understood as ethical action? It can be argued that, indeed, the willingness and desire to take decisions is a powerful form of ethical action, where the alternative is to abdicate responsibility for doing so, allowing others – a group (such as a MAPPA meeting or case conference) or an individual (such as a manager) – to take on full decision-making responsibility. In that context, the social worker simply waits to be told what action to take. This is actually not an unusual scenario and, in my own experience, I have known many social workers who are more than happy with that type of upward designation of decision-making power. Indeed, Fenton (2014a, p8) found that only 30 per cent of social workers agreed with the statement 'I would like more autonomy' and only 16 per cent agreed with the statement 'if I ever choose not to follow procedures, I don't tell my manager or supervisor', meaning that the vast majority of social workers in the study were happy with the level of autonomy they had, although, as we know, autonomy has been eroded in the statutory sector over recent years. Once again, that finding was more pronounced among younger, less experienced workers. Whittaker (2011) undertook a study looking at child protection social workers' decision practices and found that frequently, as a defence against anxiety, they tended to delegate decision-making upwards (to their seniors). Whittaker uncovered certain techniques used, beyond simple asking, for example social workers initiating a conversation about a case but not suggesting any action, to the point where the senior social worker filled in the gap and suggested what the worker should do. Whittaker also noted that this anxiety-defence strategy was less prevalent among more experienced workers, which is, again, in line with Fenton's study. He found that more experienced workers reduced their anxiety by following their own judgement. Another strategy used to reduce anxiety identified by Whittaker was the use of 'checks and counterchecks' (Whittaker 2011, p487). This strategy is as it sounds, checking and rechecking that decisions are acceptable. Whittaker's study is less clear about with whom the checks were made, but it could be suggested that, once again, the senior social worker was a key player. Finally, the third strategy used by the child protection workers was to follow a specified procedure, 'not being required to make a choice and thus incur the burden of decision-making' (Whittaker 2011, p 489). This resonates with several themes in this book, including anxiety and the difficulty social workers have in tolerating it and workers following procedures out of fear of being blamed should something go wrong. Whittaker adds some weight to this by highlighting the value and emphasis workers placed on procedural knowledge. This type of knowledge was rated as being of more value than case work 'expertise'.

So, it is suggested that workers might sometimes avoid making decisions, as above. Munro (2011, p115) adds to this by highlighting that structurally, this type of upward delegation is often actually encouraged: 'Decision-making on cases is frequently the responsibility of that manager, despite the manager not knowing the child or family very well, if at all. This leaves the social worker in an awkward predicament, holding case responsibility but with little autonomy for decision-making.' What is being suggested in this book is that rather than feeling 'awkward' about this, less experienced, younger workers actually welcome the sharing of responsibility with their first line manager. Gregory (2010) suggests that, since the change in direction towards greater managerialism and increased prescriptive practice, probation officers in her study experienced a dawning realisation 'that their autonomy was perhaps illusory. Participant "Michael" commented "what annoys me is that in so many cases where I used to be able to take decisions myself, I now have to take them to a senior"' (Gregory 2010, p2279). The workers in Gregory's study all had 12 or more years of experience. Might it be once again, then, that the older workers find the lack of decision-making autonomy stifling, but that less-experienced workers embrace it?

So what would ethical action in terms of decision-making look like? It could be suggested that social workers have an individual ethical responsibility to think through what they would *want* the decision to be, regardless of whether they are the ultimate decision-maker. Sitting quietly in decision-making fora or asking managers to make decisions with no input are an abdication of ethical action. Social workers should know, for defensible reasons (see Chapter 5), what their preferred decision would be and should be prepared to speak out, question, and argue where necessary. Even if the decision is not what the social workers would have chosen, they have acted in accordance with their moral responsibility. If ethical stress results, this may be an impetus to returning to the decision-makers to attempt once again to influence the decision.

Finding knowledge

In terms of decision-making explored above, and in terms of social work practice more widely, social workers *must* understand social justice, inequality, poverty, stereotypes, and discrimination (as per previous chapters). Without those fundamental building blocks, social workers will be hampered in terms of fully understanding the service user's situation and will be less likely to build a caring relationship or be motivated to take ethical action.

There is another aspect to essential knowledge, however, which is also vitally important: knowledge pertinent to the situation in terms of legislation, policy, and theory. Some of this should be the foundational working knowledge the social worker is obliged to acquire when taking employment in a particular agency, and some of it might be knowledge sought out for a specific situation. So, for example, if a social worker secures employment working with offenders, it is incumbent on him or her to become familiar with the legislative framework, recent policy direction (a critical understanding, of course), and the most recent theory in working with people who have offended – the desistance literature. A working and comprehensive knowledge should allow for easy access to bodies of information with which to compare practice. In terms of seeking out specific knowledge, a social worker might ask the questions: What policy supports the ethical action? What legislation? Is this an issue of human rights? Further, what research knowledge, what theory would also support my desired course of action? Can I draw on the espoused values of the agency (see Chapter 2)?

practice example

8.1

Remember Practice Example 6.1? The social worker in the example not only did not understand human rights but also had no idea of the knowledge on which the instruction to the sex offender not to socialise with others in the group was based. Theory around collusion and cycles of sex offending did not feature in the social worker's working knowledge, *even though* he was working in a specialised way with somebody who had committed those types of offences! Would you have faith that this worker was making any difference?

Another example is in relation to a student I worked with as a practice educator. The agency used an actuarial and structured clinical risk-assessment form to assess the risk of a person reoffending. The form was known in the agency as 'the pink form'. The student was meticulous in neatly filling out the form and enjoyed the idea that the form almost did the assessment for her – it gave a score at the end denoting the risk of reoffending. She was very much less interested in finding out *what knowledge* underpinned 'the pink form'. The crucial understanding of the workings of the form seemed somewhat irrelevant and just like extra work. Even knowing that she would be making judgements about someone's risk of reoffending to the court, which would in turn make judgements about the service user's freedom, did not inspire her to get a good understanding of the form. Therefore, as well as not really understanding her own assessment, the student could not explain to service users how she had come to very important judgements about them, other than by explaining that the form said so.

Both of the above examples illustrate something very interesting about the working knowledge of some social workers. There is an acceptance that knowledge *has already* been distilled and pre-packaged into working tools such as the pink form or the instruction on the work contract of people attending the sex offending group. There may be nothing wrong with that type of formulation of knowledge into usable forms, but there is a problem when social workers go no further than technically using the tool. Only in the understanding of the underpinning knowledge can a social worker: 1) critically appraise the tool and argue for not always using it, for its non-applicability in some circumstances, or for its use as supplementing rather than supplanting other forms of knowledge; 2) explain the work he or she is doing and what the tool is all about to service users, thereby practising ethically and also allowing the service user to have a voice and opinion about the tool and its use – sharing power as far as possible; 3) explain to other stakeholders such as the court and other professionals the underpinning theory.

Gray et al. (2015), in a survey of Australian social workers and evidence-based practice, found that there was an almost equal divide between social workers who preferred to appraise the evidence and apply it themselves and those who preferred to use guidelines and protocols developed by others. The use of procedures and tools is appealing, but the point being made in this chapter is that social workers must be responsible for understanding the theory and research on which the tools are based.

Gray et al. (2015) found that the social workers in their survey complained that lack of time was the biggest barrier to getting to grips with evidence-based practice. However, what is being suggested here is not

Think of a tool/procedure/guideline that you have used or seen used in a social work setting. Imagine you base a piece of practice on the tool or guideline and for whatever reason end up in a formal setting being asked to justify your practice. Rather than just saying 'I followed the procedure' and knowing nothing else, could you explain the theoretical and knowledge underpinnings of the procedure? In other words, could you explain properly *why* you practised in that way?

If you can – well done. If not, do some research now and get to grips with the underpinning thinking and theory of the procedure.

that social workers always engage in a systematic literature search to find and appraise original research before embarking on a course of action (although you might indeed do that occasionally) but rather that it is *part of the job* of a social worker to understand the evidence base that is already there for their work – and be able to critically appraise it. Once again, a general working knowledge is required, as is specific and specialised knowledge when the situation calls for it. Preston-Shoot (2012) suggests that social workers are not legally or ethically literate to a sufficient extent, in other words they do not draw on ethical principles or legal knowledge when making judgements in practice but rely on conformity to agency procedures. This leads to a stifling of ethical action and, even more worryingly, can allow poor practice to flourish. Adding to our understanding of this, Carey (2009) explores the Taylorisation of social work practice, understood as the down-grading of social work practice to scientific tasks designed by management and simply unquestioningly undertaken by social workers. Drawing on ethical, legal, or any other type of knowledge simply does not feature in this rational-technical construct of social work. These authors make a persuasive case for change, completely congruent with the key messages in this book. Social workers *must* be able to draw on knowledge, beyond tools and procedures, to implement the Practice Model.

What does knowledge mean, then, for motivation towards ethical action? It is important in several ways. The first is that it is a source of evidence for arguing for a particular course of action that might be against the neoliberal, managerial nature of the received wisdom in the agency. So actually knowing some of the research around working with families and how important relationship-based practice is, for example, might help a worker argue for a follow-up home visit. Knowing the effect of crushing isolation on people with mental health problems might inform an argument for assisting someone to become involved in a social activity and spending time on this rather than solely monitoring the person's medication. Knowing the human rights and ethical contradictions inherent in a policy denying services to asylum seekers might inform an argument for resistance. Secondly, knowledge can give a worker confidence in speaking out – in a one-to-one situation or in a meeting. Ingram et al. (2014) consider how powerful a setting a meeting can be and how a strategy often employed is for an unsure member of the meeting to say very little. Again, this is unethical if it means decisions and discussions happen without the valuable input a social worker might give *on behalf* of the service user. Finally, knowledge can contribute to moral outrage and ethical stress, as a knowledgeable social worker will be able to see where procedures and formulaic responses to people are not congruent with research on what helps families and individuals. Seeing this discrepancy can lead to ethical action.

The previous section has given an account of some of the ways that a worker can take ethical action. For social work students and/or very new workers, even understanding what feels wrong and recognising ethical stress, acquiring essential knowledge as a result, and just gradually becoming prepared for future ethical action might be good enough. All of this takes confidence and wisdom, so incrementally getting there is to be expected.

Ontological Anxiety – Coping

Turning now to the other side of the model, we are going to consider the situation where the social worker has acted in good faith, in line with his or her values, but still feels some healthy ontological anxiety due to the essential uncertainty of social work. Phillips (2009) suggests that such anxiety can be crippling for social workers who may lie awake at night terribly worried that something might go wrong. Hopefully, if a worker has made sure his or her practice was carried out with explicit defensible reasoning and in line with values as well as legislation, policy, and knowledge, his or her anxiety can be reduced somewhat, but it is probably fair to say that lingering worry will still often be experienced. How might social workers cope with that?

Supervision

Supervision has a strong tradition in social work and is usually understood as regular meetings between social worker and manager to discuss cases and the developmental needs of the worker. However, it has also been well documented that supervision, like other workings of social work agencies, has been very much affected by neoliberalism and consequent managerialism. As Lawler (2013, p101) states in relation to supervision: 'While traditionally concerned with ensuring that social work practice was in keeping with professional standards...now it meant meeting targets and adhering to organisational regulations and procedures. Lost was the reflective aspect of supervision as a learning experience.'

Chapter 5 considered Beddoe's (2010) study which explored supervisors' experiences of supervising staff. The author looked at whether practice that had indeed become 'ruled by technicist approaches in which risk assessment systems and checklists are put in place to minimise the risk of practitioners "missing something important" had resulted in supervision coming to "focus attention on micro-management and surveillance"' (Beddoe 2010, p1821). Beddoe found that the supervisors she interviewed still had a commitment to the various purposes of supervision, although she also found that the possibility of a risk and management preoccupation could diminish the quality of supervision. Sawyer (2009) adds weight to the conflicting priorities in supervision by suggesting that workers who become senior social workers are no longer 'expert craftsmen' but instead are 'expert managers' (Sawyer 2009, p443). They are concerned more with the completion of the paperwork about the work than with the actual work being done. Since the issue of caring about and helping families and individuals and attending to their welfare sits within the realm of the actual work being done, it is not a priority for discussion or quality enhancement. Again, this would be reflected in the nature of supervision as recognised by Beddoe. It can be seen, then, that increasing managerialism has eroded the supportive and ethical functions of supervision somewhat, and this means that it is a less effective space for helping social workers work through difficult ethical decisions and issues and the resultant ontological anxiety.

There is a further difficulty within supervision about whether social workers feel able to be open about concerns and anxieties and confident that they will not be judged as weak or lacking in competence. Goddard and Hunt (2011, p426) illustrate this by quoting a social worker's concerns about supervision: 'I have learned to be an isolated worker. If you open up, with personal issues and worries, then you are seen as personally incompetent.' The authors point out the dangers of supervision being concerned more with defending the agency than working in the interests of the workers and, ultimately, the service users. Bourn and Hafford-Letchfield (2011, p41) crucially suggest that supervision is important for helping workers to 'contain and work with the anxiety that naturally arises within social work'. In other words, the authors suggest that supervision should have a particular focus on the management of healthy 'ontological anxiety' (Taylor 2007). A supervisor who can 'allow' risky, responsive decisions in the best interests of service users and based on a real belief in social work values, needs to be good at dealing with the resultant, healthy ontological anxiety. A supervisor who cannot do that may well stick to the procedural, box-ticking form of supervision, of which the literature is quite consistent in its criticism.

In summary, then, it is clear that supervision *should* be an important method of helping social workers deal with anxiety but that the kind of neoliberal and managerial practice this book has explored at length might well get in the way. There is perhaps some scope here for social workers to request this type of critically reflective supervision and to make a case for why it is essential. Models of supervision that move the experience beyond the managerial can be drawn on to support this argument. For example, return to Chapter 5 and consider Ingram and Jindal-Snape's (Ingram et al. 2014) SuReCom model.

Exercise 8.3

Think about your own experience of supervision and see if you can answer the questions below, honestly:

1. Would you describe your supervision as managerial or reflective?
2. Was there trust between you and the supervisor?
3. Did you feel you would be judged as 'weak' if you raised certain concerns?
4. What did you need from supervision that you didn't get?

If you feel supervision was not as useful as it might have been, describe an ideal supervisory session. Explicitly think about the anxiety-containment element.

Peer support

The idea of getting support from colleagues was introduced in Chapter 5 when it was noted that Ingram (2015a) found that the social workers in his study rated informal support from colleagues as the most valuable of all the supportive mechanisms available to them. We will look at this in a little more detail here. The popularity of peer support may be an indication of formal supervision's inadequacies as noted above, or it might just be that people prefer the safety and freedom of discussing real issues with colleagues whom they trust. Ingram (2015b) sums up the key and unique features that a range of authors have identified in relation to peer support as follows: timing – support available on the spot; shared experience – colleagues who might well have been through similar experiences and have had similar feelings; unrecorded – informal nature and lack of formal consequences to the discussion; getting prepared for formal supervision – rehearsing the discussion in preparation for the time when it will be recorded; and a sense of belonging – sharing experiences, being listened to and cared for as a mutual 'belonging' experience.

Clearly, peer support is extremely valuable and useful but, on its own, does have drawbacks. Similarly to how covert resistance (see Chapter 6) keeps issues under the radar and hidden as opposed to exposed, faced, and perhaps facilitating change, informal peer support is unlikely to lead to changes. Therefore, peer support should be viewed as preparation for more formal discussion of issues rather than the experience remaining as an end in itself. Of course there is a place for that, but the cautionary note must be that peer support alone will not bring anything of importance to the attention of management.

Current thinking

It might well be helpful for social workers who are experiencing healthy ontological anxiety to remember that current thinking is resurrecting the idea that said anxiety and uncertainty are normal parts of social work. One consequence of the study undertaken by Morley and Macfarlane (2014), described in Research Box 8.1, was that the students, having engaged in critical thinking, felt more able to live with uncertainty and anxiety. One student said 'we're more comfortable sitting with uncertainty. We know that practice is messy and complicated and that's ok' (Morley and Macfarlane 2014, p348). It may be that understanding social work from a critical angle exposes the impossible aspiration of neoliberal social work to make positivist cause-and-effect assessments and resultant correctional or curative action. Once social work students start to question neoliberalism per se, it is easier to see the truth about uncertainty in social work. Munro (2011) as already discussed in this book, also makes it very clear the uncertainties exist and must be tolerated and that the public should understand this:

> For some organisations, the change will need a move away from a blaming, defensive culture to one that recognises the uncertainty inherent in the work and that professional judgment, however expert, cannot guarantee positive outcomes for children and families. The organisational risk principles listed in chapter three need to underpin practice. In child protection, a key responsibility of leaders is to manage the anxiety that the work generates. Some degree of anxiety is inevitable. Whilst practitioners have a key role in protecting children, their safety and welfare cannot be guaranteed. Additional anxiety is fuelled by the level of public criticism that may be directed at child protection professionals if they are involved in a case with a tragic outcome. In the review's analysis of why previous reforms have not had their intended success, unmanaged anxiety about being blamed was identified as a significant factor in encouraging a process-driven compliance culture.
>
> (Munro 2011, p107)

It is important, therefore, that social workers and students understand the healthy nature of ontological anxiety, understand uncertainty, and feel supported in this by the academic, policy, and professional communities as well as by supervisors, managers, and colleagues.

In summary, then, this section of the model might look like this:

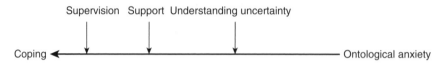

So far, this chapter has explored putting the horizontal aspects of the model into practice in more detail, and thus withstanding procedural and often oppressive neoliberal practice that simply reinforces existing inequality and hierarchy. Another barrier to the implementation of the model is the idea of *professionalism*. Chapter 2 considered professionalism in relation to implementing social justice, relationship-based practice, and ethics of care approaches, whereas the forthcoming section will explore notions of professionalism once again in relation to the horizontal sections of the model: anxiety and ethical stress.

Professionalism

As the book has already explored, the managerial and neoliberal direction of social work and social work education leads to a positivist approach to social work ethics and a rejection of a critically reflective approach (Morley and Macfarlane 2014). What this means is that rational-technical practice flourishes within a context where impersonal and distilled evidence-based practice, 'programmes' of manualised work (such as offending programmes or parenting programmes), and short, target-focused interventions abound (Ingram et al. 2014). Dependency is eschewed, and relationship-based practice is redundant. This approach produces pre-packaged knowledge, digested and interpreted and finally realised within assessment tools and procedures, programmes of work, and other standardised procedures as discussed earlier in the chapter. Agency managers and policy-makers can always point to the underpinning knowledge and justification for their processes. Add this pre-packaged, distilled knowledge to heavy workloads, targets, a drive for 'efficiency', and audits, and the consequence is unthinking, rational-technical rule-following by social workers. In Fenton's (2014a) study, heavy workloads were explicitly recognised as the reason why welfare, helping, responsive social work was prevented from taking place. Social workers saw this as an unintended consequence of the workload and as a practical, not an ethical problem. The idea that such practice was a result of the neoliberal project working as it was supposed to in a public service was completely outside their frames of reference. Any ethical objection was also, therefore, cognitively out of reach.

Morley and Macfarlane (2014) suggest that social workers have colluded with the above trajectory in order to increase their professional standing. For example, Robinson (2003) studied practitioners' and managers' perceptions of the introduction of a structured risk-assessment tool and found that use of the tool both heightened workers' sense of professionalism and credibility and, crucially, gave them a sense of security in their decisions. They could defend their assessment in the event of things going wrong. This was a consistent feeling, shared by both practitioners and managers. Again, we can see the blame culture at work, and anything that can reduce the nightmarish situation vividly described by Phillips (2009) appears to be welcomed by workers. When anxiety is felt as anathema and showing that you have followed the process properly becomes the priority, ethical stress simply is not a consideration. The job has become one that is not about values, ethical situations, or ethical difficulties.

Hearteningly, however, Robinson also found that some workers were unhappy with the de-skilling brought about by the introduction of the tool and the resultant erosion of discretion and imposition of limitations on the use of the worker's own professional knowledge. Furthermore, she found that workers adapted to the introduction of the tool in ways that allowed them to retain their professional practice by viewing the assessment tool as a supplement to their professional assessment, not as a replacement. Workers also highlighted the professional task in interpreting the knowledge needed to complete the form: a combination of technical and moral decision-making. This introduces the idea that procedures can enhance feelings of professionalism whilst simultaneously eroding that professionalism. As Morley and Macfarlane (2014) point out, colluding with this managerial shift in the name of professionalism has ironically created a less professional profession. Social work has sacrificed its value base, its explicit knowledge endeavour, and its foundational belief in radical social justice. All the elements, in fact, that assist social workers in resisting neoliberalism.

Meagher and Parton (2004) illuminate this further and highlight social work's shift in emphasis from accountability to the service user to accountability to the agency that emphasises mechanistic and impersonal practice, often in the name of efficiency. Interestingly for the Practice Model, the authors highlight that the idea of *care* was very much missing in the earlier critical literature that attempted to take a resistive stance against neoliberalism and managerialism. They suggest that social work was 'tainted' by its association with care until the resurgence of an 'ethics of care' in the academic literature. Meagher and Parton suggest that ideas of professionalism have much in common with bureaucracy, such as distance, lack of warmth, and impassivity in the face of service users' distress. This is so removed from notions of care that if social work was aspiring to that type of professionalism, care would indeed taint it, and the authors do suggest that this idea of a professional was similar to the kind of practitioner encouraged by managerialism. However, they go on to suggest that resurrecting an ethics of care and positioning it as a core part of social work practice, as advocated in this book, can counteract those particularly managerialist professional notions. As Fenton and Walker (2012, p24) state:

> As social work educators, we need to continue to emphasise that to be a professional social worker, the relationship with the service user is central... rather than this being the element that gets in the way of social work being a true profession (in terms of the bureaucratic definition), it should unashamedly be the defining feature.

So, at this point we can see that the Practice Model is compatible with professionalism, but a professionalism that avoids distant, bureaucratic, technicist mechanisms and embraces care at its heart. Liljegren (2012, p308) illuminates this further and helps synthesise the ideas in the previous section. The author differentiates between 'occupational professionalism' and 'organisational professionalism', where the former has its focus on the service user and draws on knowledge concerned with the service user's issues and the latter keeps focused on the bureaucratic structure of the organisation and looks to organisational rules and procedures as the primary source of knowledge. A good example of this occurred recently when in conversation a fellow academic told me about a teaching session with a group of social work managers. When she asked them whether a new development, about supporting children in care for a longer period of time, was a good idea, they overwhelmingly said 'no' due to financial restrictions. When she reframed the question as 'But as social workers, what do you think?' they all said 'It is absolutely a good idea, and the right thing.' The first response was characterised by 'organisational professionalism' whereas the second response was characterised by 'occupational professionalism'. In order to work out what the 'right thing' is, social workers and students *must* be encouraged to be occupational (i.e. social work) professionals and to explicitly draw on social work values and knowledge.

The ideas above are reinforced by Preston-Shoot who states that students are overly concerned with procedural knowledge and less interested in the professional knowledge required to help them understand service users and their issues. In other words, students can become 'overly identified with bureaucratic imperatives and lose sight of allegiance to social work goals' (Preston-Shoot 2011, p189), just as the managers in the above example did. Once again, the Practice Model can explicitly support occupational professionalism with its emphasis on drawing on knowledge, values, relationship-based practice, and social justice.

To sum up, this chapter has explored the horizontal elements of the Practice Model in some more detail, and it is suggested that the model, as a whole, is easily compatible with a social work definition of professionalism.

Research Box 8.2

How nontraditional placements can help foster a sense of occupational professionalism in social work students

Nontraditional placements are with agencies that 'do not define themselves as delivering a social work service' (Scholar et al. 2014, p999). Examples might be residential establishments for older people or campaigning organisations or, as in the case below, a charity delivering personal development programmes to young people.

Scholar et al. (2014) undertook a national evaluation considering students' experiences in nontraditional placements. Some students expressed concerns that I, as an educator, recognise very well, such as 'this is not real social work', 'there is no social worker around', 'it is not a statutory setting', etc.

By the end of the placements, however, there was an emphasis in student reporting on promotion of values (including a commitment to anti-oppressive practice) and a change in the way the students constructed the social work role: 'By the end of the placement, some students commented that their views of what constituted social work had changed and developed from a narrow interpretation based on the tasks involved in statutory settings to a broader perspective, expressed in terms of aims, purpose, and principles rather than specific activities or organisational contexts' (Scholar et al. 2014, p1007). In other words, 'occupational professionalism' was promoted in these placements, perhaps due to less reliance on rigid procedures and regulations that can supplant core occupational values. These placements may be a valuable source of transformational learning for students, especially if the students can be helped to recognise them as such.

---

main points

■ The ethical stress-ethical action connection can be enhanced by critical understanding and analysis, values, and strong feelings about social injustice.

■ Ethical action includes arguing and challenging, taking responsibility for decision-making, and being knowledgeable about the situation (beyond procedural knowledge).

- Some methods of coping with ontological anxiety include supervision, peer support, and being aware of current thinking around uncertainty in social work.

- Notions of professionalism in social work need to embrace ideas of care and relationship building and should eschew distant, bureaucratic, professional constructs.

taking it further

- Bourn, D., and Hafford-Letchfield, T. (2011) 'The role of social work professional supervision in conditions of uncertainly', *The International Journal of Knowledge, Culture and Change Management* 10 (9) 41–56. An excellent article to aid your thinking about some of the issues in this chapter.
- Preston-Shoot, M. (2012) 'The secret curriculum', *Ethics and Social Welfare* 6 (1) 18–36.
- Meagher, G., and Parton, N. (2004) 'Modernising social work and the ethics of care', *Social Work and Society* 2 (1) 10–27.

9 Conclusion

Overview

This concluding chapter will recap the learning journey so far. The main learning points will be highlighted, as will the development of the new Practice Model. The Practice Model will then be applied to the case study introduced in Chapter 3 and its usage will be analysed in some detail.

The model will then be applied to some current examples of what is considered good practice, leading to further critical analysis.

The Journey So Far

This book began with definitions of the main concepts that are threaded throughout all chapters, namely neoliberalism, values, and social justice. The two central themes of the book were also introduced. Theme 1 is 'reconnection to social justice' and takes as its starting point the idea that contemporary social work might actually be *losing* that fundamental connection. Evidence is presented that suggests that newer workers and social work students appear to be less critical of neoliberalism and, as a result, less connected to notions of social justice. This theme is revisited in several chapters and provides justification for the assertion that social work requires a new Practice Model that reinstates social justice as a key and indispensible principle in social work practice. Theme 2 is 'ethical stress', which is the feeling experienced when social workers, who have as a pre-requisite a robust and coherent value base, are asked to practice in a context that does not allow expression of those values. The idea is introduced that the experience of 'ethical stress' is a useful and healthy one which can provide impetus for questioning taken-for-granted practice or for taking ethical action.

Chapter 2, 'The Social Work Context', traces the development of social work from the Enlightenment to the present day. The chapter explores how we have arrived at the contemporary social work context, which is characterised by managerialism, individualisation, participationism, and privatisation, and how the neoliberal shift has contributed to that picture. The chapter then furthers the core analysis of the book and links the features of the current context to the experience of ethical stress. It is suggested that developments such as the weakening of the welfare state and the preoccupation with risk assessment and management can cause ethical stress for workers whose value-based inclination might be to help, build relationships, and understand the effect of oppression on people's lives.

Taking the reader's thinking further, Chapter 3 introduces the idea that the rise of neoliberalism has led to the 'othering' of groups of people. Several of the 'other' populations are considered in the chapter, as is how media stereotyping and pejorative reporting can skew public thinking. The point of this chapter is that social workers and students should understand the true picture and be able to see through stereotypes and hype in order to engage with service users, who might belong to an 'othered' group, in human-to-human equality. Stereotypical thinking can damage an approach based on the recognition of equal human worth and can make relationship-based practice difficult. Chapter 3 also explores how neoliberalism contributes to the perpetuation of oppressive ideas and why it may be that people accept those ideas uncritically. Concepts such as hegemony and inequality are explored.

Traditional ethical approaches to social work are covered in Chapter 4, and it is suggested that social workers and students can actually justify value-poor practice by superficially applying principles from deontology, utilitarianism, and virtue ethics. An ethics of care, however, is less easy to apply to poor practice and is, thus, suggested as the most useful approach for social work. It is introduced as forming the heart of the new Practice Model:

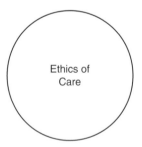

Ethics of Care

Chapter 5 looks at implementing an ethics of care in more detail. There is recognition that it is not always easy or straightforward, and applying the approach in situations where control and authority are required is considered. The experiences of ethical stress and ontological anxiety are compared and contrasted, and readers are strongly encouraged to think about the difference between those feelings, as differentiating between them is extremely important in working out what needs to happen next.

The idea that implementing an ethics of care can lead to ethical stress and ontological anxiety is introduced at this point, although these ideas are further developed in Chapter 8. Relevant concepts such as defensible decision-making, supervision, and ethical action are applied to ethical stress/ontological anxiety. This chapter builds on the first iteration of the Practice Model to include the horizontal elements of ethical stress and ontological anxiety:

Chapter 6, 'Social Justice', tackles the issue, which evidence would suggest social workers and students find very difficult, of *how* social justice thinking can be applied to social work practice. Radical social work, critical social work, anti-oppressive practice, and human rights-based practice are introduced. Themes from those approaches are teased out, and practical ideas about *how* to apply them are proposed under the suggested 'eclectic social justice' approach. Practical suggestions about application include quiet challenges, understanding leading to ethical action, advocacy, and building relationships. In this chapter the model is augmented further:

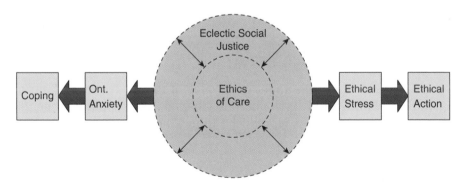

Chapter 7 glues together the ethics of care and eclectic social justice approaches by introducing relationship-based practice as an essential element of the new Practice Model. Relationship-based practice principles are explored, and connections with other aspects of the model are analysed. Limitations of relationship-based practice are considered, leading to a clear definition of 'purposeful' relationship-based practice. In this chapter, the final iteration of the model is produced:

Chapter 8 analyses further the horizontal elements of the Practice Model and looks at elements that enhance the ethical stress–ethical action connection, such as social justice understanding and critical reflection. Examples of what is meant by 'ethical action' are given, and the reader is encouraged to realise that taking ethical action might, in fact, be possible. The ontological anxiety–coping link is then interrogated further with renewed attention to supervision, peer support, and current thinking around uncertainty and anxiety. Finally, notions of professionalism are discussed, and a concept of professionalism that is congruent with the Practice Model is identified.

As can be seen above, the Practice Model evolves as the chapters unfold, and the book ultimately arrives at a workable, accessible framework for practice, which should help social workers and students reconnect with social justice in their day-to-day practice.

Applying the Practice Model

To further understand the applicatory value of the model, we will return again to the Smith family introduced in Chapter 3. As a reminder, the following practice example is reproduced from Chapter 3:

3.1 The Smith family

practice example

Meet the Smith family where the children are being neglected and alcohol use is an issue. School have referred the family, and the referral has come to the local social work team. The social worker attends the family home and sees evidence of neglect, alcohol misuse, and chaos. She introduces herself and clarifies her role as per good practice she remembers from her teaching at university (Trotter 2006). She remembers to be explicit about the authority in her role and starts off by making it clear to Mrs Smith that she needs to comply or there could be serious consequences. She also remembers her learning about active listening and relationship-based practice, but she doesn't have much time, so she listens to Mrs Smith's 'story' whilst also looking for clues and hints about levels of risk and opportunities for concrete suggestions about routines, alcohol use, etc. Finally, the social worker empowers Mrs Smith to contact the school to arrange to go and discuss the children, by finding the phone number for her. She will later check that the phone call has been made.

The social worker returns to the office and writes up her case notes, bullet-pointing all of the things she has asked Mrs Smith to do and making it clear that she left her in no doubt as to the consequences if she doesn't make improvements. At the end of the day, the social worker reflects, she must keep focused on the children's welfare as paramount. When her team manager sees her file, he comments that she has done a good piece of work today, with everything 'nice and clear'.

The social worker in this example does not feel ethical stress – she employed her values of respect (she treated Mrs Smith well), non-judgementality (she didn't leap to conclusions, but listened well) and took cognisance of Mrs Smith's right to self-determination – as long as that didn't impact negatively on the children. Her team manager says she has done good work – defensible if anything goes wrong. The social worker feels pleased – there is nothing else she should have done.

Although this case study might seem quite extreme in its managerial/neoliberal characterisation, it actually chimes with accounts, especially written accounts, given to me by social work students recently on placement. See Practice Examples 9.1 and 9.2 below for examples.

9.1

While visiting a student on placement in an establishment for homeless people, many of whom are offenders, I was given a written account of a piece of practice with a young man which exemplified the above neoliberal response. In essence the main concerns with the account were as follows:

- A factual account was given of how the young man was breaching the terms of his licence by not attending appointments as instructed.
- The student spoke about 'sanctions', about 'advising him', about giving him 'instructions', and about 'consequences'.
- She illustrated her values by talking about 'honesty' and 'checking he understood'.
- There was absolutely nothing on what the service user had to say or what he thought, felt, or believed.
- Nothing about critical understanding of criminal justice in connection with wider social justice issues.

- Complete focus on 'outer world' (behaviour management) and no focus on 'inner world' (his view).
- No attempt to build a relationship whatsoever and no mention, in any way, of care.

9.2

When I visited another student on placement in a statutory child protection team, very similar themes were apparent. The student discussed a mother struggling with two young sons:

- Once again, the account was peppered with language such as 'minimising', 'advising', and 'consequences'.
- No account of what the mother or the children thought/said/felt about the situation – what were the issues or problems from their point of view?
- So, no relationship building, no attention to 'inner world' and, yet again, sole focus on 'outer world' or behaviour management.
- No focus on social justice, and issues such as very poor housing, poverty, and struggle only became apparent after discussion.
- This student actually had heard the service user's voice and had attended to her 'inner world', but thought that the expectation of social work was that her practice was considered and documented in this clinical way, using authoritarian, controlling, and managerial language. The practice educator suggested that the student had maybe written it 'too like a report', but even this begs the question – is it acceptable to write reports in this way?

Think about reports or accounts you have written at work or on practice learning opportunities. Did you write in a 'formal' style, using jargon that you think is expected? Look out for phrases such as 'I advised', 'I warned', 'he minimised', 'consequences', and 'instructions'. Not only are those formal words, they are also authoritarian, so do you think you maybe felt you had to emphasise this aspect of your role?

Now try to recreate the written account in another style. Were you able to include information from the service user's perspective? Were you able to talk about help and support? Consider whether you think this would have been acceptable to the agency.

Clearly, then, the managerial, authoritarian way of practising reflected in the practice examples, which is anathema to the Practice Model, is widespread. Other tutors mention similar accounts given to them by students on placement, and academic literature on the current context of social work, covered in earlier chapters, would resonate with the implication that practice has become as managerial and cold as the accounts would suggest. Preston-Shoot's exploration of social work literature concludes that presence or absence of value language could profoundly affect the learning experiences of students. He draws on a study that suggests that social justice terminology, in particular, was indeed absent, even in situations where it would be expected to feature. In summary, he states that 'values were either absent from practice, or the work was described in a language that did not convey what respondents knew or believed' (Preston-Shoot 2012, p25) This chimes very well with what might have been going on in Practice Example 9.2.

To attempt to exemplify something different, we return to the application of the model, and we will consider each aspect in turn:

Ethics of care (Chapter 4)

The social worker this time would begin by being 'attentive' to Mrs Smith and her children. What is her view? What does she think/feel/want? Once the social worker has a thorough picture of Mrs Smith's and her children's views of the situation, she would take responsibility for helping where possible. Not saying 'that's not my job' and narrowing the parameters of the task to simply getting Mrs Smith to comply and make changes, but identifying what help and assistance Mrs Smith says she needs and trying to provide that. This might involve advocating for bedding, benefits, a nursery place, transport assistance, or a myriad of other examples of 'help'. Having 'competence' to provide this is the next element, which might mean arguing with a manager, going beyond the call of duty, or advocacy with other agencies/services. Again, this is *more work* than simply undertaking a narrow assessment. Throughout the interaction, the social worker would remain responsive to Mrs Smith and her family, recognising when Mrs Smith might feel overpowered or intimidated or angry and disappointed. The 'integrity of care' element of the ethics of care means that the social worker would realise how the above elements fit together and also fit into wider social justice understanding. Is Mrs Smith living in poverty? What does poverty and inequality do to people? Mrs Smith is understood as an oppressed person (in terms of gender and single mother status) and as a victim of an unfair society. The social worker also understands that her practice is taking place in a restrictive, managerial, and neoliberal social work context in which people are expected to make changes on an individual level and the influence of structural difference is considered irrelevant. Mrs Smith is simply stereotyped as 'a bad mother'. Colleagues in the office say things like 'She's not really poor, she still has money for fags and booze', with no understanding of Mrs Smith seeking pleasure and escape where she can due to her life being quite grim. The social worker, however, connects to her as an equal human being who believes she might well behave in the same way given the same circumstances. There is a distinct lack of superiority. Finally, an ethics of care requires that the social worker attend to Mrs Smith's and her children's connectedness: What are their important relationships? Do they have support systems, and if so, how can these help here?

Purposeful relationship-based practice (Chapter 7)

The social worker this time really wants to hear about the situation from Mrs Smith's point of view and, thus, attends to her 'inner world'. She demonstrates emotional intelligence and realises that having social workers visit is something that could cause Mrs Smith all kinds of negative feelings. She also demonstrates empathy – when Mrs Smith talks about loneliness and her daily struggles, the social worker tries to understand how that *feels* for Mrs Smith. The social worker wants to get to know Mrs Smith and attends to trying to do that, even if it means going back to visit in order to spend a bit more time. Through a purposeful relationship, and once the social worker really understands the situation, she can think about intervening – helping (as per an ethics of care), risk-assessing the situation, and working in partnership with Mrs Smith on the things that need to change. As covered in Chapter 4, intervention might involve aspects of authority and control – but only in so far as is absolutely required.

Eclectic social justice (Chapter 6)

The social worker in this case study subscribes to a radical social justice orientation and therefore believes that inequality and poverty are at the root of social problems. So, in this case she would try her best to alleviate some of the hardship suffered by Mrs Smith and her children and would feel anger and a sense of injustice at the situation. So, she would liaise with housing if the house was in poor condition, liaise with the benefits office if there was any way to increase Mrs Smith's income, and approach agencies that might make material provision if it was required. The social worker's role with all of these agencies would be one of advocacy, especially if Mrs Smith was viewed as undeserving. The social worker would also understand that Mrs Smith was discriminated against as a single mother and a woman. Working on zero-hour contracts, at a moment's notice, for very poor wages is the situation many women find themselves in, and a woman with children would find working under these conditions extremely difficult. Mrs Smith may also be subject to sanctions from the benefits office if she had struggled to make all appointments. The impact of these punitive measures and the concurrent austerity measures would be well understood by the social worker. Understanding, such as that exemplified in the graph below, would be in the social worker's 'working knowledge' of her area of social work (Chapter 8):

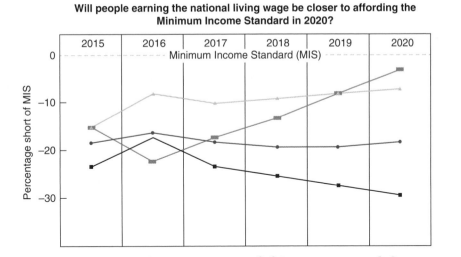

Figure 9.1 Will people earning the national living wage be closer to affording the Minimum Income Standard in 2020?

JRF (2015) from https://www.jrf.org.uk/sites/default/files/infographic/mis-2020/, reproduced with permission of the Joseph Rowntree Foundation.

Understanding the above enables the social worker to critically deconstruct the common-sense notion that if the service user 'just got a job' everything would be better. Also, in approaching Mrs Smith, the social worker would be aware of the difference in power and economic standing between the two of them and would thus consider concepts such as 'power shedding'.

This particular social worker is a member of the Social Work Action Network (SWAN) and finds that she can retain motivation and commitment to social justice, not just through her own sense of injustice, which is enhanced by getting to know people living in poverty and coming to understand their struggles, but also by reading articles and attending SWAN conferences and meetings, which help her to feel she has allies in her endeavours. This is important, because her colleagues are not always supportive.

Ontological anxiety (Chapters 5 and 8)

The social worker does what she regards as the 'right thing' and argues with her manager for resources for Mrs Smith. She has also spent time maximising her benefits and helping where possible. She has had discussions in the office with colleagues about whether she is being 'too soft as usual', and she knows that, indeed, her manager views her like this. Consequently, she has a sneaking anxiety that if something went wrong she would be judged as not being good enough or tough enough at her job. Would colleagues feel they had been vindicated in their criticisms? Would she, in fact, be one of the 'politically correct' social workers (who) were a 'soft touch' for manipulative parents, as social workers were branded in the wake of the Baby P tragedy (Ferguson and Lavalette 2009, p15)? After reflection, however, this ontological anxiety is recognised by the social worker as just that – the healthy anxiety produced by acting in good faith. To deal with this, the social worker would seek out a like-minded colleague, and they would discuss the case over a coffee. Through this discussion, she might resolve to discuss the case in supervision and advocate once again for a welfare-orientated response to the Smith family.

Ethical stress leading to ethical action (Chapters 5 and 8)

Imagine that a social work student has shadowed the social worker in the first response to this case (Practice Example 3.1). The student has a strong value base and a good understanding of the Practice Model elements. However, as she is worried about feedback from the experienced social worker, she doesn't feel able to challenge her practice, although she is very unsettled indeed by what she has witnessed. The student dwells on how she feels and decides to write about it for her university. Undertaking a critical analysis of the situation leads her to understand that she is, quite rightly, objecting to punitive, managerial, and neoliberal practice. Now that she understands this more clearly, she does some reading around this type of practice and whether there is still a place for values, relationships, and caring. She finds a plethora of academic writers who share her views. She also revisits BASW's *Code of Ethics* and, again, finds vindication for her views. Armed with this knowledge and understanding, the student discusses her analysis with her practice educator and decides to take ethical action: she asks to speak to the social worker concerned and frames her challenge in a questioning way. For example she says 'I have just been reading an article about relationship-based practice being effective, and I was wondering if you get the chance to do that. It was just that with Mrs Smith it didn't seem to feature much...' Getting into a discussion in this way might lead the student to be able to ask to return to the Smith family home to do some work of her own and thus to advocate, offer help, and get to know Mrs Smith's views. The student might also have given the social worker some food for thought...

Practice Example 9.3 illustrates some elements of the applications suggested above:

9.3

The social worker this time approaches the family with a primary task of care. She listens (and is prepared to be surprised), asks in order to really understand, finds out about Mrs Smith's and her children's relationships, supports, AND about their 'inner worlds'. The task of getting to know Mrs Smith and her children is paramount. Through the nascent relationship, the social worker begins to understand Mrs Smith's and her children's lives. She is able to express that understanding and, together with Mrs Smith, work out solutions. The social worker wants to help Mrs Smith with some much-needed essentials (like bedding) and also wants more time in order to get to know her better. Her team leader says she can have neither, simply due to restrictions on resources. The social worker experiences ethical stress about this and refuses to accept what the team leader is saying. She builds in more time (resistance), she approaches other agencies for assistance and advocates on Mrs Smith's behalf (even though some agencies do not view her as deserving), and she is thus employing the social justice values of practice. She can see that Mrs Smith is discriminated against on account of being a woman, being poor, and being in a one-parent family. She understands the stresses of living in an unequal, hierarchical society and is able to talk about some of the feelings Mrs Smith has about this. The social worker also has a construct of Mrs Smith as someone who has suffered due to an unjust society. She finds out about her childhood, her experience, and her struggles as she views them, and she links those to what she understands about structural difference.

We can see in the above example how the social worker can employ an ethics of care approach to Mrs Smith and get to know her. She can then draw on elements of the eclectic social justice approach in the new model. This is a very different practice from the earlier one.

Back in the office, the team manager is on the receiving end of the social worker's request for time and resources and is also the object of her well-articulated arguments as to why Mrs Smith should receive what she should and why she will be returning to visit the following week. Plaudits about 'good casework' are not so readily forthcoming!

So, we can see above, through detailed analysis and a more general application, that the new Practice Model allows for a form of social work practice that prioritises care, relationships, and social justice. The service user's voice is firmly at the heart of the practice. The model also allows for dealing with risk, but it recognises that risk can be reduced by help and assistance with practical and emotional issues brought about by poverty and inequality, *as well as* by individual-level behaviour change.

Application of the Practice Model to Contemporary Examples of 'Good Practice'

System redesign in the London Borough of Hackney (Munro 2011)

Highlighted as an example of good practice in the Munro report, the London Borough of Hackney redesigned its children's social care services by adopting a model based on a management framework from the 1980s. In essence the approach was a whole system redesign, making sure that different parts of the system were aligned and coherent. Although this sounds like a further example of managerialism (imported from the private sector in the 1980s), one of its clear aims was to reduce bureaucracy and increase autonomy for social workers. Rogowski (2012, p926) outlines that tension thus:

> Munro argues that cutting bureaucracy will enable social workers to spend time with families, focusing on the needs of children, in turn allowing more scope to exercise professional judgement. In particular, the Hackney reclaiming social work model is enthusiastically referred to (Munro 2011, pp. 151–66), notwithstanding it is based on a management model developed by business consultants. There is also a call for 'more determined and robust management' (Munro 2011, pp. 5), but, given that many of the problems confronting social work have resulted from such imported private sector management styles, many remain to be convinced that practitioners will see a positive difference in day-to-day practice.

According to Munro, there was some success with this model. The new social work units had time and space to get to know the families they worked with, to do more face-to-face work, and to work more collaboratively with families. All of this is in keeping with the Practice Model, as it would allow space for caring and relationship building. What is not clear in the account of the redesign is whether that extra 'space' was used for those kind of activities. Instead, there is an emphasis on evidence-based practice and the use of two particular approaches – systemic family therapy and social learning theory. So, although there is perhaps a move towards more face-to-face family engagement, and thus more opportunity for relationship building, there is also a focus on 'corrective' therapy – looking at what has gone wrong with the family dynamics and what erroneous learning has taken place. Yes, there might be a place for this, but where is help, care, and social justice thinking? The individual level of focus means that there is little space for notions of eclectic social justice, for understanding the contribution of poverty and inequality or despair and pressure. Some families might benefit more from the alleviation of those stressors than from receiving 'therapy'.

Personalisation

The concept of personalisation has been critiqued at some length in this book (see Chapters 2 and 4). Once again, there is an absence of social justice thinking in the positive accounts of personalisation. As Lymbery (2014) states, the impact of increased thresholds and tightening budgets, results of the neoliberal political shift, are not properly considered. And I. Ferguson's (2008) point that not everyone can, or wants to, 'step up' to independence is also omitted. Applying the model in this context, therefore, would mean that these restrictions are indeed highlighted and might possibly lead to ethical stress and, thus, action. Even if ethical action did not ensue, the social worker would have a critical understanding of those drawbacks that would inform his or her engagement with service users, rather than a zealous desire to promote personalisation of care.

Criminal justice social work in Scotland

Good practice ideals for criminal justice social work are set out in the *National Outcomes and Standards for Social Work Services in the Criminal Justice System* (NOAS) (Scottish Government 2010). This document outlines what it is that criminal justice social workers need to do. It operationalises the Criminal Justice and Licensing (Scotland) Act 2010 and outlines how 'Community Payback Orders' are to be implemented. The document also makes the priority work clear and outlines good practice principles. The three outcomes for CJSW services are '1. Community safety and public protection 2. the reduction of re-offending 3. social inclusion to support desistance from offending' (Scottish Government 2010, p15). Governmental direction clearly prioritises public protection work (which includes risk assessment and management), and welfare work (offering help, which would result from care and relationship-based practice) is bottom of the list. There is little mention of 'helping' in NOAS, and the standards are clear that this is the goal only when 'there is evidence that the individual is no longer a significant risk' (ibid., p51). Does this mean that the opportunity to receive help is earned by good behaviour? This would be at odds with a positive human rights agenda; a framework through which an argument for helping/welfare work to be the human right of every CJSW service user can be made (Fenton 2012b). There is little about the offender being the decision-maker in what work needs to be done, and there is little about the social worker building proper relationships with service users. Interestingly, NOAS also claims that CJSW is firmly based on social work values: 'practice in Scotland has remained firmly rooted within social work principles and values with a strong commitment to social inclusion' (ibid., p5). Is this true, given that social work values are so concerned with social justice and structural discrimination and disadvantage? There is absolutely no recognition within NOAS that the effects of discrimination and disadvantage may have had any influence upon offenders' behaviour and, in fact, when social justice is mentioned it is only in terms of the public's right to be protected. Consequently, there is nothing in NOAS to encourage workers to fight for social justice on behalf of their service users. It would seem, therefore, that NOAS is 'espousing' values (Schein 2010, Chapter 2) that actually do not reflect the reality of practice. There is no recognition of social justice for offenders, only social justice *from* offenders.

Concluding Comments

At this juncture, it is clear to see that the Practice Model may be quite difficult to apply in settings where good practice is accepted in the above form. It is also reasonable to assume that very many agencies in the statutory sector are characterised by some of the above themes and that although 'good practice' might nod towards relationships, care and values, the place of social justice thinking is marginalised. Rather than accepting this as an argument for the Practice Model not having utility, however, it can be argued that the current state of affairs renders the model absolutely essential if social work is to remain true to its value base and aims. Consider the following account by Ferguson and Lavalette (2009, p20):

> When money is tight, housing poor, living conditions overcrowded, life becomes stressful and the family home becomes a pressure cooker where parents can explode into rage at their children. The anger and frustration is more likely to be focused on the family's children if the parents are also younger and have a history of being abused themselves. The consequences are tragic, but it is the social conditions created by poverty and inequality which provide the context for the eruption of violence. It is also

here, alongside the very poorest and most marginalised in society, that social workers spend most of their working lives.

The imperative in thinking about the above account is that it 'needs to be considered with much...care and sensitivity, otherwise there is a danger of feeding into – albeit unintentionally – the long-held bourgeois view that the working-class poor make for bad parents' (S. Jones 2009, p34). S. Jones goes on to discuss the level of surveillance and scrutiny that the poorest families are subjected to, whilst the often uncaring and distant parenting of the upper echelons of society are ignored. He highlights that, for example, a group of parents from a deprived housing estate told him that they knew they were considered 'bad parents' due to where they lived, what the tabloids said about 'people like them' (see Chapter 3), what neighbours said, and judgements that would befall them if their children ever did get into trouble. This led to only trusting closest family and engendered feelings of extreme anxiety if social workers ever turned their attention on them.

Even more starkly conveyed by the parents was the psychological effect of these continual moral judgements. As outlined in Chapter 3, the effects of poverty, such as shame and loss of hope, can be overwhelming and brutalising, and the parents articulated this very clearly to Jones. These feelings are echoed by, for example, Birmingham Settlement Chief Executive Martin Holcombe. His concerns include the chronic high levels of unemployment in the area and, even more profoundly, the endemic lack of self-esteem he witnesses, exacerbated by recent media and political reporting accusing people who are struggling and in real desperation of being 'scroungers'. He states: 'The vast majority of people we see have no choice about where they are. It's not because they want to be there. The constant bashing and demonising is really depressing for people. And people are getting more and more angry about it' (JRF nd, b, np).

So, the above ideas must be tied together in a coherent and sophisticated understanding. Yes, social workers will work in the main with poor people from deprived areas, but this is not to suggest that these parents are simply bad, inadequate, or uncaring. Rather that they are parenting in extremely difficult circumstances under a disproportionate amount of surveillance and judgement, including pre-judgement and stereotyping.

If this book has helped any social workers or social work students to understand the above better, then it has done some good. If it has also helped workers, by illustrating a model for practice, to intervene in people's lives in a more caring and less oppressive manner, then even better. Here's hoping that as workers whose privileged job it is to be allowed into people's lives, we can be helped to understand that our starting point is to make an equal, human connection to those we work with – and to know without any doubt that that is the *right* thing to do.

main points

■ The Practice Model, including care, relationship-based practice, and eclectic social justice, has developed throughout the preceding chapters.

■ It can be applied to real social work situations.

■ Applying the model to examples of current practice can highlight the lack of relationship-based practice and, more frequently, the lack of social justice considerations.

■ Social workers will work with many people who live in poverty, and a sophisticated understanding of this is essential. The Practice Model can help with that.

References

Ashley, H., and Garrett, P. M. (2015) 'It's like Weber's "iron cage": Irish social workers' experience of the Habitual Residence Condition (HRC)', *Critical and Radical Social Work* 3 (1) 35–52.

Bailey, R., and Brake, M. (eds) (1975) *Radical Social Work*. London: Edward Arnold.

Banks, S. (2012) *Ethics and Values in Social Work* (4th Ed.). Basingstoke: Palgrave Macmillan.

Banks, S. (2014) 'Reclaiming social work ethics: Challenging the new public management', in S. Banks (ed.) *Ethics*. Bristol: Policy Press.

Banks, S., and Gallacher, A. (2009) *Ethics in Professional Life*. Basingstoke: Palgrave Macmillan.

Banks, S., and Williams, R. (2005) 'Accounting for ethical difficulties in social welfare work: Issues, problems and dilemmas', *British Journal of Social Work* 35 (7) 1005–1022.

Barnard, A. (2008) 'Values, ethics and professionalization: A social work history', in A. Barnard, N. Horner, and J. Wild (eds) *The Value Base of Social Work and Social Care*. Maidenhead: OU Press.

Barry, M. (2007) *Effective Approaches to Risk Assessment in Social Work: An International Literature Review*. Edinburgh: Scottish Government.

BASW (British Association of Social Workers) (1975) *A Code of Ethics for Social Work*. Birmingham: BASW.

BASW (British Association of Social Workers) (2012) *Code of Ethics for Social Work*. Birmingham: BASW.

BBC (2013) 'Disgraceful short care visits on rise, says charity'. http://www.bbc.co.uk/news/uk-24424785 (accessed 27 February 2014).

BBC News UK (2014) 'Probation union launches legal challenge over government reforms'. http://www.bbc.co.uk/news/uk–29804426 (accessed 10 Jan 2015).

Beck, U. (1992) *Risk Society: Towards a New Modernity*. London: Sage.

Beddoe, L. (2010) 'Surveillance or reflection: Professional supervision in "the risk society"', *British Journal of Social Work* 40 (4) 1279–1296.

Beresford, P., Croft, S., and Ashead, L. (2008) '"We don't see her as a social worker": A service user case study of the importance of the social worker's relationship and humanity', *British Journal of Social Work* 38, 1388–1407.

Biestek, F. (1961) *The Casework Relationship*. London: Allen and Unwin.

Bourn, D., and Hafford-Letchfield, T. (2011) 'The role of social work professional supervision in conditions of uncertainty', *International Journal of Knowledge, Culture and Change Management* 10 (9) 41–56.

Care Council for Wales (2004) *Code of Practice: Standards for Social Care Workers and Their Managers.* http://www.ccwales.org.uk/code-of-practice-for-workers/ (accessed 1 July 2015).

Carey, M. (2009) '"It's a bit like being a robot or working in a factory": Does Braverman help explain the experiences of state social workers in Britain since 1971?' *Organization* 16 (4) 505–527.

Carey, M., and Green, L. (2013) *Practical Social Work Ethics: Complex Dilemmas within Applied Social Care.* Farnham: Ashgate Publishing Ltd.

Carson, D. (1996) 'Risking legal percussions', in H. Kemshall and J. Pritchard (eds) *Good Practice in Risk Assessment and Management.* London: Jessica Kingsly, 3–12.

Catholic Herald (1978) 'The Thatcher Philosophy'. http://margaretthatcher.org/document/103793 (accessed 25 February 2015).

Clifford, D. (2013) 'Limitations of virtue ethics in the social professions', *Ethics and Social Welfare* 8 (1) 2–19.

College of Social Work (2012) *The Professional Capabilities Framework.* http://www.tcsw.org.uk/professional-capabilities-framework/?terms=capabilities%20framework (accessed 2 July 2015).

Community Care (2015) 'Social workers to face five years in prison for failing to protect children from sexual abuse, warns Cameron'. http://www.communitycare.co.uk/2015/03/03/social-workers-face-five-years-prison-failing-protect-children-sexual-abuse-warns-cameron/ (accessed 30 October 2015).

Council of Europe (1950) *European Convention on Human Rights.* http://www.echr.coe.int/Documents/Convention_ENG.pdf (accessed 12 September 2015).

Cree, V. (2013) 'New practices of empowerment', in M. Gray and S. A. Webb (eds) *The New Politics of Social Work.* Basingstoke: Palgrave Macmillan.

Criminal Justice Development Centre for Scotland (2009) *Formative Evaluation of the PSSO Constructs Programme.* http://www.cjsw.ac.uk/cjsw/files/TEP7.pdf (accessed 1 May 2010).

Crouch, C. (2011) *The Strange Non-death of Neoliberalism.* Cambridge: Polity Press.

Daily Mail (2008) 'DAVID CAMERON: There are 5 million people on benefits in Britain. How do we stop them turning into Karen Matthews?' http://www.dailymail.co.uk/news/article-1092588/DAVID-CAMERON-There-5-million-people-benefits-Britain-How-stop-turning-this.html#ixzz3bErzdt9B (accessed 18 August 2015).

Daily Mail (2010) 'Benefits couple with ELEVEN children rake in £30,000 a year and a free five-bedroom home (and now they've got another baby on the way)'. http://www.dailymail.co.uk/news/article-1303439/Benefits-couple-claiming-30-000-11-children-ANOTHER-way.html (accessed 20 August 2015).

Dalrymple, J., and Burke, B. (2006) *Anti-oppressive Practice: Social Care and the Law.* Maidenhead: McGraw-Hill.

Di Franks, N. N. (2008) 'Social workers and the NASW Code of Ethics: Belief, behaviour and disjuncture', *Social Work* 53, 167–176.

Doel, M. (2012) *Social Work: The Basics.* Abingdon: Routledge.

Dorling, D. (1998) *The No-Nonsense Guide to Equality.* Oxford: New Internationalist.

Duffy, S. (2014) *Counting the Cuts*. http://www.centreforwelfarereform.org/uploads/attachment/403/counting-the-cuts.pdf (accessed 4 October 2015).

Dustin, D. (2006) 'Skills and knowledge needed to practise as a care manager', *Journal of Social Work* 6 (3) 293–313.

Etzioni, A. (ed.) (1969) *The Semi-professions and Their Organisation: Teachers, Nurses, Social Workers*. New York: The Free Press.

Evans, T., and Harris, J. (2004) 'Street-level bureaucracy, social work and the (exaggerated) death of discretion', *British Journal of Social Work* 34 (6) 871–895.

Featherstone, B., Broadhurst, K., and Holt, K. (2012) 'Thinking systematically – thinking politically: Building strong partnerships with children and families in the context of rising inequality', *British Journal of Social Work* 42, 618–633.

Fenton, J. (2012a) 'Bringing together messages from the literature on criminal justice social work and "disjuncture": The importance of helping', *British Journal of Social Work* 42 (5) 941–956.

Fenton, J. (2012b) 'Risk aversion and anxiety in Scottish criminal justice social work: Can desistance and human rights agendas have an impact?' *Howard Journal of Criminal Justice*, DOI: 10.1111/j.1468-2311.1012.00716.x ISSN 0265-5527.

Fenton, J. (2014a) 'An analysis of "ethical stress" in criminal justice social work in Scotland: The place of values', *British Journal of Social Work*, 10.1093/bjsw/bcu032.

Fenton, J. (2014b) 'Can social work education meet the neoliberal challenge head on?' *Critical and Radical Social Work*, 10.1332/204986014X14074186108718.

Fenton, J., and Walker, L. (2012) 'When is a personal care task not just a task?' *Journal of Practice Teaching & Learning* 11 (1) 19–36.

Ferguson, H. (2005) 'Working with violence, the emotions and the psycho-social dynamics of child protection: Reflections on the Victoria Climbie case', *Social Work Education* 24, 781–795.

Ferguson, I. (2008) *Reclaiming Social Work: Challenging Neo-liberalism and Promoting Social Justice*. London: Sage.

Ferguson, I. (2013) 'Social workers as agents of change', in M. Gray and S. A. Webb (eds) *The New Politics of Social Work*. Basingstoke: Palgrave Macmillan.

Ferguson, I., and Lavalette, M. (2009) 'Social work after Baby P', in I. Ferguson and M. Lavalette (eds) *Social Work after Baby P: Issues, Debates and Alternative Perspectives*. Liverpool: Liverpool Hope University.

Fine, M., and Teram, E. (2012) 'Overt and covert ways of responding to moral injustices in social work practice: Heroes and mild-mannered social work bipeds', *British Journal of Social Work* 43, 1312–1329.

Fook, J. (2012) *Social Work: A Critical Approach to Practice*. London: Sage.

Furedi, F. (1997) *The Culture of Fear: Risk Taking and the Morality of Low Expectations*. London: Cassell.

Furedi, F. (2005) *The Politics of Fear*. London: Continuum International Publishing Group.

Garner, R., Ferdinand, P., and Lawson, S. (2009) *Introduction to Politics*. New York: Oxford University Press.

Garrett, P. M. (2010) 'Examining the "conservative revolution": Neoliberalism and social work education', *Social Work Education* 29 (4) 340–355.

Garrett, P. M. (2013) 'Mapping the theoretical and political terrain of social work', in M. Gray and S. A. Webb (eds) *The New Politics of Social Work*. Basingstoke: Palgrave Macmillan.

Gilligan, C. (1982) *In a Different Voice*. Cambridge: Harvard University Press.

Gilligan, P. (2007) 'Well motivated reformists or nascent radicals: How do applicants to the degree in social work see social problems, their origins and solutions?' *British Journal of Social Work* 37 (4) 735–60.

Goddard, C., and Hunt, S. (2011) 'The complexities of caring for child protection workers: The contexts of practice and supervision', *Journal of Social Work Practice* 25 (4) 413–432.

Gramsci, A. (1971) *Selections from the Prison Notebooks,* edited and translated by Quintin Hoare and Geoffrey Nowell Smith. London: Lawrence and Wishart.

Gray, M., Joy, E., Plath, D., Webb, S., et al. (2015) 'What supports and impedes evidence-based practice implementation? A survey of Australian social workers', *British Journal of Social Work* 42 (2) 667–684.

Gray, M., and Webb, S. A. (2013) 'Towards a new politics of social work', in Gray and Webb (eds) *The New Politics of Social Work*. Basingstoke: Palgrave Macmillan.

Green, L., and Day, R. (2013) 'To touch or not to touch? Exploring the dilemmas and ambiguities associated with touch in social care settings', in M. Carey and L. Green (eds) *Practical Social Work Ethics: Complex Dilemmas within Applied Social Care*. Surrey: Ashgate.

Gregory, M. (2010) 'Reflection and resistance: Probation practice and the ethic of care', *British Journal of Social Work* 40, 2274–2290.

Guardian (2013a) 'Gove's wrong choices over call for social work reform'. http://www.theguardian.com/education/2013/nov/13/gove-wrong-choices-social-work (accessed 10 May 2015).

Guardian (2013b) 'Margaret Thatcher: A life in quotes'. http://www.theguardian.com/politics/2013/apr/08/margaret-thatcher-quotes p52 (accessed 12 July 2015).

Guardian (2013c) 'Russell Brand: My life without drugs'. http://www.theguardian.com/culture/2013/mar/09/russell-brand-life-without-drugs p58 (accessed 17 November 2014).

Guardian (2013d) 'Benefit reforms will end "something for nothing" culture says Duncan Smith'. http://www.theguardian.com/politics/2013/oct/01/benefit-reforms-iain-duncan-smith-unemployed (accessed 5 December 2014).

Guardian (2014) 'Why are there so few male social workers?'. http://www.theguardian.com/social-care-network/2014/jul/25/why-so-few-male-social-workers (accessed 20 February 2015).

Gupta, A. (2015) 'Poverty and shame – messages for social work', *Critical and Radical Social Work* 3 (1) 131–139.

Held, V. (2010) 'Can the ethics of care handle violence?' *Ethics and Social Welfare* 4 (2) 115–129.

Hennessey, R. (2011) *Relationship Skills in Social Work*. London: Sage.

Higgins, M., Goodyer, A., and Whittaker, A. (2015) 'Can a Munro-inspired approach transform the lives of looked after children in England?' *Social Work Education: The International journal* 34 (3) 328–340.

Hollis, M., and Howe, D. (1990) 'Moral risks in the social work role: A response to Macdonald', *British Journal of Social Work*, 20, 547–552.

Horner, N. (2012) *What Is Social Work* (4th Ed.). London: Sage.

Horner, R., and Kelly, T. (2007) 'Ethical decision-making in the helping profession: A contextual and caring approach', *Journal of Religion and Spirituality in Social Work* 26 (1) 71–88.

Howe, D. (2013) *Empathy: What It Is and Why It Matters*. Basingstoke: Palgrave Macmillan.

Hudson, B. (2001) 'Human rights, public safety and the probation service: Defending justice in the risk society', *Howard Journal* 40, 103–113.

IFSW (International Federation of Social Workers) (2012) *Statement of Ethical Principles*. http://ifsw.org/policies/statement-of-ethical-principles/ (accessed 10 May 2015).

IFSW (International Federation of Social Workers) (2014) *Global Definition of Social Work*. http://ifsw.org/policies/definition-of-social-work/ (accessed 15 May 2015).

Independent (2013) 'The British public wrong about nearly everything, survey shows'. http://www.independent.co.uk/news/uk/home-news/british-public-wrong-about-nearly-everything-survey-shows-8697821.html (accessed 5 January 2015).

Independent (2015) 'Jobless must sign on every day: Government to dock money from long-term unemployed if they do not comply'. http://www.independent.co.uk/news/uk/politics/jobless-mustsign-on-every-day-government-to-dock-money-from-longterm-unemployed-if-they-do-not-comply-9294586.html (accessed November 2015).

Ingram, R. (2013) 'Locating emotional intelligence at the heart of social work practice', *British Journal of Social Work* 43 (5) 987–1004.

Ingram, R. (2015a) 'Exploring emotions within formal and informal forums: Messages from social work practitioners', *British Journal of Social Work* 45 (3) 896–913.

Ingram, R. (2015b) *Understanding Emotions in Social Work*. Maidenhead: McGraw-Hill.

Ingram, R., Fenton, J., Hodson, A., and Jindal-Snape, D. (2014) *Reflective Social Work Practice*. Basingstoke: Palgrave Macmillan.

Ito, F. (2014) 'Social work ethics and social justice: The growing gap', in S. Banks (ed.) *Critical and Radical Debates in Social Work: Ethics*. Bristol: Policy Press.

Jindal-Snape, D., and Ingram, R. (2013) 'Understanding and supporting triple transitions of international doctoral students: ELT and SuReCom models', *Journal of Perspectives in Applied Academic Practice* 1 (1) 17–24.

Jones, C. (2001) 'Voices from the front line: State social workers and new labour', *British Journal of Social Work* 31, 547–562.

Jones, O. (2011) *Chavs: The Demonization of the Working Class*. London: Verso.

Jones, O. (2015) 'Refugees are human. This simple fact seems to have been forgotten'. http://www.theguardian.com/commentisfree/2015/aug/28/migrants-humans-drowning-suffocating-safety-statistics (accessed 1 November 2015).

Jones, S. (2009) 'The myths of child protection', in I. Ferguson and M. Lavalette (eds) *Social Work after Baby P: Issues, Debates and Alternative Perspectives*. Liverpool: Liverpool Hope University.

JRF (Joseph Rowntree Foundation) (2010) 'Credit and debt in low-income families'. http://www.jrf.org.uk/sites/files/jrf/credit-debt-low-incomes-summary.pdf (accessed 24 May 2015).

JRF (Joseph Rowntree Foundation) (2014) 'Public attitudes towards poverty'. http://www.jrf.org.uk/publications/public-attitudes-towards-poverty (accessed 24 May 2015).

JRF (Joseph Rowntree Foundation) (2015) 'Will the 2015 Summer Budget improve living standards in 2020?' https://www.jrf.org.uk/sites/default/files/infographic/mis-2020/ (accessed 1 December 2015).

JRF (Joseph Rowntree Foundation) (nd, a) *About Poverty* https://www.jrf.org.uk/our-work/about-poverty (accessed 18 June 2015).

JRF (Joseph Rowntree Foundation) (nd, b) 'Austerity in the UK – Deprivation, depression and demonisation part of daily struggle'. https://www.jrf.org.uk/austerity-uk-deprivation-depression-and-demonisation-part-daily-struggle (accessed 4 November 2015).

Kemshall, H. (2002) *Risk Assessment and Management of Serious Violent and Sexual Offenders: A Review of Current Issues.* www.scotland.gov.uk/cru/kdo1/green (accessed 21 November 2014).

Kemshall, H. (2010) 'Risk rationalities in contemporary social work policy and practice', *British Journal of Social Work* 40, 1247–1262.

Kosny, A., and Eakin, J. (2008) 'The hazards of helping: Work, mission and risk in non-profit social services organizations', *Health, Risk and Society* 10, 149–166.

Lafrance, J., Gray, E., and Herbert, M. (2004) 'Gate-keeping for professional social work practice', *Social Work Education* 23 (3) 325–340.

Lansley, S., and Mack, J. (2015) *Breadline Britain: The Rise of Poverty.* Oneworld: London.

Lawler, J. (2013) 'Critical management', in M. Gray and S. A. Webb (eds) *The New Politics of Social Work.* Basingstoke: Palgrave Macmillan.

Levitas, R. (2005) *The Inclusive Society.* Basingstoke: Palgrave Macmillan.

Liljegren, A. (2012) 'Pragmatic professionalism: Micro-level discourse in social work', *European Journal of Social Work* 15 (3) 295–312.

Littlechild, B. (2010) 'Child protection social work: Risks of fears and fears of risk – impossible tasks from impossible goals?' *Social Policy and Administration* 42, 662–675.

Lloyd, R. E. (2010) 'The individual in social care: The ethics of care and the personalisation agenda in services for older people in England', *Ethics and Social Welfare* 4 (2) 188–200.

Lorenzetti, L. (2013) 'Developing a cohesive emancipatory social work identity: Risking an act of love', *Critical Social Work* 14 (2) 48–59.

Lymbery, M. (2014) 'Understanding personalisation: Implications for social work', *Journal of Social Work* 14 (3) 295–312.

MacDonald, G. (1990a) 'Allocating blame in social work', *British Journal of Social Work* 20, 525–546.

MacDonald, G. (1990b) 'Moral Risks? A reply to Hollis and Howe', *British Journal of Social Work* 20, 553–556.

MacDonald, G., and MacDonald, K. (2010) 'Safeguarding: A case for intelligent risk management', *British Journal of Social Work* 40, 1174–1191.

MacDonald, R. (2015) 'The power of stupid ideas: Three generations that have never worked'. https://workingclassstudies.wordpress.com/2015/05/11/the-power-of-stupid-ideas-three-generations-that-have-never-worked/ (accessed 2 October 2015).

Manning, R. (1998) 'A care approach', in H. Kuhse and P. Singer (eds) *A Companion to Bioethics.* Oxford: Blackwell, 98–105.

Marston, G. (2013) 'Critical discourse analysis', in M. Gray and S. A. Webb (eds) *The New Politics of Social Work*. Basingstoke: Palgrave Macmillan.

McKaskill, T. (2010) 'Neoliberalism as a water balloon'. https://vimeo.com/6803752 (accessed 1st September 2013).

McKendrick, D., and Webb, S. (2014) 'Taking a political stance in social work', *Critical and Radical Social Work* 2 (3) 357–369.

McLaughlin, K. (2008) *Social Work, Politics and Society: From Radicalism to Orthodoxy*. Bristol: Policy Press.

Meagher, G., and Parton, N. (2004) 'Modernising social work and the ethics of care', *Social Work and Society* 2 (1) 10–27.

Morley, C., and Macfarlane, S. (2014) 'Critical social work as ethical social work: Using critical reflection to research students' resistance to neoliberalism', *Critical and Radical Social Work* 2 (3) 337–355.

Morrison, T. (2007) 'Emotional intelligence, emotion and social work: Context, characteristics, complications and contribution', *British Journal of Social Work* 37 (2) 245–263.

Munday, B. (2003) *User Involvement in Personal Social Services*. University of Kent, United Kingdom.

Munro, E. (2011) *The Munro Review of Child Protection: Final Report*. London: TSO.

Murphy, D., Duggan, M., and Joseph, S. (2013) 'Relationship-based social work and its compatibility with the person-centred approach: Principled versus instrumental perspectives', *British Journal of Social Work* 43 (4) 703–719.

Murray, C. (1990) *The Emerging British Underclass*. London: IEA Health and Welfare Unit.

Nayak, A., and Kehily, M. J. (2014) '"Chavs, chavettes and pramface girls": Teenage mothers, marginalised young men and the management of stigma', *Journal of Youth Studies* 17 (10) 1330–1345.

Northern Ireland Social Care Council (2004) *Codes of Practice for Social Care Workers and Employers of Social Care Workers*. http://www.niscc.info/storage/resources/20151118_codesforemployers_updated.pdf (accessed 10 May 2016).

O'Donnell, P., Farrar, A., Brintzenhofeszoc, K., Conrad, A. P., Danis, M., Grady, C., Taylor, C., and Ulrich, C. (2008) 'Predictors of ethical stress, moral action and job satisfaction in health care social workers', *Social Work in Health Care* 46, 29–51.

Okitipki, T., and Aymer, C. (2010) *Key Concepts in Anti-discriminatory Social Work*. London: Sage.

O'Sullivan, T. (1999) *Decision-Making in Social Work*. Norfolk: Palgrave Macmillan.

Parton, N. (2014) *The Politics of Child Protection: Contemporary Developments and Future Directions*. Basingstoke: Palgrave Macmillan.

Pease, B. (2013) 'A history of critical and radical social work', in M. Gray and S. A. Webb (eds) *The New Politics of Social Work*. Basingstoke: Palgrave Macmillan.

Phillips, D. (2009) 'Beyond the risk agenda', in S. Green, E. Lancaster, and S. Feasey (eds) *Addressing Offending Behaviour: Context, Practice and Values*. Devon: Willan, 172–189.

Phillips, R., and Cree, V. (2014) 'What does the 'Fourth Wave' mean for teaching feminism in 21st century social work?' *Social Work Education* 33 (7) 930–943.

Preston-Shoot, M. (2003) 'Changing learning and learning change', *Journal of Social Work Practice* 17 (1) 9–23.

Preston-Shoot, M. (2011) 'On administrative evil-doing within social work policy and services: Law, ethics and practice', *European Journal of Social Work* 14 (2) 177–194.

Preston-Shoot, M. (2012) 'The secret curriculum', *Ethics and Social Welfare* 6 (1) 18–36.

Reamer, F. (1993) *The Philosophical Foundations of Social Work*. New York: Columbia University Press.

Reamer, F., and Shardlow, S. (2009) 'Ethical codes of practice in the US and the UK: One profession, two standards', *Journal of Social Work Values and Ethics* 6 (2) np. http://www.socialworker.com/jswve/content/view/120/68/ (accessed 13 October 2013).

Road from Crime, The (2012). DVD-ROM, Lagan Media Production for the University of Glasgow, available from IRISS.

Robinson, G. (2003) 'Implementing OASys: Lessons from research into LSI-R and ACE', *Probation Journal* 50 (1) 30–40.

Rogers, C. R. (1966), 'Client-centered therapy', in S. Arieti (ed.) *American Handbook of Psychiatry*. New York: Basic Books.

Rogowski, S. (2012) 'Social work with children and families: Challenges and possibilities in the neo-liberal world', *British Journal of Social Work* 42 (5): 921–940.

Rogowski, S. (2014) 'Radical/critical social work with young offenders: Challenges and possibilities', *Journal of Social Work Practice: Psychotherapeutic Approaches in Health, Welfare and the Community* 28 (1) 7–21.

Rogowski, S. (2015) 'Margaret Thatcher's legacy for social work with children and families: Critical possibilities?' *Critical and Radical Social Work* 3 (1) 53–65.

Sander-Staudt, M. (2006) 'The unhappy marriage of care ethics and virtue ethics', *Hypatia* 21 (4) 21–39.

Sawyer, A. (2009) 'Mental health workers negotiating risk on the front line', *Australian Social Work* 62, 441–459.

Schein, E. (2010) *Organizational Culture and Leadership* (4th Ed.). San Francisco: Jossey-Bass.

Scholar, H., McLaughlin, H., McCaughan, S., and Coleman, A. (2014) 'Learning to be a social worker in a non-traditional placement: Critical reflections on social work, professional identity and social work education in England', *Social Work Education: The International Journal* 33 (8) 998–1016.

Schon, D. (1983) *The Reflective Practitioner: How Professionals Think in Action*. New York: Basic Books.

Scottish Government (2003) *The Framework for Social Work Education in Scotland*. Edinburgh: Scottish Executive.

Scottish Government (2010) *National Outcomes and Standards for Social Work in the Criminal Justice System*. Edinburgh: Scottish Government.

Sheedy, M. (2013) *Core Themes in Social Work: Power, Poverty, Politics and Values*. Maidenhead: OU Press.

Solas, J. (2014) 'What kind of social justice does social work seek?' *International Social Work* 51 (6) 813–822.

SSSC (Scottish Social Services Council) (2004), *Codes of Practice for Scottish Social Service Workers and Employers*. Dundee: SSSC.

Stanford, S. (2010) '"Speaking back" to fear: Responding to the moral dilemmas of risk in social work practice', *British Journal of Social Work* 40, 1065–1080.

Stanford, S. N. (2011) 'Constructing moral responses to risk: A framework for hopeful social work practice', *British Journal of Social Work* 41, 1514–31.

Staunton, T. (2009) 'In pursuit of children's rights', in I. Ferguson and M. Lavalette (eds) *Social Work after Baby P: Issues, Debates and Alternative Perspectives*. Liverpool: Liverpool Hope University.

Tallant, C., Sambrook, M., and Green, S. (2008) 'Engagement skills: Best practice or effective practice?' in S. Green, E. Lancaster, and S. Feasey (eds) *Addressing Offending Behaviour: Context, Practice and Values*. Devon: Willan.

Taylor, M. (2007) 'Professional dissonance: A promising concept for clinical social work', *Smith College Studies in Social Work* 77, 89–99.

Telegraph (2010) 'We are all middle class now, darling'. http://www.telegraph. co.uk/news/politics/7053761/Were-all-middle-class-now-darling.html (accessed 5 November 2015).

Telegraph (2013) 'Michael Gove: Many social workers "not up to the job"'. http://www. telegraph.co.uk/news/uknews/10442309/Michael-Gove-many-social-workers-not-up-to-the-job.html (accessed 12 September 2015).

Thompson, N. (2001) *Anti-discriminatory Practice* (3rd Ed.). Basingstoke: Palgrave Macmillan.

Thompson, S., and Thompson, N. (2008) *The Critically Reflective Practitioner*. Basingstoke: Palgrave Macmillan.

Tirado, L. (2014) *Hand to Mouth: The Truth about Being Poor in a Wealthy World*. London: Virago.

Trevithick, P. (2012) *Social Work Skills and Knowledge: A Practice Handbook*. Maidenhead: OU Press.

Tronto, J. (1993) *Moral Boundaries: A Political Argument for an Ethic of Care*. London: Routledge.

Tronto, J. (2010) 'Creating caring institutions: Politics, plurality and purpose', *Ethics and Social Welfare* 4 (2), 158–171.

Trotter, C. (2006) *Working with Involuntary Clients*, 2nd edition. Crows Nest: Allen and Unwin.

Turbett, C. (2014) *Doing Radical Social Work*. Basingstoke: Palgrave Macmillan.

Tyler, I. (2013) *Revolting Subjects: Social Abjection and Resistance in Neoliberal Britain*. London: Zed Books.

UNHCR (United Nations High Commissioner for Refugees) (2012) *Refugees*. http:// www.unhcr.org/pages/49da0e466.html (accessed 28 September 2015).

UNISON (2009) *Still Slipping through the Net? Front-Line Staff Assess Children's Safeguarding Progress*. London: Unison.

Warner, J. (2015) 'Social work, class politics and risk in the moral panic over Baby P', *Health, Risk and Society* 15 (3) 217–233.

Webb, S. (2006) *Social Work in a Risk Society: Social and Political Perspectives*. Basingstoke: Palgrave Macmillan.

Weinberg, M., and Taylor, S. (2014) '"Rogue" social workers: The problem with rules for ethical behaviour', *Critical Social Work* 15 (1) 74–86.

Whittaker, A. (2011) 'Social defences and organisational culture in a local authority child protection setting: Challenges for the Munro review?' *Journal of Social Work Practice: Psychotherapeutic Approaches in Health, Welfare and the Community* 25 (4) 481–495.

Wilkinson, R. G., and Pickett, K. (2010) *The Spirit Level: Why Equality Is Better for Everyone*. London: Penguin.

Williams, C., and Briskman, L. (2015) 'Reviving social work through moral outrage', *Critical and Radical Social Work* 3 (1) 3–17.

Woodward, R., and Mackay, K. (2012) 'Mind the gap! Students' understanding and application of social work values', *Social Work Education: The International Journal* 31 (8) 1090–104.

Index

Advocacy, 108, 109, 115
Agency culture, 34–38
  Artifacts, 37
  Basic underlying assumptions, 37, 38, 77
  Espoused values, 37
Alkies, 50
Anti-discriminatory practice, 112
Anti-oppressive practice, 103, 110, 112, 113, 119, 159
Asylum seekers, 51–53, 141, 148
Asylums, 19
Attachment theory, 20
Attentiveness, 70–77, 84, 99, 100, 130
Austerity, 31, 36, 55, 101, 140, 164
Authority (role of social worker), 59, 99, 158, 160, 164
Autonomy (of social workers), 22, 11, 23, 40, 64, 65, 86, 87, 101, 105, 106, 111, 134, 143, 144, 168

Banks, S., 3, 4, 32, 34, 62, 63, 67, 69, 70, 78, 88, 115
Banks/bankers, 47, 58
BASW, 2–10, 14, 17, 22, 74, 84, 91, 102, 103, 166
Benefits, 6, 10, 28, 31, 32, 48–50, 56, 163–166
Benefits Street, 50
Beveridge, W., 20
Blaire, T., 49

Blame (of social workers), 34, 35, 66, 82, 83, 87, 88, 102, 106, 110, 126, 144, 151, 153
Bureaucracy, 23, 118, 153, 168

Cameron, D., 5
Capitalism, 43, 46, 104
Carers, 8, 20, 123
Carey, M. and Green, L., 63, 64, 67, 69
Carson, D., 90
Case Con, 105
Case conferences, 92, 143
Challenging/challenges, 84, 106, 115, 159
Chavs, 15, 45, 54, 112
Child abuse, 99, 101
Child protection, 36, 40, 77, 89–91, 101, 107, 134, 135, 143, 144, 151
Class (social), 42–45, 49, 51, 55–57, 61, 67, 74, 104, 105, 110, 171
Code of ethics, 2, 4, 6, 10, 17, 22, 65, 74, 102, 166
College of Social Work, 7, 10, 91
Connolly, P., 57, 106, 166
Competence, (ethics of care and) 71, 72, 76, 85, 88, 96, 100, 163
Compliance culture, 32–33
Conservatives, 30, 46
Consumerism, 21, 24–26, 48
Corbyn, J., 44
Criminal justice, 11, 32–34, 71, 77, 107, 130, 161, 169
Criminals and rioting thugs, 52–54

Crisis response, 36
Crouch, C., 42, 43, 58
Culture (of organisation), 12, 34–39,
 67, 68, 71, 83, 85, 87, 94, 96, 97,
 151, 153
Cuts (in services), 3, 26, 31, 32, 36, 44,
 58, 120
Cygnor Gofal Cymru/Care Council for
 Wales, 10

Dalrymple, J. and Burke, B., 111
Debt, 48–50
Decision-making, 80–92, 101, 105,
 143–145, 153, 155, 159
 Defensible Decision-Making, 85–92
Deontology, 3, 15, 19, 62–66
Deserving/undeserving, 19, 53, 164, 167
Deviant social work, 109
Dignity, 4
Direct payments (see also 'Self-directed
 support'), 26
Disability, 110, 119
Discretion, 81, 105, 106, 115, 116,
 119, 153
Diversity, 9, 102
Doel, M., 4, 20, 25, 30, 128
Domestic abuse, 100
Dorling, D., 55
Duncan-Smith, I., 49, 56

Economics, 42–45, 56
 Free market economy, 44
 Keynesian economics, 42, 43, 56, 61
 Monetarism, 44
Emotions, 92, 122–127, 137
Employment, 18, 27, 49, 145
Empowerment, 1, 10, 64, 75, 108, 109
Enlightenment, 18, 19, 157
Etzioni, A., 23
Evidence-based practice, 135, 146,
 152
Exclusion (see 'Social exclusion')

Ferguson, I. 1, 2, 12, 17, 24, 26, 30, 33,
 44, 66, 110, 117, 122, 169
Finding knowledge, 145–148
Fook, J., 111

Freedom, 2, 33, 83, 95, 113, 114, 146,
 150
Furedi, F., 33, 55

Garner, R., Ferdinand, P. and Lawson,
 S., 42
Gate-keeping, 12, 35–38, 40
Genuineness, 81, 122, 132, 133
Gilligan, C., 70
Global definition of social work, 1, 6
Gove, M., 28
Gramsci, A., 57

Hennessey, R., 121–123, 128, 130, 132,
 137
Horner, N., 19
Howe, D., 123, 124
Human rights, 1–4, 9, 10, 15, 52, 103,
 110, 113, 114, 117, 119, 143, 145,
 148, 159, 170

Illegals, 51, 52
Inclusion (see 'Social inclusion')
Individualism, 14, 18, 27–29, 30, 33,
 34, 40, 45, 122
Inequality, 5–8, 16, 22, 27, 28, 34, 36,
 47, 51–55, 58, 61, 100, 102, 104,
 113, 116, 119, 135, 140, 152, 158,
 163, 164, 168–170
Ingram, R., 126, 127, 131, 137, 150
Ingram, R., Fenton, J., Hodson, A. and
 Jindal-Snape D., 25, 64, 93, 108,
 143, 148, 150, 152
Inner world, 122–124, 128, 130, 132,
 134, 162, 164, 167
Integrity of care (ethics of care and),
 71, 73, 76, 77, 85, 96, 163
International Association of Schools of
 Social Work General Assembly, 1
International Federation of Social
 Workers (IFSW), 1

Jones, O., 5, 7, 45, 49–51, 56, 104,
 129
Junkies, 15, 50, 51, 122

Kilbrandon Report, 20

Lansley, S. and Mack, J., 46, 47, 61
Labour Party, 44
    New Labour, 5, 27, 44
    Third Way, 44
Levitas, R., 5, 27, 53
Liberty, 42, 113, 114
Living wage, 165

Managerialism, 2, 3, 18, 21, 23, 25, 26,
    40, 45, 66, 80, 86, 91, 120, 122,
    144, 149, 153, 154, 158, 168
MAPPA, 108, 143
Markets, 2, 3, 5, 18, 21, 26–30, 42–44,
    73, 103, 120, 139
Marxist, 22, 104
McLaughlin, K. 9, 52
Moral underclass discourse (MUD), 27,
    53
Morale, 107
Morality period, 19
Munday, B., 20, 21, 24, 26
Munro Review of Child Protection,
    36, 40, 89, 90, 101, 107, 131–136,
    144, 151, 168
Murray, C., 45, 61

National Health Service, 20
National Insurance, 20, 43
New Public Management
    (see 'Managerialism')
Northern Ireland Social Care Council,
    10

Okitipki, T. and Aymer, C., 112
Older people, 74, 77, 79, 118, 155
Ontological guilt, 12, 81–87
O'Sullivan, T., 87
Outer world, 122, 124, 132, 133, 136,
    162

Parenting, 135, 152, 171
Participationism, 18, 20, 21, 26, 27,
    30, 32, 33, 40, 158
Parton, N., 2, 33
Peer support, 94, 95, 150, 151, 156, 160
Political action, 22, 114, 115
Poor Laws, 19, 128

Poor people, 26, 31, 34, 45, 48, 49,
    104, 171
Poverty, 5–10, 16, 20, 24, 27, 31, 36,
    46–61, 72, 100–105, 109, 116,
    118, 134, 140, 145, 162–165,
    168–172
    Absolute poverty, 46, 104
    Relative poverty, 46, 47, 50
    The working poor, 50
Prevention, 36, 40, 107
Privatisation, 18, 25, 27–35, 40, 45,
    106, 122, 158
Probation service, 13, 29, 30, 86, 98,
    107, 113, 144
Professionalism, 16, 21–25, 132, 138,
    152–156, 160
    Occupational professionalism, 155
    Organisational professionalism, 155

Reamer, F., 63
Redistribution (of wealth), 8, 9, 22, 55
Reflective practice/reflection, 25, 26,
    30, 52, 54, 60, 71, 81, 83, 85,
    92–95, 99, 101, 104, 112, 115,
    119, 124, 141, 143, 149, 150, 160,
    161, 162, 166
Refugees, 51, 129
Responsibility (ethics of care and), 70,
    71, 74, 76, 84–87, 95, 96, 99, 109,
    115, 130, 163
Responsiveness (ethics of care and),
Risk assessment, 25, 33–36, 63, 86, 92,
    134, 136, 158
Risk aversion, 11, 12, 33–36, 80, 82,
    85, 86
Risk management, 89, 93, 109, 143
Rogers, C., 103, 157, 170, 229

Schein, E., 37, 60, 77, 112, 170
Scroungers, 6, 48, 49, 56, 61, 103, 128,
    171
Seebohm Report, 20
Self-directed support (see also 'Direct
    payments'), 26, 31, 118
Semi-profession, 23
Sheedy, M., 9, 11, 17, 39, 58, 114
Social democracy, 42

Social exclusion, 10, 11, 27, 51, 63, 67, 102

Social inclusion, 7, 10, 27, 78, 169, 170

Social Work Action Network (SWAN), 95, 106, 117, 120, 141, 142, 165

Scottish Social Services Council (SSSC), 10

Supervision, 37, 68, 92–96, 101, 148–150, 152, 156, 159, 160

Thatcher's Children, 11, 13

Thatcher, M., 43, 46, 49, 55

The Charity Organisation Society, 19

The Spirit Level, 28, 61

The SuReCom model of supervision, 93

Thompson, N., 112

Thompson, S. and Thompson, N., 143

Tirado, L., 48, 49, 61

Trevithick, P., 122, 129, 130, 133, 137

Tronto, J., 70–74, 78

Trotter, C., 59, 69, 160

Tyrbett, C., 20, 43, 53, 104, 105, 108, 109, 115

Tyler, I., 45, 51, 53

Unemployment, 42–44, 49, 51, 57, 102, 145

Utilitarianism, 15, 19, 62–65, 67, 158

Virtue ethics, 15, 62, 67–70, 78, 95, 158

War on Want, 20

Webb, S., 27

Welfare state, 3, 20, 31, 32. 35, 40, 158

Welfarism, 14, 20, 21, 49

Wilkinson, R. and Pickett, K., 6, 28, 29, 34, 47, 51, 55, 61, 102, 113

Workhouses, 19

Working-class, 42, 45, 61

World view (developing a), 41, 96, 114, 138

World War I, 20

World War II, 20, 42

Younger social workers and students, 11, 13, 32, 33, 41, 42, 139, 144